The Ethical School

Conflicts often arise between regulations, making it difficult for school management teams and teachers to resolve situations with appropriate dignity and respect to all concerned. This book will help teachers reflect on their own ethics, guiding them to make more reasonable decisions in their own schools, and thereby gradually transforming schools into more cohesive and caring communities. It presents provocative actual case studies and discusses possible responses from three traditional ethical positions – consequences, consistency and caring. These provide a scientific base, a rational base and a responsive base for ethical decision-making. It is argued that none of these positions is adequate in itself to provide an ethical response, although consideration of all three will keep a school balanced and open to changes.

The book covers such everyday problems as censorship, inclusivity, school uniform, punishment, personal gain and confidentiality, and argues that care and respect for others, equity, rational autonomy and concern for long-term benefits are more important for a school community than short-term power and control.

Educational management series
Series editor: Cyril Poster

Recent titles in this series include:

The Ethical School

Felicity Haynes

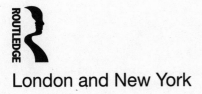

London and New York

First published 1998
by Routledge
11 New Fetter Lane, London EC4P 4EE

Simultaneously published in the USA and Canada
by Routledge
29 West 35th Street, New York, NY 10001

Typeset in Palatino by Routledge
Printed and bound in Great Britain by Page Bros (Norwich) Ltd

British Library Cataloguing in Publication Data
A catalogue record for this book is available from the British Library

Library of Congress Cataloguing in Publication Data
Haynes, Felicity.
    The Ethical School/Felicity Haynes
          p.   cm.
    Includes bibliographical references.
    1. Teachers – Professional ethics – Australia – Case studies.
I. Title.
LB1779.H39   1988
174'.937 – dc21   97–25911
                                                                      CIP

ISBN 0–415–14185–0

This book is dedicated to T.A. (Bert) Priest, who was shrewd enough to see the need for reflective practitioners in education long before the term became fashionable and who first encouraged me to enter the ongoing ethical debate in postgraduate classes at The University of Western Australia.

Contents

Case studies

Illustrations

Preface

It is a privilege to be a part of the ongoing realm of existing things and processes. When we see and conceive of ourselves as a part of those ongoing processes, we identify with the totality and, in the calmness this brings, feel solidarity with all our comrades in existing.

We want nothing other than to live in a spiral of activities and enhance others' doing so, deepening our own reality as we come into contact and relation with the rest, exploring the dimensions of reality, embodying them in ourselves, creating, responding to the full range of the reality we can discern with the fullest reality we possess, becoming a vehicle for truth, beauty, goodness, and holiness, addding our own characteristic bit to reality's eternal processes.

R. Nozick, *The Examined Life*

Every society and every cultural group tends to accept without question a number of beliefs. These are taken for granted, instilled in the young as part of their education, and presupposed in the process of forming further ideas. Under the pressure of change directed from both political leaders and academic theorists, many educators have little time or opportunity to reflect on what they are doing and why. The main purpose of this book is to help students in university education departments reflect on the ethics of their practice, to allow them the opportunity to discuss and debate the propriety of their actions in dialogue with people who may hold assumptions very different from their own. If, after examination, they can adequately defend their actions against opposition, then they can act with rational assurance instead of unthinking acceptance, in other words as autonomous persons. If they cannot, then they may have to suspend judgement, change their plan of action, or modify their framework of belief in ways that may well change the way they act in all situations.

Is this inquiry into the ethics of educational practice a theoretical or a practical one? Well, both, because it deals mainly with questions about the criteria or standards of moral judgement in private life or within a professional institution. What makes a good thing good? What makes an unjust situation unjust and how can an educator help to make it more just? Can the criteria or standards be tied up in a coherent, and prefer-ably a simple, scheme? The criterial structural framework of consequences, consistency and care that is used in this book owes much of its origins to philosophical theories that have been constructed and debated through the centuries. To understand which criteria to apply in a certain situation, it is helpful to know the theoretical framework within which those criteria are considered to be important. So there are many references to the writings of other philosophers throughout the book. While the examples in this book are drawn from education, the process of thinking about the ethical aspects of one's practices applies equally well to all other professions including law, management, business, medicine and journalism. It could indeed serve as a practical introduc-tion to moral philosophy for anyone interested in the subject. The views of traditional philosophers are presented here, not as an academic exer-cise, but as examples of reflective and literate people who have disagreed with each other in the past. They present the frames of reference from which the criteria for judging whether an act is moral or not have been drawn, and even the criteria for *deciding* whether a situation is an ethical one or not. The final chapter is an attempt to ask the general philosoph-ical questions about the status of moral issues, where they stand in our systems of knowledge, and how we could mark progress in our moral development as professional educators.

The situations described in this book are neither contrived nor fanciful. They arise from the accounts of educators currently working in educational systems and have formed the basis of discussion among very lively postgraduate students in education at The University of Western Australia since 1992. My gratitude goes especially to Mark Antulov, Ruth Bairstow, Monica Butler, Maria Camporeale, Alf de Bono, Simon Gipson, Jo-Anne Hine, Victoria Morgan, Stephen O'Brien, Janet Phillips, Greg Ryan-Gadsden, Stefan Silcox and Chris Somers for their contributions and friendship and to all those future students who will help me to examine and refine the ethics of my own ideas and actions.

Chapter 1

Introduction

The unexamined life is not worth living.
                                        Socrates

WHAT MAKES A SITUATION UNFAIR?

Most of us can remember a situation in our own educational experience
that made us feel angry or upset because it seemed so unfair. It may have
been someone punished when they did not deserve it, or someone not
punished when others similarly misbehaving had been. Reflect on that
situation and ask yourself what it was about it that made you see it as
unfair. How did you know it was unfair? Many of the situations that are
perceived to be unfair involve the unequal distribution of goods or
power. Others involve a requirement of consistency or equal treatment.
Some appear to lack consideration for other people and are seen to be
unfair because they are selfish actions, or abuse a power relation. Others
may depend on unequal recognition of merit. The features that you
consider significant or salient may well reflect your basic ethical position.

If you ask other people around you to discuss their own memory of a
case of unfairness and ask what their situation has in common with
yours, you may find it very difficult to find core concepts that tie
together a notion of unfairness. The word is an ethical one and is one of
those words that, like the rules of our native language, we acquire
without understanding the rules for using it. We start from a shared
understanding of fairness and try to imagine a different conception of
the same situation. The reflective teacher must have enough intellectual
awareness to stand aside from personal subjectivity and analyse the
possible different responses to the situation.

As professionals, teachers are faced with such a plurality of cultural,
professional and political injunctions, each jostling the other for priority
and each providing counter-defences against the other, that there is no
time for them to reflect on what they ought to do in a given situation.
Nor even if they have time to reflect do there seem to be any objective

standards of ethics or fairness to which they can appeal. It is easy for them to escape into a belief that objective standards, either in the subjects that they are teaching, or in ethical behaviour, are nothing but historical artefacts and slide from that into a relativism that allows every person to have their own set of ethical values over which there can be no resolved discussion.

Relativism has its values. We can use it to tolerate anything and everything. In this multicultural mass-media global culture, we are encouraged to make space for previously marginalized voices, to value identities other than that of the colonizer. We can use relativism to dismiss difference as irrelevant to our own world-view. It can lead to a cynicism available only to the economically self-sufficient and the politically comfortable that shuts itself away from recognizing oppressive practices. It can lead to a terror of exercising independent judgement, so that one takes refuge in the rules of others, the dominant local conventions. The most dangerous, and most common, reaction is that teachers faced with making an ethical decision are unable to react spontaneously to such a situation. They are paralysed by what Derrida has called an aporia, of not knowing how to go on. There is often a retreat to the conventional rules, the sanctions of the system.

Ironically ethics is often considered irrelevant to any large system, whether corporations or state education departments, in which accountability counts profits, efficiency and performance criteria as the measures of efficiency and effectiveness. Ethics surfaces in documents of social justice and anti-discrimination legislation but there is little attempt to tie these into other aspects of education policy such as increased class sizes, or punishment. Ethics is often invisible within an economic rationalist framework of increased efficiency and control. Yet a view of ethics as professional power-sharing lies at the heart of devolution. With the growing size and diversity of schools and school systems, the increased possibility of law suits and the increased demand for public accountability, there is a need to reaffirm that education is continually about human beings interacting responsibly with each other rather than about those with power controlling others or those without power acting like automata with neither time nor incentive to make autonomous decisions.

REFLECTING ON ETHICS IN SCHOOLS

I am not going to present a single philosophical theory of ethics in this book. I do not intend to analyse the ethical views of great philosophers such as Aristotle, Plato, Augustine, Hume, Locke, Mill, Kant, Moore or Wittgenstein, and offer only an extremely brief résumé of their writings in the final chapter. Many philosophers have discussed the matter and I have provided a glossary at the back to help with unfamiliar terms that I have borrowed from their discussions. According to Strike and Ternasky (1993: 4), philosophers have in the past worried more about the structure of ethical arguments or the meaning of ethical terms than about what is right and what is wrong. Readers will need neither philosophical nor legal training to mount arguments about the correct way to proceed morally. This is a philosophical book only in that it encourages critical reflection about the way persons interact and what it means to be a good person. I want readers to develop a disposition to reflect on their own situation, to draw up their own structures to fit their activities and strivings into a pattern that will allow them to see and understand the old components of their lives differently, and perhaps to understand where their own ethical values come from, so that they can react confidently and appropriately to ethical situations in schools.

It sounds a little harsh to say, with Socrates, that the unexamined life is not worth living. However, as Nozick (1989: 15) reminds us, when we guide our lives by our own pondered thoughts, then it is our life that we are living, not someone else's. In this sense, the unexamined life is not lived as fully. Reasons are essential to that reflection, but as we have seen in thinking about the unfair situations we have experienced, feelings also play an important part. It is often difficult to know how to reflect critically. I present my own reflections for consideration, but I do not aim thereby for the reader's consent – I ask simply that they be considered.

I use this book to argue that ethics is relevant to anyone who ever asks the question 'what ought I to do?' or 'would this be right?' It is of relevance to anyone who ever makes moral judgements about others, who ever praises or condemns other people's actions. It is of particular importance in education because not only are teachers and administrators beset with moral questions, but now, more than ever, they are responsible for the moral well-being and education of their pupils, the future generation.

However, it may not be useful to urge teachers to pay attention to ethics if I cannot explain what holds all those different notions of unfairness together. I cannot offer a systematic ethical theory without running the risk of being labelled modernist, dogmatic or insensitive to other cultures. Just as teachers of English struggle with the imposition of Standard English and the literature they grew up with and loved on complex multicultured classes, so anyone who tries to impose a systematic frame of values runs the risk of unethically excluding minority groups. This book offers a framework consistent with postmodernism within which educational administrators can develop their own reasonable structure. This structure will help them to argue from their own moral point of view with those who would normally dismiss ethical considerations as irrelevant to their concerns.

WHAT OUGHT I TO DO?

I said that ethics is relevant to anyone who ever asks the question 'what ought I to do?' or 'would this be right?' To ask the question indicates that there can be no morality without a choice between alternatives: there would be no moral problems if a person's behaviour were completely determined by external agencies. Morality concerns values. A moral choice is a decision for the better alternative; an immoral choice is a decision for the worse alternative. Morality is not concerned with the behaviour of floods or behaviour towards bricks and mortar (Barrow 1981: 169). It is concerned with behaviour that is the result of a decision about conduct among and in relation to sentient persons.

When we say 'you *ought* to do something' or 'I *should* do something' there is always a value component embedded in the statement, but it may be a legal value rather than an ethical value. Law and morality are distinct, particularly from an ethical point of view. It may be legal to insist that all children ought to attend class, but is it ethical when one child is in mortal fear of being bullied by the teacher? A legal act, for all the moral intentions underlying its framing, may be immoral in its execution. It is illegal for a 10-year-old child to stay away from school without permission, but there may be circumstances in which it is ethical, for instance if that child is the sole care-giver of an ill parent. Whether any law is ethically significant is a separate question. This disjunction does not mean that the law carries no moral weight. Laws are usually sanctioned on moral grounds. Compulsory education is legislated to prevent exploitation of children and truancy.

The 'What ought I to do?' question may also be a prudential one. A prudential decision usually considers what is in *my* best interests. 'I ought to lose weight' has no consequences for anyone else other than me, nor does it fit easily under the general principle of benevolence or non-maleficence, unless at the same time I donate the money I save by eating less to the starving children in Africa. If redistributing unequal wealth is my reason for losing weight, then dieting can take on a moral dimension, but once again, the ethics of the action have a different significance from the prudence of the action. Ethics presumes that in considering what I ought to do, I take into consideration the rights and interests of others.

IS THERE A DIFFERENCE BETWEEN ETHICS AND MORALITY?

In ordinary language, morality is often associated with personal life, particularly sexual habits and rules. Most philosophers use the word 'ethics' to mean the philosophical study of morality, making it a higher order of reflection. Ethics is usually held to differ from morality in going beyond asking the practical question 'What ought I to do here and now?'

to examine such moral questions within a broader, more schematic or theoretical perspective. That is one way of making the distinction between ethics and morality. Ricoeur (1992: 169–239) distinguishes between the ethical aim and the moral norm. The first is based on an Aristotelian heritage in which ethics is defined by its aiming at the 'good life' and the second by a Kantian orthodoxy where morality is defined by the obligation to respect the norm. He (Ricoeur 1992: 170) argues that

- in order to be moral one must first be ethical;
- the ethical aim must pass through the 'sieve' of the norm; and
- whenever the norm leads to impasses in practice, it is legitimate to appeal to the aim.

Ethics on Ricoeur's distinction is not a 'science of morality'. It does not pretend to answer questions, nor to lay down a comprehensive rule of conduct, but to examine moral questions with a view to determining the good life. The first and last chapters of this book are mainly concerned with ethics, and the intervening chapters are concerned with moral practices in schools that raise ethical questions, often by presenting impasses or confronting our moral assumptions. Throughout the book, 'ethics' and 'morality' can be seen as two interconnecting ends of the same spectrum, starting with the general abstractions and moving through the immediate and practical back to the theoretical, so that the reader can judge current norms against current aims, to consider ways of improving them for a more ethical society.

CONCEPTS AND CONCEPTIONS OF ETHICS

'Persons' is a cultural construct linked to legal, political and ethical concerns. In earlier centuries slaves or women were regarded more as possessions than persons, and were similarly excluded from ethical or legal rights. Consider whether animals could be said to behave morally or ethically. Would they have to be considered persons? Self-aware? Rational? Do you consider that all the people in your school have an equal right to personhood? Normal citizen rights are denied to criminals and psychotics, but not to students under 18 or animals. Should this be the case? Imagine that you are organizing an international culture tour and a student comes up saying that they cannot go because they cannot get a passport. An Australian hermaphrodite was denied a birth certificate, and therefore voting rights and a passport, because the doctors could not call her/him either a male or a female. This essentially denies that individual the rights of personhood and, interestingly enough, removes him/her from the province of state control.

A great deal of what it means to be a person is to understand that there are good and bad ways to share the world with other persons, whose intentionality is like our own in that they too have world-views, self-concepts, projects, needs, desires, claims and so on. The sophistication required to see oneself as separate from and yet similar to others would seem to require at least language and a basic rationality that connects the concepts. Our languages are also ways of making sense of shared practices, and over time, abstract concepts evolve which bind those understandings and practices together so that, for instance, societies develop a word 'murder' to distinguish intentional and sanctioned killing (as in war, capital punishment or euthanasia where it is allowed) from that which is not sanctioned, or 'bullying' to identify certain intimidatory processes that go beyond playful tussles.

These very concepts themselves make some basic presumptions that good and bad are in some way distinguishable, and that such a distinction ought to be maintained and constantly refined (Kovesi 1978). As humans who command language, we set up schemata or frames or structures of meaning which represent the objective world, and tie things in that objective world together formally through rational connections. In ethics, we build up a rational frame composed of concepts such as good, honesty, justice, merit, blame and bullying, which help us to see connections between certain types of action and practices and for which often tacitly we generalize rules for good and bad behaviour through social agreements.

If you find Ricoeur's distinction between ethics and morality a little confusing, a related idea was expressed by John Rawls (1971) as the basis of his theory of justice. He proposed that ethics, the study of moral rules to determine the good life, is best understood as a concept embodied in a number of alternative conceptions. Even the a-rational and non-verbal newborn baby pulls together various sensations to develop notions of hunger, discomfort and pain. Humans seem to share a concept of fairness, even across cultures. But as you may have discovered when discussing different cases with colleagues, what we mean by 'fairness' differs from person to person. We need concepts to pull our ideas together. Conceptions, in a nicely punning way, are the concepts made flesh, the way we use them everyday. Some concepts, like 'furniture' or 'vegetables', tie physical things together; others, like 'intelligence', may tie together other concepts or ideas, such as 'cleverness' and 'success' – but in both cases they gain their meaning in experiential contexts.

Rawls argues that the concept of justice transcends cultural traditions, but its conceptions do not. Because conceptions of justice are so tightly connected with practices, they vary from one culture to the next, and sometimes within the same culture. Conceptions are sets of beliefs and motivations that more or less systematically cohere around a few central properties or core features that need not be the same for every person, place or era. What the several conceptions of fairness have in common is not their core features, but only the overall function of the concept. I would not be tempted, as Lawrence Kohlberg was, to go out and seek empirical evidence that ethical concepts such as justice are universal, but it does make sense to assume that humans generally have a social need to divide actions into fair and unfair actions, and to that extent moral concepts are universal. A notion of honesty, for instance, is a logical and practical prerequisite of language. If we could not assume that people could normally be trusted to tell the truth, then speech would be useless.

Kovesi (1978) discusses at some length the place of these moral notions in our language, dividing all our concepts into formal and material elements. What makes an action 'bullying' as opposed to 'exerting power'? The material act of exerting power over someone need not be defined as bullying; if it happens in a socially sanctioned setting such as sport, or the classroom, even if the behaviour is in each case equal. There has to be an element of coercion for the moral term to be used appropriately. Kovesi (1978: 14) would say that the element of moral disapproval, that is, an appeal to the concept of 'not-good', is the necessary formal element of bullying, while the material act of exerting power is necessary but not sufficient to provide the ethical element. The simple way of saying this is that 'bullying' is a moral notion, while exerting power over another person is not. There are even formal elements of moral disapproval in the word 'dirt' which in our culture make the same material element of sand 'dirt' when it is on the floor, but not when it is on the beach, or custard 'dirt' when it is on your shirt but not when it is in a full plate. To put this another way, 'dirt' and 'bullying' are abstracted ethical concepts, tied to culturally specific specifications of behaviour or practice called 'conceptions' which are linked to moral norms like wiping feet on entering a house or behaving with courtesy to weaker persons.

Since the 1970s we have become aware that we define actions within schemata or frames or structures which give them meaning (Kuhn 1972; Berger and Luckmann 1967). Most of our concepts are an essentially contested matter, which is always open to debate and contention by people coming from different social contexts, because they will 'see' the same behaviours under a different ethos, or in a different way. They will have different conceptions of the concept. Ethics is similarly an essentially contested concept. This apparent relativism is a feature of postmodernism. In postmodern theories and critical theory, we are urged to expose our own assumptions or those of others to constant critical scrutiny. This is not to deny the importance of looking for the facts within a particular frame of reference, like researching into the relation between self-esteem and substance abuse in schools, which will require fixed definitions of self-esteem and substance abuse, usually within a psychological theory. But such stability is now commonly viewed as a temporary state, a deliberate setting aside of any alternative conceptions which might be present but would interfere with the exactness required of scientific research.

All concepts, even those we take for granted as 'self-esteem' and 'intelligence', are essentially contestable; that is, they can be taken aside and exposed to questioning within a particular frame. The lack of an essential or grounded meaning for 'good' or 'bad', however, does not make ethics a random or an anarchistic matter. It still has a common function which is to define the ways in which human beings can best work together in a social community, even a sub-community like a school. What makes ethics more than a matter of mere 'intuition' or haphazard choice is that it is connected by these common concepts, which means that we can talk about our different conceptions by using a vocabulary of shared concepts, showing by examples what we mean by our conceptions. This book offers a rational conception of morality because I assume that we can discuss our different conceptions and understand those differences through elaboration and justification.

ALTERNATIVE CONCEPTIONS OF MORALITY

Beck (1994: 21) and Nozick (1989) assume the existence of certain eternal ethical verities. Traditional views of philosophy present the two main ethical positions as those of the Aristotelians versus the Platonists, the utilitarians versus the Kantians, or perhaps the consequentialists versus the deontologists (Stout 1988; Strike *et al.* 1988; Frankena 1963). I will present these positions very briefly in the final chapter. I do not want to deny their importance in structuring the way that we think and talk about moral behaviour. However, I believe that in a postmodern era, it is not useful to treat them as oppositional theories, but as theories that simply pick up different aspects of morality. The discussion about essentially contested conceptions of morality, including the rational conception of morality I am offering here, is necessarily conversational and tentative (MacIntyre 1981:6–8).

Wren (in Noam and Wren 1993: 80) identifies six current conceptions of morality:

- the teleological conception of morality which conceives of morality as an overriding concern for some objective, large-scaled good or value, such as the happiness of humankind, beauty or the glory of God
- the juridical conception of morality which thinks of morality in terms of systematic laws, obligations and universally reciprocal connections between rights and duties
- the self-actualization conception of morality, which regards human life and social relationships in terms of the self and its qualities, be they stable (the static version, which stresses virtuous dispositions) or changing (the dynamic version, which stresses development)

- the proceduralist conception which emphasizes the structural aspects and procedures of either deliberation (the intellectual version) or choice (the voluntarist version) in moral decisions
- the intuitionist conception of morality, in which moral values and principles are thought to be directly perceivable, in the same fashion that self-evident propositions or primitive sense qualities are immediately apprehended
- the romantic conception of morality, which rebels against most or even all social institutions and other structures as enslaving, puerile and ultimately immoral, and conceives of morality as liberation into a kind of cultivated artlessness.

Most teachers and administrators will identify with at least one of these, but it is more likely that they will profess to sharing more than one. Wren (1993: 81) reduces them to two major groups which he calls, rather oddly, the deontic and ethical forms of morality, the first being more extra-moral, a social function, and the second more intra-moral, reflecting the personal domain. The central features of the deontic group, he says, are keyed to the notion of right action (relatively impersonal features such as justice, judgements, criteria of fairness, duties, rights, claims and so on) and it therefore includes the juridical, proceduralist and intuitionist conceptions. The teacher who identifies with this will probably place more emphasis on the development of students as good citizens with a sense of civic duty. The ethical group (teleological, self-actualizing and romantic) is so called because its central features are keyed to the various personal notions of the good (such as happiness, self-actualization, personal excellence, authenticity, autonomy and other forms of human flourishing) – notions that characterize the ethos or character of one's culture as well as one's self but will probably be favoured by the teacher who seeks students' personal happiness.

On reflection, the distinction between ethical and deontic moralities is useful for certain purposes but too dualistic to maintain as an absolute distinction, because it does not account for the inter-dependence between the intra-moral and extra-moral. It does not allow for the fact, to use our earlier terminology, that concepts are built up from conceptions, and conceptions make sense only in terms of concepts. I would prefer to refer to the private and public aspects of morality, but am wary of setting up as artificial a dualism as that between the intra-moral and extra-moral. Private and public, intra-moral and extra-moral, ethical and deontic aspects of morality, while they may be separated out temporarily for discussion, do not exist independently of each other but build on each other. An autonomous or self-actualized person must have a personal commitment to public duty for it to be meaningful for them. They are two interdependent aspects of ethics, like the two sides of the same coin.

We can move in two different directions to tie the two faces together – towards the arena of practice (which Wren would call extra-moral) or towards the notion of the responsible self, the intra-moral aspect, which directs action.

Many philosophers these days prefer to present tripartite theories of philosophy which seem to lend themselves more easily to a conversation about differences rather than a conflict between them. Beck (1994) names caring as the central concern of ethics, but says it is justified by both deontological and consequentialist arguments. Strike and Ternasky (1993: 13–66) distinguish an Aristotelian perspective, a liberal democratic tradition and a feminist perspective. Robert Nozick (1989: 151–6) similarly points to three basic stances to value questions: the egoistic, which approximates to Wren's intra-moral or ethical position; the absolute, which corresponds partly to the deontic or extra-moral position and which Nozick favours as being the closest we can approximate to a concept; and then the relational, which connects the first two stances.

If morality is rational, then we as rational and reflective human beings will try to fit it into a coherent structure so that we can more easily see how different aspects fit together. But we can put it into such a structure only from a particular stance or point of view, through our own conceptions, no matter how general or universal we try to make it.

By describing moral behaviour as a deliberate decision among alternative values, I locate it in the person's intentions rather than in the act itself and therefore my own stance focuses more on the dialectic process than Wren's, Beck's or Nozick's. I believe that we are continually making meaning, and that our structures are continually undergoing refinement and change. Behaviour that has become habitual may well not mark a change in meaning, but I can exhibit the same behaviour in a specific situation after a period of twenty years for very different reasons. The values that govern a decision are frequently quite different from those that announce themselves in the act. As I said, exerting power may or may not be classified as bullying, meaning that the moral dimension of the same act is constantly open to question. A student may be polite to a teacher, not because he respects the teacher, but because he wants to win some favour or privilege which the teacher can bestow, so the same behaviour can be ethical or unethical, depending on how one views it. As we shall see in examples throughout the book, behaviour is often highly ambiguous in its moral message. Some people argue that because one can never observe a private intention, morality must rest in some more public domain, whether it is social purpose or public acts. That is why moral acts should in principle be justifiable, because as a social act they are constantly negotiable.

Only certain kinds of reasons can count as moral reasons (Warnock 1971; Peters 1973) and they are mostly those that deal with the interface between the public and private aspects of personhood, the individual and the social. When we look out at the world we are aware of everything on the outside of our face as being external to us, even the behaviour and intentions of other people. This is what Wren (1990) called the extra-moral conception. As persons, we are at the same time self-conscious, aware of what is going on internally within us, 'behind the eyes' as it were, and no one else can see what is going on behind our eyes – the intra-moral conception. There is a way of describing moral behaviour through this external gaze or objective focus as if it was separate from us, and yet another focus which looks at our intentions, our internal structures of beliefs which we could term 'subjective' as, like our personal experience of pain, it can be known only to others by inference and generalization from external actions and shared social practices.

Think of the difference between a mistake and an accident (Austin 1975), or between a hope and an expectation (Illich 1972). I see a student in the playground and call out 'Tom!' but it turns out to be William. I have made a mistake, which is a subjective experience. If, on the other hand, I accidentally bump into a student, and the student, thinking I am chastising her, bursts into tears, I would have described her reaction as a causally described objective event, an accident. In the former, one's subjective reasons for acting or one's intentions are considered; in the latter, a more externally focused prediction of the objective consequences of one's actions. The distinction is often inbuilt into much of our language without our realizing it but it is not one that we will use again in this book until the conclusion.

A TRIADIC TAXONOMY OF ETHICS

Following this rather idiosyncratic use of 'subjective' and 'objective', two aspects of which are closely tied to traditional philosophical 'theories' of ethics usually referred to as deontology and utilitarianism, this book proposes a slightly different and very tentative taxonomy of approaches to ethics which incorporates three aspects as jointly necessary to consideration of any ethical action. While the main framework of the taxonomy is initially triadic, I will argue throughout the book that for moral growth and maturity it takes the form of an evolving spiral in which there is no prior value or end point. The taxonomy consists of the following:

1 Consistency: a 'subjective' aspect in which one internalizes practice to see it as intentional. Here ethical action is deliberate, chosen, shaped and made justifiable by the personal coherence of internalized rules, meaning and values.
2 Consequences: the 'objective' aspect of ethics which sees practice as

externalized individual or social behaviour, in terms of its causes and consequences.

3 Care in which the carer attends to the cared-for in a special mode of non-selective attention or engrossment which extends outward across a broad web of relations. It is a holistic and responsive making of reciprocal connections in order to help others in a special act of receptivity.

Consistency – the subjective model of ethics

Any theory or frame that holds that there are degrees of being ethical, or that one's actions can be more or less ethical, must presume some form of hierarchy or developmental model. The one with which most educators will be familiar is the Piagetian or neo-Kantian model proposed by Lawrence Kohlberg (1981,1984). He developed the Piagetian notion of thought as interiorized action, leading from concrete to formal operations, from egocentrism to rational autonomy. This model suffers from the common criticism of Piagetian theory (see Thomas 1992 and Siegal 1991) that in focusing on the self-legislating moral subject who constructs their own rules and schemata, it ignores the social and cultural aspects of development. However, it serves our current need to focus on the interiorized or 'subjective' aspects of ethics.

As a good Piagetian, Kohlberg believed that moral judgement and moral behaviour were conceptually as well as causally reciprocal, two moments of a single personal unity, and that moral unity was the cognitive career of an individual subject or self. This is consistent with a constructivist epistemology, in which language is tied to and built up from interacting with a physical reality. Each individual moves through reflection on disturbances to equilibrium from an egocentric and concrete level to a universal and abstract level of reason, through the three distinct levels of moral development – pre-conventional, conventional and post-conventional (see Table 1.1) (Kohlberg 1981, 1984; Sommers 1989).

Teachers will be familiar with this rational developmental model because it underpins most national curricula, requiring students to abstract from the particularity of their circumstances to the universal principles apparently underlying each subject area. For Kohlberg's moral development, the principle of respect for persons defines the moral sphere. The more consistent one's actions are with one's self-constructed principles, the more ethical one is. The principle of respect for persons is one of justice, requiring the subject to consider all persons as morally equal, which is also a matter of consistency. It means that you must do unto others as you would they should do unto you, a notion that Kant and Hare refer to as universalizability.

Table 1.1 Kohlberg's levels and stages in moral development

Levels	Basis of moral judgement	Stages of development
I	Moral value resides in external, quasi-physical happenings, in bad acts, or in quasi-physical needs rather than in persons and standards.	*Stage 1* Obedience and punishment orientation. Unquestioning egocentric deference to power or a superior, or a trouble-avoiding set. Objective responsibility.
Pre-conventional	Good and bad defined in terms of the physical or hedonistic consequences of action – punishment, reward, or exchange of favours.	*Stage 2* Naively egoistic orientation. Right action is that instrumentally satisfying the self's needs and occasionally others'. Awareness of relativism of value to each actor's needs and perspective. Naive egalitarianism and orientation to exchange and reciprocity. Fairness is interpreted in a physical, pragmatic way. 'You scratch my back and I'll scratch yours.'
II	Moral value resides in performing good or right roles, in maintaining the conventional order and the expectations of others.	*Stage 3* Good-boy orientation. Orientation to approval and to pleasing and helping others. Conformity to stereotypical images of majority or natural role behaviour, and judgement by intentions.
Conventional		*Stage 4* Orientation to 'doing duty', showing respect for authority and maintaining the given social order for its own sake. Regard for the learned expectations of others.
III	Moral value resides in conformity by the self to shared or shareable standards, rights or duties.	*Stage 5* Contractual legalistic orientation. Recognition of an arbitrary element in rules or expectations for the sake of agreement. Duty defined in terms of social contract, general avoidance of violation of the will or rights of others, and majority will and welfare.
Post-conventional		*Stage 6* Conscience or principle orientation not only to ordained social rules but to principles of choice involving appeal to logical universality and consistency. Directing agents are conscience, mutual respect and trust as part of the principle of justice or equal respect for persons.

On the rational consistency view, lying is always wrong, whatever the circumstances. Universalizability means that whenever one uses the term 'ought', one must be ready to apply it to all similar situations, for all persons. Whatever one person is morally obliged to do in a particular situation, all others in comparable situations must also be obligated to do. This has been criticized because it is abstracted away from the complexities of real and experienced situations. Generalizing from one experience to the other is the most usual way that we make meaning, and we encourage students to do it in schools, but it can be dangerous if the conceptions so formed become rigid and closed on the basis of past experiences, for instance in racial stereotyping or a definition of a student as stupid.

Consequences – the objective view

There are problems with the efficacy of any system which become logically consistent without contradictions, because, as Gödel pointed out in his attack on formal logical systems, such a system becomes self-justifying and circular, an idealistic system of principles which may have no direct relation to our practices (Bourdieu 1977; Toulmin 1972). If ethics were only a set of ideas, of conceptions or principles that hang together, we would not know what to do when those principles came into conflict. You might believe in a principle of honesty, but if a parent comes to you and asks whether a child should be promoted to the next class, you might have to hesitate before saying outright that the child could not manage intellectually. Those who believe that ethics is a matter of building a consistent system of rules or principles cannot evade this problem by building a more complicated system of qualifiers into the system, or by ranking the rules in some hierarchical and abstracting structure to resolve conflicts between them, for that only pushes the resolution of issues back to a more abstract set of ideals.

 The consequences approach places its emphasis on what can be observed and agreed upon intersubjectively and, like utilitarianism, it focuses on the scientific or measurable aspects of morality. It is also a teleological view – that is, it does not start with rules but with goals. Actions are assessed by the extent to which they reach those goals. Such an ethics is not relative or subjective, but will judge lying as bad in some circumstances and good in another, depending on its consequences. It looks at cause and effect rather than at principles.

Many educators tend to operate using a consequentialist position for most of their decisions (Kirby *et al.* 1992). Robin Barrow (1975) focuses almost exclusively on this consequentialist view of ethics and it is he who also offers some fairly exclusive criticism of utilitarianism. Peter Singer (1983) has espoused a view of ethics that is self-confessedly utilitarian: it has as one of its main features an expanding circle of concern for the consequences of one's action. A short summary of utilitarianism is that it attempts to provide a felicific calculus for each action, that is, it will draw up all the possible beneficial consequences, weigh them against the possible harmful consequences and carry out the action that promotes the greatest happiness or well-being for the greatest number of people. It is called 'objective' because it promotes the belief that such a calculus can be agreed upon, that different people can see the consequences of any action as if they were real in the world. It has been criticized for reducing persons to atomistic items, for presumably all people count as one, but it is the dominant one in use in schools, especially for accountability purposes.

If one believes, as I do, that the objective and subjective aspects of each action or intention are different views of the same behaviour, along a continuum, then the traditional dualisms dissolve. We look at an action from one of these points of view for certain purposes, and one is not *essentially* more appropriate than another. An objective theory of ethics is not inconsistent in its movement up a hierarchy with Kohlbergian ethics because, from the subjective point of view, a young child starts with an immediate egocentric and concrete concern for pleasure and pain as immediate benefits and costs and builds up from that calculus to a wider awareness of short-term and long-term consequences to a concern for abstract consequences. From an objective perspective of the same action or intention, the person is moving towards rational decision-making by shifting from the consequences of behaving in a certain way to the more conceptual consequences of breaking or following a rule. At the level of autonomy, being inconsistent with principle is on a Kantian account logically impossible for any individual (thus the categorical imperative) and physically uncomfortable because it indicates a lack of integrity and thus 'pulls at the conscience'. From an objective or scientific point of view, inconsistency would make any individual action difficult to explain, because it would be less predictable. The objective view of a person would value consistency not for its internal coherence, but because, like a logical theory, it allows someone to predict what the consequences of any familiar sequence of events would be for a particular person who is consistent in their behaviour.

The consequential point of view by itself is inadequate as a foundation for ethical behaviour, if it presumes that the greatest good for the greatest possible number could be discovered independently of any conceptual structure or idealistic structure. Such a structure is necessary to provide the criteria for good or bad consequences. Consequentialism requires an abstracted and coherent system of rules to avoid the reductionism and oversimplification of empiricism (Bourdieu 1977). As Kant said, percepts without concepts are empty, and concepts without percepts are blind.

The two sit side by side, the right-hand extra-personal side offering an objective way of looking at the world, the left-hand side offering the 'subjective' or inter-personal route of intentionality and reasons. They are not mutually exclusive, but different aspects of the same things, two sides of the same coin, like a paper folded in half, with a different description on each side of the paper.

We can superimpose the utilitarian notion of development over a Kohlbergian model, and say that as the concern with the physical reality moves further away from physical punishment or consequences to conceptualized sanctions according to rules and principles, the 'objective' aspects of morality become more and more internalized into a 'subjective' conceptual schema which constitutes a moral self. When Lipman (1985: 27) speaks of universalizing, he reminds us of the compatibility of consistency requirements with consequentialism:

> Let's say you are considering doing something, and you wonder if it would be the right thing to do. One test that has been offered is the test of what is called *universalization*. Simply put, you could say to yourself *'What would happen if everyone were to do what I am now considering doing?'* Then, according to this view, if you would not be willing to live in a world where everyone else were to do this, you should not do it yourself. On the other hand, if you would want a world where everyone felt obligated to act this way, then the action you contemplate is the right action for you and you should do it . . .
>
> Notice that when one universalizes, one does not avoid the test of consequences. When it is asked, 'wouldn't it be better if everyone were to act this way?' presumably one means, 'wouldn't the consequences of everyone's doing this be better than the consequences of their not doing it?' Another way of putting this would be to say that when one does not universalize, the test of consequences applies merely to one's own specific, singular act. When one universalizes, the test of consequences applies to the *rule* of one's actions, and that rule is one to which everyone must conform.

Table 1.2 indicates how, as a person internalizes the rules that they construct both through concrete operations and the acquisition of social practices through language, the physical consequences of their actions become less and less easy to distinguish from the linguistic and logical structures of knowledge and belief. What counts as a consequence becomes more and more abstract as it is forced to cover a wider and more complex set of actual and possible circumstances.

Echoing my earlier concern that 'theories of ethics' might often over-simplify what is a fairly complex web of related concepts, Kleinberger (1982) pointed out a shift in Kohlberg's hierarchy in what counts as the proper focus of moral judgement. It begins by looking at the beneficent

Table 1.2 The compatibility between consequences and consistency

Subjective – internal consistency	Objective – consequences
1. Punishment and obedience – personal immediate pleasure/pain	Short-term consequences to one's own self, often immediately physical
2. Instrumental relativist	Considering the short-term consequences of an action in a small sphere (the Canter method)
3. Interpersonal concordance or 'good boy – nice girl'	Consequences within a small social group which imposes sanctions against anti-social behaviour
4. Society-maintaining	Social cost/benefit of breaking or maintaining the law; counting the social costs of any action – accountability within a social system
5. Social contract	Maximizing the social good
6. Universal ethical principle – do unto others as you would they should do unto you	The greatest good for the greatest possible number

consequences of behaviour under given circumstances. It then shifts to overt behaviour in conformity with moral norms and duties. At the post-conventional stage, it focuses on morally meritorious motives and reasons for acting. Kleinberger concludes that there is no point in empirically measuring moral stages. Your answer as to whether a person is ethical or not will depend on why you are looking, or what you are looking at. A parallel situation would be to try to measure a student's progress in literacy throughout their formal schooling. The criteria shift dramatically from writing and spelling correctly at early primary level to mastering niceties of style and complexities of genre in post-compulsory schooling.

The interesting aspect of Kleinberger's conclusion is that although he isolates out different markers of morality, the different aspects are still tied to a developmental model of self, a growth towards autonomy (in Kohlberg's phrase) or a growth towards personhood. That construction of self can be aided by interaction with a physical reality, but it also becomes an initiation into what others think of us through the social sanctions of praise and blame and the narratives that we construct of ourselves as our own self-construct develops. In education, this aspect of personal growth is rarely taken into account for university entry or exam results, but it is often noted both in report writing and the awarding of school prizes. The development of an autonomous and transcendental self that can move beyond social conventions is presumed by both constructivist and principled ethics. This construction of self is not acceptable to those postmodernists or behaviourists who believe, for very different reasons, that the self is either a myth, a ghost in the machine (Dennett 1984, 1987) or another self-interested construction of the liberal tradition (Foucault 1972).

If teachers believe in a collective aim of education rather than an individualistic aim, they will be inclined to believe that the distinction between physical consequences and conceptual consistency becomes less easy to make. Enculturation into a particular social community's progress on the hierarchy makes the consequences become less physical and more conceptual and they become less distinguishable from the internalized structures or schemata that shape any individual's construction of reality. The described reality becomes the reality. When you believe in the greatest good for the greatest number of people, the consequences for your own person are fairly unimportant in the universal scheme of things. Kohlberg makes one of the measures of having reached the sixth level of autonomy, where one acts on principle rather than self-interest, that one will sacrifice one's own life for the sake of a principle. This model of increasingly abstract concepts which enable people to manipulate formal concepts, such as ethical principles, without having to experiment with them physically to see what the consequences are, will be familiar to any teacher who has struggled with the national curriculum, especially a curriculum that has an autonomous citizen as one of its main objectives. So why can't we just look at the objective and subjective aspects of ethics along this developmental model and fit all our ethical judgements into that?

The hierarchical model which combines consequentialism and a move towards logical consistency is inadequate because it is still basically a modernist model of the moral subject. Writers such as Foucault and Derrida have done much to deconstruct the assumptions that our logical models are a guarantee of truth. To put it rather pompously, one can only arrive at the 'truth' of maximizing benefits or of universalizability within a frame of transcendental arguments which presume categorical imperatives, moral laws that cannot be disobeyed. I should explain that I am not criticizing the subjective model for its cultural constraints. While Kant was a devout Christian and saw no need to further justify the foundational principle of justice, the definitive notion of universalizability or always treating others as you would like them to treat you is not limited to a Christian view. Confucius said, 'What you do not like when done to yourself, do not do unto others.' The prophet Muhammad said, 'Do unto others what you'd love to have yourself.' In Buddhist doctrine this becomes: 'Hurt not others in ways that you yourself would find hurtful.' The Koran preaches that you cannot attain righteousness until you give others of what you love to have for yourselves; and finally the Talmud says, 'What is hateful to you, do not do to your fellow man.' These are all universalizability principles that would seem, like concepts, to transcend cultural values.

What is limited for both the consequentialist and the consistency position is that their strength in providing an impartial and distanced form of cognitive accountability is also their weakness. A bit like Rawls and Quine, and certainly like Piaget, they presume that *thinking within* a coherent system of abstract ideas will help us settle our disputes. But in a complex world, competing coherent systems will require ongoing negotiation for the competing merits of different conceptions of ethics which could each be consistent with their own abstracted concepts but are incompatible with one another (Lyotard 1988).

Let us presume that an Aboriginal teacher and a senior ministry official disagree about the ethics of a specific educational practice, that is, counting as enrolled at school those Aboriginal students who have temporarily gone walkabout. They can agree about the value of justice and maximizing benefit, but their own cultural practices and understanding about those basic shared concepts will be so different that a rational resolution of their differences will not be engineered by logical argument alone. What happens to empathy or concern for others' feelings?

Moral sensitivity appears to be as central to moral behaviour as moral rationality and knowledge. Simone Weil (1951: 115) wrote:

> In the first legend of the Grail, it is said that the Grail . . . belongs to the first comer who asks the guardian of the vessel, a king three-quarters paralysed by the most painful wound, 'What are you going through?'
>
> The love of our neighbour in all its fullness simply means being able to say to him: 'What are you going through?' It is a recognition that the sufferer exists, not only as a unit in a collective, or a specimen from the social category labelled 'unfortunate,' but as a man, exactly like us.

Such sensitivity seems to be a necessary part of becoming moral. Any teacher or parent knows the difficulty of imparting such sensitivity in the young. There are no algorithms or quick-fix rules. It takes a lot of work, a bit like music practice or sports practice. Many of the same things have to be pointed out more than once and transfer to different but similar situations is not always immediate. A certain amount of practical knowledge of cause and effect, the probability of good and bad consequences, is required for the acquisition of any concept and that accrues rather slowly over time; similarly with understanding the likely feelings, wishes, needs, etc., of other people. People with the best of intentions often do terrible or thoughtless things because they do not realize the physical or psychological consequences of their options. Sometimes they do not even consider or realize all their options. This is what Hannah Arendt (1978: 4–5) referred to as 'the banality of evil', where German soldiers carried out their orders without thinking about them. The many daily actions and reactions that form conscience, knowledge, habits, ideas, factual knowledge, feelings and all the things that go into the way you behave, operate as a holistic impression, almost an intuition, a right-brain feeling. Hearing people talk about feelings and how one should be sensitive to the feelings of others can help to raise certain matters above the threshold of awareness. Equally one has to have experienced ethical sensitivity before one can really understand what it could be.

Care – the function of responsibility

Ethical sensitivity seems closely related to care. The two great comprehensive ethical systems – Kant's ethics of duty and utilitarianism – put enormous emphasis on human rationality. Care, argued Gilligan, is not a matter of logic or justice, but more a matter of caring within a circle or web of responsibility. She says (1982) this different construction of the moral problem by many women may be seen as the critical reason for their failure to develop within the constraints of Kohlberg's system regarding all constructions of responsibility as evidence of a conventional moral understanding. Kohlberg defines the highest stages of moral development as deriving from a reflective understanding of human rights. The morality of rights differs from the morality of responsibility in its emphasis on separation rather than connection, in its consideration of the individual rather than the relationship as primary. Gilligan illustrates this difference between separation and connection with two responses to interview questions about the nature of morality. The first comes from a 25-year-old man, one of the participants in Kohlberg's study:

[*What does the word morality mean to you?*] Nobody in the world knows the answer. I think it is recognizing the rights of the individual, the rights of other individuals, not interfering with those rights. Act as fairly as you would have them treat you. I think it is basically to preserve the human being's right to existence. I think that is the most important. Secondly, the human being's right to do as he pleases, again without interfering with somebody else's rights.

[*How have your views on morality changed since the last interview?*] I think I am more aware of an individual's rights now. I used to be looking at it strictly from my point of view, just for me. Now I think I am more aware of what the individual has a right to.

Gilligan (1982) quotes Kohlberg's comment on this man's response as illustrative of the principled conception of human rights which exemplifies his fifth and sixth stages.

Moving to a perspective outside of that of his society, he identifies morality with justice (fairness, rights, the Golden Rule), with recognition of the rights of others as these are defined naturally or intrinsically. The human being's right to do as he pleases without interfering with somebody else's rights is a right prior to social legislation.

In the same study, Kohlberg interviewed a 25-year-old woman, a third-year law student:

[*Is there really some correct solution to moral problems, or is everybody's opinion equally right?*] No, I don't think everybody's opinion is equally right. I think that in some situations there may be opinions that are equally valid, and one could conscientiously adopt one of several courses of action. But there are other situations in which I think there are right and wrong answers, that sort of inhere in the nature of existence, of all individuals here who need to live with each other to live. We need to depend on each other, and hopefully it is not only a physical need but a need of fulfilment in ourselves, that a person's life is enriched by co-operating with other people and striving to live in harmony with everybody else, and to that end, there are right and wrong, there are things which promote that end and that move away from it, and in that way it is possible to choose in certain cases among different courses of action that obviously promote or harm that goal.

[*Is there a time in the past when you would have thought about these things differently?*] Oh yeah, I think that I went through a time when I thought that things were pretty relative, that I can't tell you what to do and you can't tell me what to do, because you've got your conscience and I've got mine. [*When was that?*] When I was in high school. I guess that it just sort of dawned on me that my own ideas changed and because my own judgement changed, I felt I couldn't judge another person's judgement. But now I think even when it is only the person himself who is going to be affected, I say it is wrong to the extent it doesn't cohere with what I know about human nature and what I know about you, and just from what I think is true about the operation of the universe, I could say I think you are making a mistake.

[*What led you to change, do you think?*] Just seeing more of life, just recognising that there are an awful lot of things that are common among people. There are certain things that you come to learn promote a better life and better relationships and more personal fulfilment than other things that in general tend to do the opposite, and the things that promote these things, you would call morally right.

Gilligan notes:

This response also represents a personal reconstruction of morality following a period of questioning and doubt, but the reconstruction of moral understanding is based not on the primacy and universality of universal rights, but rather on what she describes as a 'very strong sense of being responsible to the world.' Within this construction, the moral dilemma changes from how to exercise one's rights without interfering with the rights of others to how 'to lead a moral life which includes obligations to myself and my family and people in general.' The problem then becomes one of limiting responsibilities without abandoning moral concern. When asked to describe herself this woman says that she values 'having other people that I am tied to, and also having people that I am responsible to. I have a very strong sense of being responsible to the world, that I can't just live for my enjoyment, but just the fact of being in the world gives me an obligation to do what I can to make the world a better place to live in, no matter how small a scale that may be on.' Thus while Kohlberg's subject worries about people interfering with each other's rights, this woman worries about 'the possibility of omission, of your not helping others when you could help them.'
    ... [A feminine fifth] autonomous stage witnesses a relinquishing of moral dichotomies and their replacement with a 'feeling for the complexity and multi-faceted character of real people and real situations.' Whereas the rights conception of morality that informs Kohlberg's principled level (stages five and six) is geared to arriving at an objectively fair or just resolution to moral dilemmas upon which all rational persons could agree, the responsibility conception focusses instead on the limitations of any particular resolution and describes the conflicts that remain.

Women, Gilligan argued, often choose to react to a situation by trying to assess what action would cause least harm to all within the web of proximal relations, such as a family or a known community. They *respond* to the needs of others. Men tend, because they had been socialized into defining themselves as separate from other, to argue hierarchically in terms of their own rights, which is why Kohlberg had placed justice at the peak of his hierarchical model. Thus it becomes clear why a morality of rights and non-interferences may appear frightening to a woman in its potential justification of indifference and lack of concern. The ethic of care is not unconcerned with individual rights, the common good or community traditions, but it de-emphasizes these concepts and recasts them in terms of relation. From a masculine perspective, a morality of responsibility may appear inconclusive and diffuse, given its insistent contextual relativism, and it may appear that the structure of logic or cause gives a necessary shape to the ethic of care.

Buber (1961) distinguishes between two modes of meeting or ways of encountering other entities. We can meet each other in the I–thou mode, which is the way of relation, but we cannot live in that mode all the time (see also Noddings 1993: 47). Weil (1951: 115) describes this way of looking as attentive: 'The soul empties itself of all its contents in order to receive into itself the being it is looking at, just as he is, in all his truth. Only he who is capable of attention can do this.' It is neither possible nor desirable to inhabit the holistic care attitude all the time. It is just necessary to be aware that it is there, and to be open to it. We normally shift back into the I–it mode, in which we observe others or listen to what they say by assimilating it to pre-selected schemata.

Unlike those who propound the subjective and objective views of morality, Gilligan is not attempting to offer a new, fully developed moral theory. The psychology of women that has consistently been described as distinctive in its greater orientation towards relationships and interdependence implies a more contextual mode of judgement and a different moral understanding.

Richard Peters (1981: 111) suggests that the weakest aspect of Kohlberg's theory was not its inference of the moral inferiority of women, nor its neglect of other basic moral principles such as promise-keeping or truth-telling, but the omission of empathy, which requires more depth of description (lower-level content) and situational judgement than Kohlberg's hypothetical examples. Peters wanted to retain 'morality' as a classificatory term by means of which a form of interpersonal behaviour can be distinguished from custom, law, religious codes and so on.

He makes the following point about any moral system in which justice is regarded as the fundamental principle:

> When we talk about what is just or unjust, we are applying the formal rule of reason – that no distinction should be made without relevant differences, either to questions of distribution, when we are concerned about the treatment which different people are to receive or to commutative situations, when we are not concerned with comparisons but with questions of desert, as in punishment. In all such cases some criterion has to be produced by reference to which the treatment is to be based on *relevant* considerations. There must therefore be some further evaluative premise in order to determine relevance. Without such a premise, no decisions can be made about what is just on any substantive issue. In determining for instance what a just wage is, rele-

vant differences must be determined by reference to what people need, to what they contribute to the community and so on. To propose any such criteria involves evaluation.

(Peters 1981: 112)

This is a curiously postmodern concept from a philosopher whom many have dismissed as being locked into a traditional analytic framework. His writing is similar in this respect to Lawrence Blum who offers an ethic of 'altruistic responsiveness'. Blum (1980) notes that moral decisions are seldom made once and for all. They need to be made over and over again. Using the example of his three-and-a-half-year-old son Ben, who noticed a pin and took it to his mother, explaining that it might hurt his baby sister, Blum concludes that Ben felt a natural sense of connection with his sister, and did not need to appreciate or apply moral standards. 'All that is necessary is that the child understand the other child's state, believe that the other child will be made better off by her action, and have some altruistic sentiment or motivation toward the child' (Blum 1988: 319).

It throws the base for logic back to a community's shared values. Martin Heidegger (1927: 227) posited that *Sorge* or care as an ontological attribute is a prerequisite to reasonableness. When Gilligan (1982: 12) accuses Erik Erikson (1964,1968) of drawing up his eight-stage hierarchy of psychosocial development from a masculine model and for not incorporating in his hierarchy the gender difference, she does not recognize that he incorporates what he describes (in Gilligan 1982: 98) as a women's identity through intimacy rather than separation into his very first stage of child formation which is driven by a Heideggerian disposition to care. Caring about what happens in and to the world is a necessary prerequisite of any kind of serious inquiry for Erikson. The emphasis on contextuality and narrative moves the care frame outside an objectively measured one or a logically constructed one and is centred in the personal response. To care is to inhabit a Habermasian life-world, to be aware rather than reflective (Habermas 1990: 207).

Gilligan (in Gilligan, *et al.* 1990: 321ff.) similarly modified her initial differentiation from Kohlberg on the basis of gender differences to it being an ethic of responsibility or care as opposed to a Kohlbergian ethic of justice, or principles. In her different description of moral development,

> the moral problem arises from conflicting responsibilities rather than from competing rights and requires for its resolution a mode of thinking that is contextual and narrative rather than formal and abstract. This conception of morality as concerned with the activity of care centers moral development round the understanding of responsi-

bility and relationships, just as the conception of morality as fairness ties moral development to the understanding of rights and rules.

(Gilligan 1982)

Because the ethic of care focuses on response to the situation, it is more grounded in the perceptions of situations than the abstracted reflection and measurement of them required by either the consistency or consequences model. The strengths of the consistency and consequences approaches, namely that they invoke important forms of cognitive accountability, are at the same time their weakness in placing too much emphasis on rationality and too little on the immediate response, a way of seeing which is personal. While caring uses distinction as an instrument, it does not depend upon it for their meaning. A recognition of the differences in women's and men's experience and understanding expands our vision of maturity and points to the contextual nature of developmental truths. An ethic of care depends upon a different procedure from an ethic of consistency or consequences in moving beyond constructed theory (Hekman 1995: 3–8).

Does proposing care both as a prequisite of good thinking and judgement and of impressive teaching entail that care is in and of itself a form of thinking or judgement? Is another word for it 'thoughtful'? At least the notion of caring is less obviously logical and abstract. As Gilligan and Noddings present it, it is situational, responsive to context. What do we mean when we advise someone to take care? How is it related to the more sentimental notion of caring? The thesaurus indicates that care is related to anxiety, responsibility, being anxious, being careful. This is a common thread throughout many of those who write about the need for an ethical community to be a caring one (see Bateson 1994; Frankfurt 1988; Fuller 1992; Noddings 1984; Nussbaum 1990).

I will argue that the ethic of responsibility is needed for ethical practices to be meaningful because it is a holistic response rather than a distanced or analytic one. This ethic of responsibility or care picks up the etymology of responsibility as responding (Buber 1961), that is, it is one in which one responds to the concerns of others, not out of a sense of duty but out of a feeling of responsive mutuality. The apparent gender differences are more illusory than useful and the ethic of care or responding to the world situationally and holistically is as much an agent of conceptual development as it is a different manner of conceptualizing morally. The ethic of care is not superior to the consistency or consequences aspects – they are all necessary components of a dialogical and relational process of moral growth.

We need to understand the connections as well as the tensions between our desire for consistency, consequences and care. To illustrate their interdependence, I should like to borrow a metaphor from Lacan

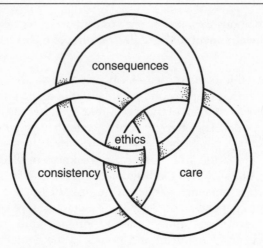

Figure 1.1 The Borromean knot of ethics

(1975: 112), that of the Borromean knot – interlocking rings such that when any one of the rings is cut, the entire interlocking system falls apart (see Figure 1.1).

What the Borromean knot particularly emphasizes is the fall from privilege of any one of the rings that constitute the knot. Neither consistency, consequences nor care provides adequate foundation for ethical decisions, but jointly they constitute the base for ethical decision-making. When we go through discussion of various cases, imagine what might be the ethical limitations of staying inside only one or two of the frames or circles.

For Noddings at least, the care perspective is the driving force behind the dialectic. It is whatever is responsible to the world of things and other persons at any given moment of personal growth. It might be simplistic to call this holistic driving force the self. This construction and evolution of a morally mature self in relation to others will be one of the features of this book which will argue that moral growth is possible only through continually dialectic reflection on the subjective and objective aspects of understanding.

THE USE OF DRAMATIC NARRATIVE

Our understanding of concepts, even those of consequences, consistency and care, rests, as we have argued, on our personal conceptions of it, and those personal conceptions are grounded in our shared agreements, our social practices, social codes, laws and practices which are an eclectic mixture of language, emotions and behaviours. To avoid notions of fixed or absolute structures, or of delivering ultimate truths, philosophers such as Plato, Sartre and Nietzsche grounded their philosophies in dramatic dialogues. I shall follow their example and move away from a scientific or logical approach which is limited by describing from either an objective or a subjective point of view. Narratives provide an opportunity to elicit moral reflection outside consolidated categories of reason (Haraway 1992; MacIntyre 1981).

The case studies I present in the following chapters are 'true' in the sense that they are grounded in particular instances that have happened, and they present the voices of the teachers and students concerned in the situations. The moral relationships they present are therefore not idealized or completely abstracted, as those in the carefully constructed 'cases' given, for instance, in Strike et al. (1988) seem to be. They arise from the stories volunteered and collected in graduate classes or from newspaper accounts, and the questions raised will invoke passions and imagination as well as reason.

The narratives or dramas will involve traditional conflicts between such issues as self-interest versus altruism, the law versus higher principles, efficiency versus persons, which Australian educators face daily. Often they will involve conflicts between different ethical values. It is a mistake to describe these conflicts as moral dilemmas, because dilemmas presume the choice is an X or Y decision and that to choose either will have undesirable consequences. The narratives are dramatic because they present the conflicts to be still resolved in one of any number of ways. This pragmatic approach urges conscious action based on deliberation and reflection, and the reflection is relational and holistic as much as rational or scientific.

Our ability to reason is an important factor in leading us away from arbitrary subjectivisms and an uncritical acceptance of the values of our society. As Singer concedes, it is an essential component of our moving away from a simply personal base to consider the Other, the basic ethical stance. Reason makes it possible for us to see ourselves from a wider perspective because

> by thinking about my place in the world, I am able to see that I am just one being among others, with interests and desires like others. I have a personal perspective on the world from which my interests are at the front and centre of the stage, the interests of my family and friends are close behind, and the interests of strangers are pushed to the back and side. But reason allows me to see that others have similarly subjective perspectives, and that from the point of view of the universe my perspective is no more privileged than theirs. Thus my ability to reason shows me the possibility of detaching myself from my own perspective and shows me what the universe might look like if I had no personal perspective.
>
> (Singer 1993: 229)

Romantics may argue that we could be mounted on what Singer (1993: 225) called an escalator of reason. He argues that, even though we need to step on it to help us survive and reproduce, if we step on it unthinkingly we may end up somewhere that creates a tension with other aspects of our nature. To that extent Singer supports Kant's picture of a tension between our capacity to reason and our more basic desires. So we have to maintain contact with our personal integrity, whatever it is that drives what we focus on to reason about, our bundle of changing values.

Like symbols in art forms, narratives reverberate within the personal as shared experiences which make meaning out of the world. They are part of *our* story as educationists, and as humans we are continually constructing and interpreting similar stories in our lived experiences. Through such stories, social change can be effected as previously silenced moral voices can be heard and analysed through the traditional ethical frames of consequences and consistency as well as care. This book encourages conversations about the issues raised here, because through conversations a community of inquiry can be set up (Burbules 1992).

This book therefore is about both personal commitment and moral reasoning, designed to help educators in particular to reason about their own practices. In the final chapter we will ask again whether reasoning about ethics allows for progress in ethics. In the intervening chapters, we will try to show how stepping on an escalator of reason does not necessarily lead away from consideration of personal commitment in relation to physical and personal consequences in what Singer calls the universe. We will use reason to discuss possible responses to ethical situations and the reasons for those responses. It is an evolving and expansive spiral of concern which reflects back onto a lived world, rather than escalating inexorably to a given conclusion.

Presenting a framework within which many people have traditionally made their ethical choices is not meant to constrain or thwart possible ethical choices. It is meant to be liberating by helping people to understand their own reasons for the ethical choices they must make daily, by thinking about them. It is my belief that ethics is founded on reasonableness, and that an educational administrator will be ethical to the extent to which they give serious consideration to these three aspects of any situation:

- What are the consequences, both short and long term, for me and others, and do the benefits of any possible action outweigh the harmful effects?
- Are all the agents in this situation being consistent with their own past actions and beliefs? That is, are they acting according to an ethical principle/ethical principles that they would be willing to apply in any

other similar situation? Are they doing to others as they would they would do unto them?

- Are they responding to the needs of others as human beings? Do they care about other people in this situation as persons with feelings like themselves?

Chapter 2

Beyond power

He never wants anything but what's right and fair; only when you come to settle what's right and fair, it's everything that he wants and nothing that you want. And that's his idea of a compromise. Give me the Brown compromise when I'm on his side.

Thomas Hughes, *Tom Brown's School Days* (1857: Pt 2, Ch. 2)

I repeat . . . that all power is a trust – that we are accountable for its exercise – that, from the people and for the people, all springs and all must exist.

Benjamin Disraeli, *Vivian Grey* (1826: Bk 6, Ch. 7)

The consequences, consistency and caring model that I developed in the preceding chapter still needs to be applied to lived experiences before it can be fully understood. If Kant, Rawls and Nozick each see the central notion of ethics to be a principle of justice or equity, and Bentham, Mill and Singer see it to be setting goals that maximize happiness, and Gilligan , Blum and Noddings see it to be preventing harm to others in a network of relations, it is only a concept of ethics that holds these three ways of looking at human action together. We may still have different conceptions that place different weightings on such aspects of ethics as honesty, abuse of power, equal respect for persons, scrupulously following the law, applying ethical principles, thinking of others.

What will be required throughout this book is for you as reader to reflect on your own presumptions and reactions to various situations and to develop the capacity to imagine yourself in the position of another. Notice that the act of imagining the point of view of another is not a Piagetian formal operation, but it does minimally require an awareness of the way you would act and an ability to distance yourself from it. When you were remembering the unfair situation, could you construct the thought experiment that would allow you to describe the same situation as fair? Would this ability to see things from another person's point of view have affected your actions in any way?

Kant would argue that we need a concept of fairness to understand what ethical practice means, and that the concept of fairness is a necessary organizational principle for ethics, much as time, space and causality are for scientific knowledge. However, both consequentialists and feminists would argue that there is nothing innate or *a priori* about such concepts. They are built historically out of social practices, and that is why different cultures build up different conceptions. Such concepts arise out of practices. For the consequentialists these practices arise from observing behaviour and associating words with such behaviour. Others, like Foucault, say that even observing something as a practice carries its own social assumptions. The problem of practices of power did not consist for Foucault in 'trying to dissolve them in the utopia of a perfectly transparent communication, but to give oneself the rules of law, the techniques of management, and also the ethics, the *ethos*, the practice of self which would allow these games of power to be played with a minimum of domination' (Foucault 1986: 129). Appealing to the Greek idea of *ethos*, Foucault goes beyond Kant in asserting that ethics is less about the provision of reasons than about practice, a way of being. For the Greeks a person with a good *ethos* was a person who was practising freedom (Foucault 1986: 117). However, even to engage in practice, practice in contrast with behaviour, requires a certain amount of self-awareness in relation to the other or the immediate community. This self-awareness involves understanding the 'rules' that one has constructed for oneself. His ethical position is not inconsistent with Gilligan's. Ethics is both a discourse and practice because language is a way of life embedded in history and culture. Remember Kovesi's contention that ethics itself was a formal sort of scheme within which ethical concepts were related.

Foucault's definition of the self or subject as an act of self-creation allows the self to be capable of resistance against the prevailing institutionalized power. While Kohlberg had allowed for a post-conventional stage, his fifth and sixth stages were, from a subjugated feminine ethic, still conventional within a prevailing masculine power structure. In Foucauldian terms, the resistant subject is one that refuses to be scripted by the dominant discourse and turns instead to subjugated knowledges. Foucault says that resistance to the dominant discourse arises at the site of repression. It is necessarily local because repression itself is always local and specific. He (Foucault 1980: 81) claims that it is not necessary to appeal to universalistic concepts of truth and knowledge in order to ground political action. He does acknowledge, however, that something created is always created out of something given (Hekman 1995: 85). The resistant discourses of feminism and the resisting feminist subject, for instance, were fashioned from our discursive configurations: they could arise in no other way. They arise out of our practices and our discourse about them.

RULES AND POWER

Let's place this abstract leap into poststructuralist thought in a context with which you are more familiar. The following story was told by a teacher and has been left deliberately open-textured; it is a typical and relatively ordinary occurrence which may be ethically disturbing to many teachers. It was not designed to elicit a particular response or to give an advantage to one perspective over the others, but to illustrate a 'resistant subject' who still remained tied to existing practices.

In the following case study, and in all others in this book, major decision points will be starred (★) marking possible cross-references to other starred points in the book, but also marking decision points at which a different decision might possibly be made. Teachers using the book as a basis for discussion may pause at these points to invite suggestions of possible actions. I will follow this first narrative with a number of questions which may help you to reflect using consistency, care and consequences orientations. But as the book progresses to develop other moral topics in education, these focusing questions should become less and less necessary as you learn how to ask questions about your own reactions to the situations described and imagine different possible positions.

2.1 Following the rules

An Italian teacher, Maria, in a small Catholic private school is going out to her car at the end of a hot and busy day. She is small and attractive, popular with most students. She sees a group of three large Year 12 students scuffling near the car park with a small Chinese Year 8 boy. At a distance it looks like a friendly game, but as she gets closer she sees that the boy is bleeding from a cut on his face and is clearly frightened and upset. There is a crowd of boys and girls gathered round watching with some fascination. She recognizes the leader of the group as a champion rugby player, Tony, who has been in one of her classes, and goes up to tell him to stop, to leave the small boy alone.★ The aggressors pause,★ the small boy runs off crying, and the group turn to face the teacher, aggressively. She is slightly afraid. The thought momentarily crosses her mind that it would be more prudent just to leave quietly. The young boy is safe, and she is outnumbered.

Maybe she should go back and fetch Jim, the physical education teacher, to help her control the mob. She is considering the consequences to herself of interfering, which is a reasonable appeal at level one of Kohlberg's scale. However, she knows that she must also consider the consequences of not interfering for all other weak people, not only those in her school. She is therefore also considering the utilitarian or consequentialist principle of the greatest good for the greatest number of people.

This assessment of the number of people affected is not just a rational consideration. She also feels angry and decides to follow her feelings. She steps forward and in a loud voice tells the group as a whole that bullying is not allowed in this school and she will not tolerate such behaviour.★ The immediate response is not one of guilt or apology. Instead it is more aggressive.

'Fuck off, you interfering bitch,' says Tony and advances towards her. The audience gasps. Swearing is explicitly forbidden in the school and there is a general requirement of respect for all persons in the contracts that post-compulsory students have had to sign. The penalty for lack of respect to teachers is suspension for a week. She tells the three boys to report to her the next morning in her office, fearing that further confrontation at this point will not be in anyone's interests and that it is best to allow the situation to cool down overnight.★ She retreats to her car, shaking.

At home that night she reflects on her best course of action. The principle of equity requires her to apply the school regulations equally, without fear or favour. She writes up the report with all details of the interaction and the involvement of all three boys and presents it the following day to the deputy principal. Normally the deputy principal would then contact the community liaison officer who would report it to the boys' parents and have the principal enforce automatic suspension. This may well have the consequence of keeping the group violence under control, in the school yard at least. But the community liaison officer reports back to Maria that Tony in particular is known to have a violent family history. If Tony's father hears of his actions, he will thrash the boy. Indirectly, suspension, with the subsequent parental punishment, would encourage the same kind of abuse of power that she was trying to prevent. Indeed the more she thinks about it, any possible action that she takes under the school regulations involves her in perpetuating control by those in power against the weaker. Even to require detention is the imposition of punishment by someone with more power. The consequences of such punishment may well be to perpetuate the violent cycle. Tony will try to overcome his own feeling of powerlessness by exerting power over those weaker than him before his group of friends, and even if in the short term the violence is prevented, the situation that causes it is not being addressed and may well cause similar bullying in the streets. Appealing to the rules against swearing and implementing the normal disciplinary measures may not have the best consequences for Tony at least.

This is not just a decision based on considering the consequences. At the same time she has to consider whether her actions are consistent with her fundamentally ethical principle of minimizing harm, and the consequences of not following the legal process through. How can she make Tony an exception to the rule? Because the action was so public, it cannot be ignored without undermining the smooth running of the school. She is aware that it would be inconsistent to punish the other boys and not punish Tony.★ Tony appeared to be the leader in the aggression and it would be unfair to impose sanctions on the others and not him. She is an authority figure, but the trick here seems to be that she cannot use her authority to bring about a change in attitude and behaviour. Somehow the boys have to be helped to exercise self-control rather than have that control externally imposed. And that is partially because her professionalism as a teacher requires her to care about the boys. That does not mean that she has to like them, but she takes on responsibility for their future welfare as well as her own and that of the small boy.

How can she demonstrate that care? She decides to take a personal approach to try to make them responsible for their actions. When the boys come in, she first of all tells them that she had been afraid of them, and felt insulted and powerless when she was sworn at. She says that she also felt angry because she deserves more respect than that, not because she is a teacher, but because she is a person. She asks them to imagine or remember a situation in which they feel powerless, to imagine how they would feel if they were being sworn at or hit by someone more powerful than they were, knowing that at least one of them, Tony, would have known many such experiences. In this, she is showing that she understands how they feel and that they may have had reasons for acting as they did but that its consequences are to inflict the same hurt on others that they have experienced themselves. She could ask them to think of a way out of the vicious circle, making them responsible for finding a solution.

However, she is worried that this might be a little like asking a child at one stage of development to think at a higher stage. Clearly in their bullying, the boys had not shown any capacity to empathize with other people. There may need to be an intervening stage in which the consequences of breaking the rule need to be reinforced.★ She decides that Tony at least should be suspended from normal classroom activities, consistent with the school regulations, but that there would be no need to inform his parents if she herself took on the responsibility for his suspension. That is, Tony should be constantly with her, sitting at the back of other classes that she took, sitting with her when she is on duties other than teaching. When she was on yard duty or at staff meetings, Tony was to be supervised by other teachers or the youth education officer. He was informed of the reasons for this decision and accepted this as being fair. He was 'punished' for his behaviour consistently with the rules, but avoided the extra penalty that a normal application would have incurred for him.★ He respects Maria in a way that would not have been likely if she had confronted him or stuck to the letter of the law. He begins to learn what fairness and respect for persons involves.

Any narrative, even when describing a 'real' situation, will pick out what seem to the narrator to be the most important features of a situation. Are you as a reader left wondering about certain facts of the situation that were not mentioned? Would the provision of further details have made a difference to what you would have done in Maria's situation at any ★ point? What made those details relevant to your decision? What did other people want to know? Why do you think they need other details? If your decision was different, how would you justify it to Maria?

Maria has made Tony an exception to the rule. Do you think that this is fair or that her 'soft' interpretation of the rules is fair? Consider under what different circumstances the rules could be equally sidestepped, or more easily sidestepped? Would it have been fair if Maria relaxed the rules simply because she had a soft spot for Tony? Could she have justified that sort of decision by appealing to the ethic of care? No, she has to have a reason which treats Tony impartially even where the treatment is unequal. In other words, she must appeal to principle as well as her feelings. What is her rule for singling out Tony for special consideration? She could take into account the predictable consequences and decide that if Tony's father would react in such a way as to do further harm to Tony, then the punishment was not justified in its stricter form. Would it make a difference if Tony's father did not engage in any physical abuse, but was known simply to have a violent temper which involved verbal abuse only? It would be less likely that the deputy would have known about it, and therefore these consequences, while less potentially harmful, might not have been taken into consideration at all.

It was Tony alone who swore at her, who transgressed by breaking the rule about showing respect for the teacher. We do not know here whether there was an explicit sanction in the school against bullying, nor what the incident was that led to the attack on the smaller boy. So there seems to be a superficial case for punishing Tony more, not less, than the others. What do you think the consequences of this would be? Would the other boys consider it unfair that Tony received a lesser punishment than them for doing more? If Maria does impose the heavier penalty, she runs the risk of Tony just swearing at her again and, worse, of continuing to bully others. Think of similar circumstances in school or society where an attempt to control behaviour is met by defiance. Is the problem solved by increasing control?

Let us look at a few other differences that could have been relevant to a different decision.

To what extent can a teacher allow students to decide their own fate? Would it work? Is it the teacher's role to impose penalties consistently for breaking rules? Is it fair to be inconsistent? Can you imagine a case when it is unfair always to follow the rule rigorously? Should the decision about penalties be left to a deputy principal or someone who is distanced from the immediate situation? Or is it better to have someone who was there, and involved?

Would your decision have been any different if Tony had been a prize-winning art student who did not have a record of violence? If he had been female?

How would you have reacted to Maria's decision:

1 if you were Maria?
2 if you were the principal?
3 if you were Tony?
4 if you were one of the other boys?
5 if you were a student afraid of being bullied?

Maria has considered the consequences of her action at each point and has borne in mind the interests of others. She has considered that in other similar cases where an abuse of power might be the consequence of following the school rules, she would act similarly, so she has considered consistency. Even while she sees the need to impose the school rule in the interests of both the small boy and all future possible victims of bullying, the most salient feature is for her the welfare of all of the students. This seems to be one of the requirements of teaching as a service profession. It is, or should be, what Ruddick (1980, 1989) calls 'the work of attentive love'. All frames of consistency, caring and consequences have been considered, but we have yet to consider whether this is enough to make Maria's action ethical.

BULLYING AND HARASSMENT

The story of Maria begins with an incident that most of us would call bullying. What are the criteria that allow us to describe an incident as bullying? Abuse of power begs the question because 'abuse' is also ethically loaded. Bullying usually involves intimidation where superior strength is made into a salient reason for a weaker person to do something against their will. It need not be physical or verbal abuse and can be carried out quite subtly through body language. In the more subtle cases particularly it requires a reciprocal relation to be built up, almost a form of complicity in which the bullied must pick up the signals of the bully, must recognize the power inequality even where it may not be real. There are several similarities with the complexities of sexual harassment. A pinch on the bottom does not in itself constitute harassment, especially if it exists in a context of playfulness, affection or trust. If a person is already feeling threatened by any display of power or sexuality, the pinch becomes a marker of bullying and harassment. In school administration, many staff may feel harassed by a line manager who is simply trying to balance the books and prevent retrenchment. But it is clearly bullying if a boss makes lower-status staff carry out impossible tasks to make them feel as though they ought to resign. The victim is less to blame than the person misusing power. Sometimes there really is a misuse of power. Yet the issue is not simply initiated by the powerful. It requires the victim to accept the role of victim. It requires shared meanings.

In the context of Maria's decision not to perpetuate power by legitimate punishment, you might like to consider how far she can move beyond power in a school situation. McLaren (1993: 167) considers that schools are designed to be constant sites of dominance, describing a Canadian school graphically:

Simply because teachers do not punish students in the form of malfeasant thrashings or physical mutilation . . . this does not obviate the fact that students experience strong debilitating feelings of enchainment. Students often appeared as anguished configurations against the sterile landscapes of formica and cement. They were transformed into bodies subjugated and fragmented, distilled to shadows, and pushed to the margins of acceptability. Pain was made legible in the body postures and facial expressions of the students; it was inscribed in the tight mouths, clenched jaws, hunched shoulders and angry glares – typical gestures of the student state.

To return to the question that I posed at the beginning of this chapter, if there is power imposed within the school by teachers on students, is it unfair that students do not have equal power? Both Maria and the principal are confronted by a rule system that does not meet their distinct needs, nor apparently does it meet the needs of the students. What would be the consequences of burning the rule book? Why do we have rules? To share power, or to control?

RULES AND REGULATIONS

Even in a devolved school system, equal voices are still not heard. How free was Maria to change the rules? The constraints of accountability severely constrain the moves that an autonomous principal or teacher can make. An efficient school is not necessarily an ethical or an equitable one, nor is one in which some make the rules and others simply follow them. The professional administrator does not act automatically. He or she acts voluntarily, consciously, with free will. Nel Noddings (1993: 52) cites an instance from when she was a secondary mathematics teacher where there was a rule that those students who were absent without an excuse should not be allowed to make up the work they had missed: that is, these students were to receive a zero grade for the days they had missed. Noddings chose to ignore the rule. It seemed to her that teachers should be encouraging the students to do the necessary work, and that penalties discouraged them, especially where some students may have doubted the worth of what was being presented anyway. Because her students knew that she would insist on them doing the work, and that she would credit them for having done it successfully, there was little incentive to miss classes. It was easier for them to attend class and do the work on time. 'Participatory decision-making' has been one of the rhetorical markers of devolution, but it assumes professionality and personal autonomy, the possibility of thinking for oneself. Ethics works most successfully in an open community of inquiry in which each of the participants has an equal voice.

Charles Handy in *Understanding Organisations* (1986) says that most administrative stress arises where there is role incompatibility and here 'the most clear cut examples exist in the ethical issues where company practice and standards may differ from a man's [sic] personal standards'. Most administrators, especially in education, agree upon goals in a large system and are then required, as professionals, to work towards those goals. This is the viewpoint of the consequentialist. An unthinking application of the regulations does not necessarily count as a moral decision.

Where the public goals and the expectations to meet those goals clash with an internalized set of moral values such as honesty, loyalty, peer pressure, responsibility and reward, is there a practical guide to which professionals can appeal? Or must they appeal to the more idealistic values such as preventing harm or promoting the welfare of others?

In the introduction, I suggested that the caring aspect was the one that could offer a situational and responsive critique of the intellectual structures that had partly formed it. Nel Noddings (1993: 52) raises this point explicitly:

Is it not ethical – or at least professionally reprehensible – to ignore a school rule? Not always. Indeed we might argue that sometimes it is morally unacceptable to follow a rule. Advocates of many different ethical theories would agree with this. But some would insist that one must break the rule openly, accept whatever penalty comes with the violation, and thereby demonstrate to the community that one's moral sense challenges the law. This course of action requires a form of moral heroism. Acting within an ethic of care, teachers might behave this way – if for example, the rule was tremendously important and strictly enforced – but more often caring teachers just do what they judge best for their students.

There is a caution here and its mention should lead to lively discussion. It is always risky to ignore the rules of the group to which we are accountable. If disobeying the rule might lead to chaos or harm, carers would probably do better to follow the rule. But one must remember that following rules and orders can lead to dreadfully immoral behaviour. How do we decide? There is no foolproof answer to this question, but from the perspective of care we ask 'What is best for this student? Will doing what is best for her or him hurt other students? What effect will my decision have on the network of relations on which we all depend?' Asking such questions we are led sometimes to follow the given rule, and sometimes to fight it publicly, even at the risk of considerable personal sacrifice. Often however, we simply ignore it, knowing that we cannot fight pitched battles over every bit of bureaucratic nonsense, but that we can lose our moral sensitivity by acquiescing to rules instead of caring for each student in each situation.

Piaget spent much of his life trying to discover how children created and conformed to rules in general, how they internalized them. He (Piaget 1932) identified two stages of moral development. The first, heteronomy, is characterized by an attitude of unilateral respect for authority and acceptance of rules as absolute and sacred. At the second autonomous stage, rules are not deemed sacred and they can be modified if a change in them is considered necessary for the advantage of the group as a whole. My triad of consequences, consistency and care is an attempt to outline a procedure that will lead developmentally to moral autonomy. One of the aims of this book is to help the ethical administrator to become autonomous rather than heteronomous. Part of what it means to be a professional is not to be someone who follows the rules automatically, but someone who is competent and intelligent and ethical in their practice, and who obeys the basic ethical requirement that any social rule should be considered in the light of the needs of people who are likely to be affected by it with no partiality towards the claims of any of those whose interests and needs are at stake. Yet the professional is also bound by legal and professional requirements articulated out of a need by various people over time, even where it is as apparently petty as a requirement for a teacher to wear either a tie or stockings to class.

USING JUDGEMENT THROUGH A PROFESSIONAL CODE OF ETHICS

What sort of administrative system best fosters the rationality and self-awareness necessary for an ethical agent? It would probably be one in which administrators decided among themselves on a code of ethical practices, and what those meant. Western Mining Corporation Limited (WMC), a wealthy international private industry, recently asked a group of its employees to set out a code of conduct. They provided a set of core values as follows:

> We value people and treat them with dignity.
> We respect the law and act accordingly.
> We conduct ourselves with integrity and are fair and honest in our dealings.
> We use WMC's assets (including funds, equipment and information) responsibly and in the best interest of WMC.
> We are responsible for our actions and accountable for their consequences.
>
> (Western Mining Corporation Limited 1995: 2)

These were to provide strategies for practice in the workplace, not to tell people how to conduct their lives outside their relationship with WMC, nor to influence anyone's personal beliefs. It was built on a set of shared values and was intended to help corporate activity by outlining the values that should guide employees when they ask themselves 'What is the right thing to do?' The booklet in which these values were printed also contains a brief elaboration of what these core values mean as a code of conduct, including under the first core value a responsibility for maintaining a safe and equitable work force, and under the second core value, 'we operate in countries with many different laws, customs and business principles. We recognise these but do not compromise the principles embodies [*sic*] in this Code.' There are also thirteen pages of illustrative examples to help employees identify situations where they might need to seek advice from a Code of Conduct Advisory Committee established within the company.

Many professional communities have drawn up a code of ethics to make more specific the moral code that specifically applies to their situation. The code must be idealistic and at the same time practical, so that it can apply reasonably to all educational administrators. In some professions, in medicine particularly, the code has become so detailed that it almost takes the place of law. But a code of ethics is not as finely tuned to detailed particulars of precedent as the law. The school administrator does not have the time to subject every ethical judgement to the same study of precedent and juridical decision.

A code of ethics is a slightly more specific social heuristic, a strategy that gives general guidelines for educational practices in particular and is open to a much wider interpretation than the law can allow. It often arises from a particular historical context and can change according to historical changes in practices. We cannot study practice in terms of social structures alone. As Giddens (1984, 1991) says, practices are a product of action and history, and also produce action and history.

An educator's code of ethics (adapted from the American Association of School Administrators' *Statement of Ethics for School Administrators*) might look like the following:

The educational administrator:

- makes the well-being of students fundamental in all decision-making and actions
- fulfils professional responsibilities with honesty and integrity
- supports the principle of due process and protects the civil and human rights of all individuals
- maintains professional confidentiality at all times
- implements the governing board of education's policies and administrative rules and regulations and/or pursues appropriate measures to correct those laws, policies and regulations that are not consistent with sound educational goals, ensuring that where possible no person shall be disadvantaged by a change in regulations
- pursues appropriate measures to overcome apparent injustices and unethical practices
- avoids using positions for personal gain through political, social, religious, economic or other influence
- maintains the standards and seeks to improve the effectiveness of the profession through research and continuing professional development

- honours all contracts until fulfilment, release or dissolution mutually agreed upon by all parties to contract.

This could be a much longer list if the codes were more specific, but specific cases are generally subsumed under a broader rule. For instance, the American code has the requirement that the administrator accepts academic degrees or professional certification only from duly accredited institutions, but this is covered by the second requirement of honesty and integrity and the eighth one of maintaining standards. The principles are deliberately general even though this makes them difficult to comply with in specific circumstances where different codes may come into conflict. These codes are more specific than the very broad ethical principles of beneficence and non-maleficence on which they are founded, but they are not yet closely enough related to practices to be called conceptions. The code operates at an ethical level rather than a moral one.

Given a specific moral situation in a school, how do you decide which code to follow where different codes come into conflict? What rules, strategies or codes of ethics does an autonomous educational administrator follow in an ethical situation? Is there any pattern, any consistency in the justifications offered by administrators for following one part of a code of ethics rather than another? Can you imagine a situation in which it could be unethical to follow the fifth code above by following *too* rigorously the guidelines that make an administrator accountable to the Education Department?

Strike and Ternasky (1993: 2) describe the code of ethics for teachers of the National Education Association as 'platitudinous and perfunctory' and say there is little evidence that it is taught or that most teachers are aware of its existence. Even if it could be universally agreed upon, what would its relation be to the universal values of beneficence, or non-maleficence, or to the values of honesty, loyalty, equity, rights? Strike and Ternasky would bypass the codes of ethics, saying that laws, regulations and rules are simply means to the end of promotion of ethical values and therefore must be applied ethically. The codes, however, do provide guidelines to the implementation of ethical values even when they are as broadly defined as those of WMC. The more specific they are, the more useful they are as a guide to behaviour. The detailed medical code of ethics is highly specific, giving substance and meaning to the ethical values.

Kant said that there were maxims that had to be distinguished from cultural law, maxims that drive one of Kohlberg's subjects at any stage, whether it is reciprocity, or following the rules, or obeying a social contract. Kant also believed in an objective principle, that is, the universal principle or moral law or categorical imperative, valid for every rational being, and the principle by which it ought to act, i.e. a categorical imperative which cannot be disobeyed. 'There is . . . only one categorical imperative. It is: Act only according to that maxim by which you can at the same time will that it should become a universal law' (Kant 1969). Kant believed that a foundation for social behaviour existed prior to human existence and thought. He also believed that a human cannot begin to formulate language without an innate concept of good and bad, or time, or cause. But this innateness may be no more than an attempt to explain by genetics a logical requirement of language and action, that we have a central concept of a distinction between good and bad behaviour, and that we must have respect for persons, or be honest, or respect other people's property because we have evolved a set of social practices and assumptions which embed core ethical values that develop the basic distinction between good and bad behaviour. For Erikson, these were an innate capacity to care. For Kant, they are logical laws, known prior to experience.

CORE ETHICAL VALUES

OVERARCHING VALUES

Non-maleficence	*Beneficence*
Do no harm	Promote human welfare
Risk no harm	Prevent harm
	Remove harm

UNIVERSAL VALUES

Sanctity of life	Dignity of life
Respect for persons	Honesty
Justice	Equality
Freedom	Reparation
Promise-keeping	Loyalty
Confidentiality	Privacy
Property rights	Functional welfare
Public welfare	

These 'universal' values may be an understanding that we have picked up in whatever culture we inhabit to allow us to detect conflicts in codes of ethics that operate at the next more practical level. Maria may or may not have been aware of the code that makes the well-being of students paramount, but she was aware that this moral 'rule' conflicted with her professional responsibility to obey the rules of her contract as a teacher.

In the case studies that follow, I will focus on situations where various codes conflict. The clash of codes makes one aware of one's own moral priorities in a particular situation. To apply rules ethically that are in accord with the categorical imperative or the overarching values named above will always require judgement, interpretation and responsibility. Such judgement can be built up along a developmental matrix founded on an increasing knowledge of consequences, growing autonomy, integrity and an awareness of an expanding social experience. The ethical matrix so formed is not spontaneous, intuitive or logical but reasonable and built on evidence, a notion of good reasons and caring about others.

In the opening paragraphs of this book, I mentioned the construction of concepts from conceptions, and the need for formal notions or concepts, such as ethical notions of 'murder' or 'bullying', to provide the structures for frames within which certain actions become relevant to the way we ought to behave. In looking at the theoretical frames of consistency, consequences and care and the way they shape descriptions of and justification for actions, I implied that our actions somehow depend upon our purposes. In the consequentialist agenda, because it focuses on goals, is the assumption that we usually justify actions as a means to an end. In the consistency framework, though to a lesser extent, when we give a reason for doing something, we justify our actions by referral to intentions. These intentions, such as saving Tony from harm, operate as the ends that justify the means, even when we are operating in the subjective frame of giving our intentions as a reason for acting.

When Maria is asked why she did not punish Tony in the normal manner, she might well reply, because I care about him as a person, in which case care is the end that justifies her means. If she replies that she did it to be consistent with the principle of not doing harm to others, then her ends are those of principle, and she justifies her actions as the best way, or means, to further that end. Even while her conclusion was ultimately based on *feeling* respect for Tony as a person, Maria had to consider or think about her actions, to consider what the point of her actions was. In the next chapter we will look a little more closely at the relationship between means and ends in educational contexts and whether the ends can justify any means.

Chapter 3

Ends and means

Love thyself last . . .
Still in thy right hand carry gentle peace,
To silence envious tongues: be just and fear not.
Let all the ends thou aims't at be thy country's
Thy God's and truth's

Shakespeare, *Henry VIII*, III.ii.444

We argue about what is 'training' and what is 'education': how about the proposition that I want my daughters to receive sex education but not sex training?

Kessell (1992)

MEANS–ENDS RELATIONS

There has been less debate in recent years as to what the aim of education is, and perhaps this is unfortunate. Kessell's epigraph illustrates how abstract goals even like education or training can influence what and how we teach in lessons about sex. In similar ways, our goals or ends do make a difference to the way we interact with other people, even when those goals or purposes are not overtly expressed. When people remark that the end justifies the means, they may be saying that, in certain cases, their goal or purpose (the end) may seem so overwhelmingly important to them that they are warranted in using any means in order to obtain it. On this interpretation, any behaviour, no matter how odious, illegal or unscrupulous, can be justified if it is a means to the desired end. This is possible within the consequentialist programme, as action is justified by the long-term consequences being seen to be of greater benefit than possibly painful short-term consequences. In other words, though the maximizing of benefits may incur short-term losses, usually to others, the end justifies the means because of the greatest happiness of the greatest possible number. On a felicific calculus, the short-term costs are cancelled out.

Another interpretation of the expression 'The end justifies the means' is much less sinister; according to this interpretation, when we are asked for our *reason* for using a means, we simply cite the end or purpose that we have in mind (Lipman 1985: 35). In discussing any matter in which the end justifies the means, we should be prepared to ask 'Do you mean regardless of other consequences, or do you mean having taken other consequences into account?' The latter is, according to the openly reflective and self-conscious view of ethics presumed in this book, the more ethical way to proceed.

3.1 Does the end justify the means?

The following questions are presented as warm-up exercises for considering the relation of means to ends:

1 'Punishing wrongdoers is a top priority with me, so I'm punishing all the students in this class. That'll get the miscreants! The end justifies the means.'
2 'I want good results so badly that I'll stay up studying till 2 am every night to get them. The end justifies the means.'
3 'Frank is misbehaving badly in class. Send him out of the classroom immediately, even though he will suffer in missing the lesson. The end justifies the means.'
4 'Frank is misbehaving badly in class, but his parents have just separated and he is desperate to have someone take notice of him. Send him out of the classroom immediately, even though he will suffer in missing the lesson. The end justifies the means.'
5 'Frank is abnormally hyperactive today. A dose of Ritalin will stop him interrupting others. The end justifies the means.'
6 'Freedom is a value so desirable that we have to impose compulsory education and even compulsory subjects on them from 9 am to 4 pm daily, so that they can learn how later to make informed choices which enable them to be free. The end justifies the means.'

THE WELL-BEING OF STUDENTS AS AN END

In the previous chapter, Maria took pains to show that she cared about Tony's well-being. For many teachers, this felt or experiential dimension is possibly the most important ethical dimension of being a teacher, more important than the amount of information or skills they transmit. The American code of ethics for educational administrators places the well-being of students as paramount. It seems difficult, if not impossible, to imagine a school in which all the teachers do not show a concern for their students' well-being, and if we were to come across one, we would judge it as an unethical school. But if we are to use the concept of the well-being of students as an end, or even *the* end, of education, we need to understand it a little better. What does 'well-being' mean and is it the same as happiness?

Many schools all over the world are being encouraged to redefine their brief in terms of providing the country with a skilled workforce. Education and training are viewed as being synonymous, and schools that are funded by the taxpayer are urged to justify public expenditure by contributing in real terms to national productivity. Many politicians believe that the end of education is to produce industrially literate workers. In this way problems of economic efficiency, overseas competitiveness, unemployment and social justice can all be addressed and resolved. Furthermore this will contribute to the well-being of each individual, with greater chances of promotion and varied career paths. So from a consequentialist position, to treat the student as a means to the end of national productivity could be seen to be ethical, even when taking the consequences for the student into account.

If we look at this matter from the consistency position, further education does not mean a more equitable distribution of resources over a wider base; it simply means a redistribution of resources within the same patterns of poverty and wealth. The greatest good for the greatest number cannot be argued for if the rhetoric about a commonwealth is based on false premisses which in reality continue to reinforce any inequities embedded in the ideology. The act or policy becomes unethical if it is done out of self-interest or maintaining power. Maximizing benefits has to be universally applicable rather than self-directed.

Look at the assumptions underlying the first code of ethics, namely that we should aim at the well-being of students. Is that the point of education? Is well-being the same as happiness? In 1561 happiness was described, rather circularly, as 'the state of pleasurable content of mind, which results from success or the attainment of what is considered good' (*Shorter Oxford English Dictionary*, 1965 edn: 864). As with most dictionary definitions, we have to have a clear understanding of the words used in the definition and unless we can spell out what 'good' is, this definition does not get us very far. Happiness equals well-being. We may have to step further back to decide what, if anything, is the point of living, and whether well-being or happiness is limited to earning an income or achieving success.

The importance of the well-being of students is directly related to the American Constitution which defends each person's right to life, liberty and happiness, and to Bentham's emphasis on what he called a felicific calculus, the indicator of benefits and costs of any action. There is a problem with this, raised by Elizabeth Telfer (1980: 19). You cannot presume, as Aristotle and Mill did, that because happiness is based on an aggregate of all the things that a person pursues for their own sakes, everything a person seeks is sought either as part of or as a means to their happiness. Such an argument presumes that happiness or well-being can be aggregated, and that it is just a sum of parts associated with goods that one strives for.

On this view, pursuing something 'for its own sake' is construed as pursuing it because one has a positive attitude to it – but you would not pursue it unless you believed that it would please you – at least at some time. Mill believed (in a theory that became known as psychological hedonism) that everyone's sole final aim was to be pleased with life as a whole rather than separate items in it. But we can think of many counter examples to this, for instance the person who believes that the purpose of life is to strive for something – anything, which may not be happiness. Or that person may do things just because they feel like it with no further end in view at all. Again, as Telfer says (1980: 22), a person can do something for the sake of some narrow and specific end which they regard in isolation without relating it to any wider context – like taking driving lessons so that they will pass the driving test, without any particular idea of why they want to pass the driving test.

However we describe the aim of education, it is ultimately the justification of a particular form of human life, and will undergo revision as social values change. These things are learned and the form of learning appropriate to them involves conceiving of ends, deliberating about them and about the means to them. The activities that constitute people as agents – able to take initiative and accept responsibility for what they do – seem to me to be an inherent part of education and therefore its end. We want people to think for themselves which is the best path for them to take. For Skinner, a consequentialist, such a goal of autonomy is valuable because it contributes to well-being. He wrote a novel about the mythical inhabitants of Walden Two who simply exist in a pleasurable world without pain or the need for decision-making. Mill (1975: ch. 2) says that if happiness is to have the quality of *human* happiness, it cannot be divorced from decision-making or autonomous activity – 'If a person possesses any tolerable amount of common sense and experience, his own mode of laying out his existence is the best, not because it is best in itself, but because it is his own mode.'

I will assert here and argue later in this chapter that Bentham and Mill were right in assuming that it is necessary to look at the consequences of one's actions and that any tolerable theory of the standard or standards of right action must include as an element the probable consequences of action in terms of well-being of individuals or the commonwealth, even where such a reckoning can never be precise. But it must also be considered alongside the autonomy of any person to decide which beneficial consequences outweigh others.

I suggested in Chapter 1 that one end of ethics is to share power, or at least to guard against the abuse of power. In any classroom of about thirty children, with different backgrounds, levels of achievement, temperaments, interests and expectations, packed often without reference to their own desires into not very comfortable classrooms, it is not surprising that many will want to rebel, to create their own disturbances and assert their own autonomy. To what extent should the well-being of each student be considered, how far must it be curtailed in the greater interests of the class as a whole, and by what means?

Let us take the example of a recently defined phenomenon, that of attention-deficit hyperactivity disorder. Western Australia has one of the highest prescription rates of Ritalin for attention-deficit disorder children in the world. What ethical considerations could one have for prescribing the drug? For many children its main benefit is that it controls their individual need for activity and distraction sufficiently to let them concentrate on the task in hand and learn something. For teachers it has the benefit of 'slowing down' student activity to a level nearer the norm of obedient compliance and sitting still, enabling teachers to spend more time with more normal children. In those respects, it is ethical because it contributes to the greater well-being of all those in the classroom. Where I suspect it becomes less ethical is where it is used simply to deprive children of their autonomy. It uses a physical means to subdue them and this amounts at a metaphorical level to a deterrent punishment which makes them prisoner, not leaving them free to choose whether or not to disrupt the class. In that case the well-being of the student is at risk. Because it therefore makes the children less powerful, less able to express themselves, it becomes less ethical, reducing them to a means to the end of getting the whole class through a programme in the fastest possible time. Here we seem to be in the situation of justifying short-term non-autonomy on the grounds of long-term gain for the school programme. Getting through the programme becomes the end to which student understanding has become subordinated.

Similar issues arise in the administration of punishment, particularly in schools. If, as Kant maintained, it is unethical to treat any persons as a means to an end, then how far is one justified in giving short-term pain on the grounds of long-term gain? To what extent is a teacher shouting or being sarcastic to students a more ethically justified means of control than physical pain? Why? What are the criteria for deciding when a teacher's raised voice is ethical or not? Is it only when it is in the greater interests of the class or school?

THE ETHICS OF PUNISHMENT

Most teachers would be familiar with the following 'punishments', but there would be less agreement over the misdemeanours for which each is appropriate.

1 The offender's name is written on the bulletin board.
2 The offender serves between one and five hours' detention.
3 The offender is to be thrown out of the classroom and referred to the vice-principal for further action.
4 The offender hears a lecture on the importance of the rule.
5 The offender must write why they did it, and why it is important that they never do it again.
6 The offender must apologize to the entire class.
7 The offender gets double homework for two nights.
8 The offender loses library privileges for one week.

We can consider them all as a means to the end if we use them to beneficial effect. Some might argue that punishments may stop short-term misbehaviour but are ineffective for long-term change and will, in most cases, only make matters worse. Making clear the consequences of rule violation is more logical and natural and helps the rule violator to learn acceptable behaviour from the experience. Their intention is instructional rather than punitive because they are designed to teach the students the positive or negative effects of their behaviour. I do not disagree with this at a behavioural level. Punishment is often a form of retribution, using fear as its main motivator, and therefore can be unethical. But we need also to focus on the intention, why we wish to prevent recurrence of the offences. Then we are looking not only at the consequences but at the ethical 'ends' of blame and just desert.

Benn (cited in Kleinig 1981: 232) offers the following five criteria for punishment which allow us to apply the term consistently in different contexts:

1 it must involve an 'evil, an unpleasantness, to the victim';
2 it must be for an offence (actual or supposed);
3 it must be of an offender (actual or supposed);
4 it must be the work of personal agencies (i.e. not merely the natural consequences of an action);
5 it must be imposed by authority (real or supposed), conferred by the system of rules (hereafter referred to as 'law') against which the offence has been committed.

Kleinig, appropriately in my opinion, argues (1981: 233–6) that this is philosophically myopic, because it confuses punishment with penalization, ethics with legality. Hockey players can invoke a penalty for breaking a rule, but they are not thereby being punished. Because ethical punishment is inconsistent with victimization, persecution, discrimination, vengeance, or even therapy, there must be some normative component that underpins the notion of punishment, particularly in schools. Kleinig claims that this normative component is the notion of autonomy, and that on one score at least, punishment can be viewed as compatible with the ends of education by recognizing, and indeed affirming, the personhood of the person being punished: it treats the person as a subject to whom justice is due. In this it is different from the therapeutic aim of prescription of drugs for inappropriate behaviour.

Moral wrongdoing involves a breach in the relationships that are appropriate to human beings and punishment ought to express the loss that some breaches involve (Kleinig 1981: 239). However, in bureaucratic structures including schools, both offences and their punishment are usually depersonalized and justified on consequentialist grounds. It is meted out by any justice system, including a school, in order

- to obtain a beneficial result
- to discourage the offender from further offending
- to act as a deterrent to others who might contemplate offending
- to discourage the victim from personally inflicting retribution
- to prevent vendettas.

It is usually justified as an unpleasant means to one of these ends, and these ends in turn are justified by an appeal to maximizing happiness. The main point of this chapter is to have teachers consider to what extent the end can justify the means. There are many institutions in the world that still follow the British tradition of public caning for misdemeanours. An Australian teacher on a short-term teaching contract in a former British colony which imitates many other features of education in Victorian England witnessed the public caning of a student and was horrified. The following is taken directly from a personal letter to the author dated 26 April 1994.

3.2 Is caning in schools justified?

Well I had a whole new life experience today. I witnessed my first public caning! Well I don't mean saw, because I ran out the door as the boy 'assumed the position'. But boy o boy did this disturb my karma for the day. I found it really disturbing, and I had to go and hide to gather my breath, and my wits! I don't approve at all, and I want to say something about it. I mean there are reasons to believe that the (locals) are not wrong in this, BUT . . . I mean, I said to one of my classes after, that it was the sort of thing I would have expected to see on a movie, not ever in real life.★ I must ask that next time there is this little plan afoot, they let me know so that I can stay away. I guess it depends on how mad you are with the boy,★ and that depends on whether it was you who was on the receiving end of his nefarious activities.★ But, I still don't approve of the public nature of this activity. I spoke to the principal after, and she agreed that it doesn't work,★ but then no-one has ever presented a solution that does. Is the whole thing improved by the fact that this treatment is especially reserved for boys?★ It might be a good one to set for one of your classes. It was only one stroke (are we impressed by this?) and the offender was quickly removed for more counselling (a euphemism for a good talking to, again).★

This was followed by a public humiliation of another boy, but I wasn't around to watch this so I can't supply details. Does it work? I don't know. What other alternatives are there?★ W.A. kids have been burning down schools. I think this tells us of their anger at becoming the new dispossessed, and I think that the case of the James Bulger murder gave us a new understanding of the evil that kids can do. All in all I think I prefer to spend my time watching soppy movies, as I have no stomach for institutionalised violence.★ It's all too hard. Got any ideas?

As I said, this whole experience is remarkably like stepping into a time warp of how things used to be twenty or thirty years ago. I remember from my own school days, a deputy caning a boy in his office. The P.A. system was housed in the same office, and whether it was inadvertent or deliberate, he left it switched on while the sound of the cane descending brought silence into every classroom in the school. But then it was like a radio play, not quite so immediate as this. I can't get over the image of the boy standing from among all the students, and walking forward with his sloppy grin,★ to stand with hands outstretched to grip the edge of the stage, bum to audience . . . and I left. Nearly 400 spectators, all under 16!

The public humiliation of an offender is not new to other countries. Singapore made international headlines in 1995 for its caning of an American youth, Michael Lay, for spraypainting cars. Richard Court, the premier of Western Australia, quotes (1996: 1) approvingly the penalties imposed for even minor misdemeanours such as littering where the penalty can consist of a fine and a compulsory cleaning up of a public area wearing a brightly coloured bib that pronounces to all the world that the offender is a litterbug. The system of legalistic/punitive regulation in many Asian countries is consistent with a consequential focus in which individual rights are minimal. Even though punishment does not result in the happiness of the individual student being punished, it is usually justified in terms of the long-term consequences of the child's suffering. It is a means to the greater end of social happiness.

Any protesting teacher who questions the various means of social control in the classroom and to what ends the means are justified by the goal is a resistant subject, in Foucauldian terms, who refuses to be subjugated by the dominant local discourse. Such a resistant subject, often a level-five person on the Kohlbergian scale, could find at least three major problems with a consequentialist defence of corporal punishment. The first is that the consequences are not always beneficial. Repeated caning results in boys becoming hardened to violence. Corporal punishment is simply expected. There can be also regressive behaviour as children try to adapt to the routine. Tough 13-year-old boys start behaving like babies. They try to retreat to the comfort zone of being young children protected by their mother. Later some displace their aggression and anger into bullying and violence on the sports field.

If punishment is justified solely by reference to its consequences, there seems to be no clear reason that punishment should be restricted to offenders. Public humiliation, for instance, of anyone who was different or who disagreed with the dominant hegemony would be justifiable in the interests of the state. A Japanese graduate spoke of the slap of love given to control those who had not offended, as a lesson to others about authority. She had been beaten in class because she was the best behaved, to show the class that anyone could be punished, and she did not think this was unjust. We are close to arguing here that the end justifies the means.

In an article justifying the introduction of caning in schools, Court said:

> In many of our close Asian neighbours punishment is hard, swift and effective. At the same time, the role of the family is strong, personal responsibility is emphasised and government welfare systems are usually seen as an insult to families . . .
>
> In the past, petty juvenile crime was dealt with swiftly, normally by parents, local community leaders or, if this was not possible, by the police. Basic tenets of our society such as responsibility, respect and discipline began in the home, and were reinforced at school. Self-respect and respect for other people and their property were the values ingrained into society . . . In a school system, where our

teachers are reporting problems with discipline and where there is a growing disrespect for authority and other people's property, something has to be done. It was in this light that I gave my response on corporal punishment.

If we agree that the end of a school is to increase personal responsibility, then we can agree that caning might be one way to reach that end. If we also see the welfare of students as critically important, we might see the need for corporal punishment, detention, tongue-lashing and deprivation of privileges as relatively unproductive and negative in comparison with other means which might obtain the same ends more positively. What we see as salient consequences depends to some extent on whether we see the end of education as training or as education. It is dependent on our prior sets of values, the conception or the concept of ethics that drives our actions. There would, I suspect, be universal ethical disapproval of anyone who inflicted pain on another simply to gratify his or her own pleasure.

One of the teacher's concerns about the caning described above was that in his public humiliation the child was being degraded as a person. An educational policy that was simply consequentialist and did not care about autonomy, self-actualization and self-esteem was to her immoral because it was contradictory. She was also concerned that repeated caning did not seem to have the desired effect. But would it be justified if it did? In a Machiavellian world, there would be little wrong in ignoring the well-being of an individual. 'Whether the action is evil or not can only be decided in the light of what it is meant to achieve and whether it successfully achieves it.' Not only are successful governments always ready to act ruthlessly to attain their ends, according to the Prince, but the acquisition and maintenance of power by government can be justified no matter how evil the consequences of their actions. The assertion of power over non-compliant material would be justifiable in ensuring the authority of the school, especially if all decisions by the rules were for the ultimate benefit of the state. Where that argument becomes unethical is when a government cynically uses it to maintain power out of self-interest, aimed at the sustaining of power by the incumbent political party because it appears to provide illusory short-term solutions to endemic social and economic problems. If this is true, it is an unethical policy because it treats students as means to ends.

This leads us back to the questions posed at the beginning of this chapter. The consequentialist does not condemn any serious attempt to maximize value merely because the consequences of the attempt turn out to be less than ideal. 'What is important, morally speaking, is that one conscientiously attempts to determine the most favourable action, and then with equal seriousness attempts to perform this action' (Beauchamp and Childress 1984: 48). The question remains – what is to count as the most favourable action? To which end? How can we know whether, for instance, the authority of the state is aimed at desirable ends? The notion of any end is value-laden.

If the means–end argument offered by consequentialists will not offer resolution, we might argue on the grounds of consistency that it is inconsistent to hurt children physically, if we are also trying to teach them that no person shall be subject to torture of any kind whether physical, mental or emotional, nor shall any person be subject to cruel, inhuman or degrading treatment or punishment. Punishment seems an inseparable part of any consistent moral schema in which justice and personal responsibility are valued and pursued. Paul Wilson (1971: 113) says that 'the elimination of punishment from social relationships would only be possible along with the elimination of the whole moral order of life'. Maria's problem in the previous chapter was that she wanted to move beyond punishment as power for its own sake, as an end that justified any means. Kleinig raised the further question of the appropriate severity of punishment meted out in schools. Most Australian schools now ban any form of corporal punishment, but still many school-based punishments fail to reflect a proper sense of the seriousness or triviality of particular offences. You might like to consider recent punishments in your school that seem inappropriate. Illegal drugs on school grounds can warrant immediate expulsion, but are often totally ignored. A girl who could not afford a compulsory school uniform was barred from meeting her hero, the then premier Bob Hawke. These punishments constitute a confusing or unintelligible response to situations in which there are different levels of blame, and the resulting puzzlement or anxiety can interfere with the learning of educational consequences. Punishment, at least the belief in its propriety, seems inseparable from a social order in which justice and personal responsibility are valued and pursued. As Kleinig says (1981: 240), what is upheld as the 'normal order of life bears the strong imprint of a particular social formation, and so what comes to be affirmed in punishment may not be much more than the conditions necessary to support a fundamentally unjust and coercive status quo'. We need always to be considering whether the means justifies the end, even in such extreme situations as the use of electric cattle prods to modify the behaviour of autistic children.

We need to reflect on to what extent, for instance, the classroom method of assertive discipline is an instrument of control in using pleasure and/or pain to modify student behaviour to desirable ends and to what extent it can be used to guide the child towards making their own judgements, that is, towards full autonomy. Animal experimentation in science classes might serve as another example. Is the educational cost of using virtual reality or plastic models worth the ethical gain in demonstrating to students that animals are not simply means to human ends? Other case studies can also be redefined as means–ends debates by looking at the relative value of short-term and long-term consequences.

DOES THE END JUSTIFY THE MEANS?

The distinction I made in Chapter 1 between ethical and legal matters was also present in the earlier discussion about the different status of codes, rules, regulations and laws. The constraints are there for a purpose, towards the end of the smooth running of the school. There usually is an ethical base underlying them to maximize happiness and minimize harm. One of the reasons for the discomfort in witnessing caning is that there appears to be a contradiction in the morality of imposing the rule, just as it might have been unethical for Maria to carry out the letter of the law on Tony. But if we abhor any violence towards children, we generally believe that laws should be followed. When are we justified in speaking out against what we consider to be an unethical rule? It would seem that we have a moral obligation to try to change what could be seen to be an immoral law, especially in the frame of Kohlberg's hierarchical develop-ment to a post-conventional stage. To what extent are we justified in breaking some laws in order to overturn others that we consider immoral, or does that involve us in inconsistencies that prevent us from doing that? Can a desire to change an immoral law justify civil disobedience; in other words, does the end sometimes justify the means?

The consequentialist argument that the end justifies the means does not always work as a good argument for punishment because, as I have shown, there is no way of deciding whether the bad consequences outweigh the good outside existing presumptions about the end of education, and the argument may be used to enforce power rather than justice. Peter Singer describes (1979: 182) the slogan 'the end never justi-fies the means' as a 'simplistic' formula. The difficult issue for him is not whether the end can ever justify the means but which means are justified by which ends. He asks whether such ends as equal consideration of interests irrespective of race, sex or species, liberal abortion laws, volun-tary euthanasia and the reduction of absolute poverty, could justify the use of any means that may bring about the desired end. On the matter of civil disobedience, he claims (Singer 1979: 182–200) that breaking the law, even with violence, is justifiable if the end can justify it. He gives as his example the action of the Animal Liberation Front (ALF) in 1979 in raiding fur farms, releasing the animals, damaging the laboratories used for animal experiments and holing boats about to be used for seal-hunting expeditions, saying that their ideals were identical to those of the RSPCA, and therefore conventionally ethical ones. They simply chose an illegal way of drawing attention to ethical wrongs.

3.3 Can one justify breaking the law on ethical grounds?

Imagine a scenario where a group of school students break the law and justify their actions on the grounds that the law is wrong. It may be that they wear black armbands as a protest against racist policies in a school that has banned political slogans or it may be more serious such as the open use of marijuana or heroin in an attempt to change the drug laws. Is punishment justified in such a situation?

Are we under any moral obligation to obey the law, if the law protects and sanctions things that we hold utterly wrong? On the consistency model, the conflict between individual and society will be decided in favour of the individual, even, as we shall see later, in the case of whistle-blowing. We should do what we think is right, as our conscience dictates, as we autonomously decide we ought to do, not as the law directs. While Singer, from a consequentialist point of view, says that he does not have much faith in the subjectivity of conscience, he does not deny the importance of consistent reasoning:

> 'Following one's conscience' means doing as one's 'internal voice' prompts one to do. However, to follow one's conscience is to abdicate one's responsibility as a rational agent, to fail to take all the relevant factors into account and act on the best of one's judgement of the rights and wrongs of the situation. The 'internal voice' is more likely to be a product of one's upbringing and education than a source of genuine ethical insight.
>
> (Singer 1979: 185)

'Following one's conscience' could also mean doing what, on reflection, seems right and what seems unobjectionable – in other words, exercising rational judgement. On the face of it, it would seem reasonable to obey the law. Singer (1979: 186–8) argues that although human beings are social in nature, they are not so social that they do not need to protect themselves against the risk of being assaulted or killed by their fellow human beings. Laws and settled decision procedures are designed to generate more speedy and economical resolutions to disputes than violence. He claims that there are two consequentialist reasons for obeying the law, namely, not encouraging others to similarly disobey established decision procedures and saving the community the expense of enforcement. However, these are neither universally applicable nor conclusive.

They are not, for instance, applicable to breaches of the law that remain secret. If, late at night when the streets are deserted, I cross the road against the red light, there is no one to be led into disobedience by my example, and no one to enforce the law against so crossing. But this is not the kind of illegality we are interested in.

Where they are applicable, these two reasons for obedience are not conclusive, because there are times when the reasons against obeying a particular law are more important than the risks of encouraging others to disobey or the costs to the community of enforcing the law. They are genuine reasons for obeying, and in the absence of reasons for disobeying, are sufficient to resolve the issue in favour of obedience; but where there are conflicting reasons, we must assess each case on its merits in order to see if the reasons for disobeying outweigh these reasons for obedience. If, for instance, illegal acts were the only way of preventing high numbers of painful and unnecessary experiments, or of prodding governments into increasing overseas aid, the importance of the ends would justify running some risk of contributing to a general decline in obedience to law.

(Singer 1979: 186–8)

Consistency does play an important part in this argument. Why, for instance, does the ALF balk at injuring people? Because to inflict harm deliberately on people would weaken their case that others should not harm animals.

BLAMEWORTHINESS

The notion of intentional disobedience usually carries with it notions of both responsibility and blame. The student who was caned was guilty of breaking the rules and therefore was shown to have 'deserved' the punishment. People who take a self-righteous stance against the law are usually prepared to accept the consequences of their action. We have not yet considered the consequences for someone who invokes a legal penalty, but is not wholly responsible for their actions.

Kelley (1996: 7) outlines the case in America of Guinevere Garcia, who was orphaned and sexually abused before she was 6, an alcoholic at 11 and pregnant at 16 with a daughter whom she suffocated with a plastic bag after learning that welfare authorities were going to foster the child with her grandmother and the uncle who had abused her. Her two-week-old marriage to a 60-year-old man whom she met on a prostitution call ended in 1991 when he told her that he gave her money and attention only in return for sex and she shot him dead. The prosecutors described her as 'a walking catalogue of crime . . . a criminal storm that affects everyone who comes in her path'. Garcia accepts responsibility for her actions and has said that she deserves to die, but those who oppose the death penalty continue to fight for her right to life. Sentenced to receive a legal injection, Garcia was given a stay of execution on 16 January 1996. Is this a concession to her well-being or not?

We seek consistency in the application of our laws, and if she knowingly took the life of another person, then she deserves to be executed. Perversely, if she wants to be executed, would it constitute a punishment, and is it more of a punishment to keep her alive? To what extent is she finally tranquil because she does accept responsibility for her decisions, seeing it rather as something that is just happening to her?

I spoke earlier about the differences between a penalty and a punishment, the latter having connotations of blame and responsibility which the former does not. Perhaps the question to ask in the case of Garcia is: to what extent does she deserve the death penalty? To what extent can she be blamed for her actions?

The death penalty, horrific as it is, is justified as an unpleasant means to the end of deterring deliberate killing of other people. In Garcia's case it was not deterrent enough. But if it is to be seen as a means to an end, then the penalty must be imposed, to make other people fear the consequences of harming others, even though in this particular case it seems unbelievably harsh.

We could find many similar but less extreme examples within the school environment. To what extent can the girl who could not afford to buy a school uniform be blamed for not wearing one to school, and to what extent did she deserve to be deprived of another pleasure, namely seeing the prime minister in person? To what extent does it serve the public or private good to imprison repeated drug offenders, or car thieves, many of whom come from deprived homes in which they have not been brought up to consider the rights or needs of others? Is Kleinig right to distinguish as he does between penalty and punishment with only the latter connoting blame?

To what extent does blame assume responsibility? Aristotle (1969: 52) stresses that we do not blame individuals for bad actions that are involuntary. What happens when an action that has very bad consequences is undertaken by a person who is not responsible for their actions? When courts exonerate a person who is temporarily insane or drunk, they are removing blame. But they still hold people responsible for drinking while driving and will impose legal sanctions on those who offend, particularly if they repeat the offence. A contentious issue is that of recidivists who are repeatedly arrested for stealing cars and deliberately inciting police chases. Do we want to blame them, especially when they are usually juvenile offenders? If they are high on drugs, we may want to let them go free, but should they be held responsible for taking the drugs? If the offenders argue that they were stealing the car as a means to their own pleasure, we quite properly discount that as an inappropriate means to an end because their action disregards the well-being of those they affect. Another way of saying this is that they are not considering the long-term possible consequences of their behaviour, the risk to those police who are trying to apprehend them or to those innocent bystanders who accidentally get in the way of a high-speed chase. In that case we will assume that they are responsible for their actions, and blame them accordingly. They are choosing to treat other people and their property as means to a personal end, and even if the end is a desirable one, it is unethical to do this. But what do we say if they have had an upbringing or an education that has never encouraged them to consider consequences of their action or the well-being of others? In that case do we blame society instead?

The cases in this chapter have ascribed different levels of responsibility to the agents. That might be seen as begging the consistency position. To what extent is the ALF responsible for its actions? Is it equally to blame for its actions? For the Greeks, 'blameworthiness'– moral or otherwise – did not entail the sort of personal guilt that we now associate with moral responsibility. It was a much more social and political matter of what others thought, a mixture of communal standards and luck, of existing moral and social practices of accountability and praiseworthiness in an environment that influenced certain actions.

We have to ask whether any intention or deliberate choice to pursue certain means to reach those ends is the same as the social pressure that in an impersonal consequentialist account influences one to behave in a particular way. We have to be wary of setting up a false dichotomy between 'society' causing us to behave in a particular way, and us being wholly responsible for our actions. In most cases it is a mixture of deliberate and freely chosen actions, and the constraints of the pressures of the social environment or life-world that we inhabit. Such an ongoing dialectic between the subjective and objective aspects of ethical behaviour places a different perspective on the use of guilt as a means of social control, because it means that we as educational administrators must take a certain amount of responsibility for placing pressure on some people to conform to rules. We must decide whether conformity to the rule *is* ethical.

Conversely we must decide how far we accept conscience as a matter solely of individual decision, and how far actions are undertaken in the light of social pressure as well. There is a fine line between teachers blaming external factors such as working conditions, parental influence or lack of financial support for poor teaching rather than taking responsibility for their own teaching capacity. While they should not take on the burden of guilt for matters beyond their control, if they intend wholeheartedly to bring about their educational ends, they will take on the responsibility of changing those conditions as far as possible to further those educational ends.

ACCOUNTABILITY AND ASSESSMENT

I have been trying to show how punishment may be ethical if it considers the well-being of students, the consequences of painful deterrents, the consistency of assigning blame and responsibility. It may not appear that the assignment of grades is an ethical matter, but in this discussion of means and ends I want to raise the issue of treating assessment of students as a means to an educational end or an end in itself. In many aspects of education, including punishment, examinations and disciplinary areas, what was previously a means to a broader end becomes an end in itself as attention becomes focused on short-term goals.

In the global move towards accountability, a system of payment by results is being advocated in which a class's performance on basic literacy and numeracy is tested at the beginning and end of each school year, and the teacher is promoted, allocated good or bad classes, or demoted, depending on the improvement or otherwise of the class as a whole, assuming that the test results provide adequate evidence of the merit of the teacher. There are all kinds of ethical questions embedded in this practice, as there are in any kind of monitoring of teacher performance against standard measurements of changes in children's ability. To what extent is improvement in an individual child 'caused' by the teacher, and how much influenced by external factors such as natural maturation, additional paid tuition or happier home environment? The consequences of valuing teachers' work on the basis of the apparent consequences of their teaching may well be, on a utilitarian scale, extremely detrimental to the well-being of the individual student in a teacher's care. Teachers who consider the short-term rewards may well inflate the grades of their class without considering the longer-term consequences for either the children or the teacher who takes that class the following year.

Louis Schmier (1995) presented for discussion a hypothetical case of a student getting a C+ for the course when she had received Bs and B–s on all her tests, the term project/paper and final exam. The professor explained that the course syllabus stated that attendance would influence 10 per cent of the final grade. Because the student had an unreasonable number of unexcused absences, he had imposed the stated penalty. The student argued that she had demonstrated her competency by working well outside class, using library resources and the notes of a friend. The end of the class had been demonstrably achieved. She had chosen to help with a charitable welfare agency instead of attending class. The professor believed that academic requirements had a higher priority than social welfare. Moreover the student understood the requirements of the course as laid out in the syllabus and had therefore been penalized fairly for not meeting them.

Teachers' reactions to this position were mixed. Some considered that the student should have negotiated with the professor for a special contract before the course started. Others, promoting consistent application of rules, would have refused the request. Some thought that the professor could modify the grade only if the purpose of the class was to teach character development, but that this should be more explicit. Otherwise the earned academic grade should stand. Another teacher suggested phrasing the attendance policy in such a way that drew attention to natural consequences rather than penalties, even though this was more complicated. He would say, for instance, that anyone who misses three or more of his classes is not likely to be able to earn an A. Additionally, anyone who misses no more than one class will earn an extra half-grade (B– to B, C to C+, etc.). Anyone who does not read the assignments but attends all classes, takes good notes and tests fairly well can probably earn a B. Anyone who does not do well on tests and flunks them all can still earn a C to a B if they read assignments, attend class, participate in class and do a B paper or better. Anyone can earn an A– if they get C–s or better on all tests, read assignments and participate in class, miss no more than three classes, and get A on the final paper; or they get A grades for all tests and earn a C or better on the final paper (and, of course, miss no more than three classes). This policy does not require a contract and takes up no more than a page in the course outline. He claims that this is equitable because it recognizes different preferences for learning and rewards attendance rather than penalizing non-attendance. You might consider whether this is an ethical exercise of power, given that one of the themes of this chapter has been the awarding of punishment and penalties. Consider also under what circumstances it could be considered appropriate to try to change, from a weaker power base, some rules and laws that currently apply.

You might like to imagine a conversation about assessment criteria that might take place in your own staff room. What reasons do educators give for their assessment policies? How are they related to care for the individual student, the consistency of their actions or the consequences with which we have been mainly concerned in this chapter? Teachers often have to formulate strategies that will accommodate exceptions. However, what some consider a relevant factor in reaching their ends, others consider irrelevant. Disagreement may be as much about ends as about grades. Many teachers confuse the means and ends of assessment; the grade has become an end in itself rather than a means to an educational end. Similarly in other examples used in this chapter there will be many readers who believe that conformity to the rules and standards is the major end of schooling, in which case they will tend to emphasize the training aspects of their practices.

The relationship between ethical codes and school regulations grew closer in Germany in the early 1980s, where school assessment and grade promotion practices came increasingly under the jurisdiction of state administrative law, with the effect that teachers found these elements of their practice subject to legal action. They tended to respond either by forms of compliance that caused their assessment practices to become more bureaucratic and intrusive, or by pretending to comply with the law while going on as before. When they adopted the former strategy (like a work to rule) their relationships with students were correspondingly bureaucratized, a result that Habermas argues is educationally dysfunctional.

> If one studies the paradoxical structure of juridification in such areas as the family, the schools, social-welfare policy and the like, the meaning of the demands that regularly result from these analyses is easy to decipher. The point is to protect areas of life that are functionally dependent on social integration through values, norms and consensus formation, to preserve them from falling prey to the systemic imperatives of economic and administrative subsystems growing with dynamics of their own, and to defend them from becoming converted over, through the steering mechanism of the law, to a principle of sociation that is for them dysfunctional.
>
> (Habermas 1987: 372–3)

We may see similar confusion between means and ends arise in the following chapter between the rules for wearing school uniform and tidy dress itself as a means to an end. It may be that such issues can be resolved only by dialogue between those who differ rather than by fiat from the teacher, which may alienate students from participation in the school ethos. Ends can be achieved by a wide range of means, and the matter still remains unresolved that some means are more ethical than others. To ignore the possibility of ongoing negotiation and take refuge in the stated legislation is to move towards a legalistic rather than an ethical consideration of matters. The problem of deciding which means are more ethical is so contentious that many take refuge in the law or regulations to resolve disputes.

In this chapter, I have tried to look at the complexities of separating out means and ends in education, with a particular focus on the ethical code of considering the well-being of students, collectively and individually. The relationship between the well-being of each student and the longer-term welfare of the school and eventually the community has resulted in a focus on various forms of social control, particularly our notions of punishment and penalties. I have argued that punishment, unless simply defined legalistically, has ethical implications of blame and worth built into it, and the consequent ethical requirement of choice and negotiation with those in power requires consideration of the appropriateness of the ends as well as the means. Legislation is not there to be imposed as an end in itself even in the awarding of grades. It is a matter to be discussed by all parties, negotiated if possible through to a resolution that meets the wishes of all relevant parties, and in so doing continues the ongoing dialectic between the well-being of the student and the community. I will resume this point in the next chapter on equity. The issues of looking at ends as long-term consequences of short-term means have been raised in this chapter in the light of the consequentialist aspects and will be refined in Chapter 8 in the broader context of care and consistency.

Chapter 4

Equity and the construction of difference

As agents of class domination, school rites courted catastrophe: they appeared to be a crucial contingency in the reproduction of inequality. This conclusion, of course, needs to be investigated further, but it is admissible if we accept the fact that the rites of instruction reified the classroom world according to the tenets of an oppressive dominant culture. Forms of instruction and teaching practices generally constituted an inadvertent ritualised reaffirmation of ethnic stereotypes and the daily remaking and reconfirmation of class division.

McLaren (1993: 227)

The world is not what I think, but what I live through. I am open to the world, I have no doubt that I am in communication with it; . . . I can never completely account for this ever-reiterated assertion in my life.

Merleau Ponty (1962: 177)

In the second chapter we began to analyse the relationship between rules and ethical codes. The rules of a Catholic co-educational school in Western Australia are so detailed that they cover over nine legal-size single-spaced pages. Their rules (Sacred Heart College 1993: 55) for wearing school uniform will be familiar to most parents of children at private schools. The winter uniform for boys consists of a school shirt, a tie (worn correctly with shirt top button done up), a school jumper (not a windcheater), brown school trousers (not jeans, cords, etc.), fawn socks, dark brown leather shoes and a blazer (optional). Girls must wear the same tie and shoes, with the optional blazer, and are required to wear a blouse, a regulation fawn skirt and fawn stockings (long socks are *not* permitted). It is worth noting the tone of some of the further detail provided, especially the label of 'offender', for those who transgress:

(iii)(a) Boys' hair may not be longer than down to the collar and must be neat.
(b) Girls with long hair must have it tied back, both in and out of class for hygiene and safety reasons.
(c) Hair ribbons and plain combs may be red, brown or white in colour.

(d) Hair styles for both girls and boys must be of a generally conservative nature.

Styles which follow the latest fads (e.g. tails) or which are considered
extreme, are not permitted.
   Hair colour is to be natural. Dyes, rinses are not acceptable.
   Any flouting of hair regulations will result in the offending student
being asked to remain at home until his/her hair style or colour is
acceptable.

(iv) No T-shirts are to be worn under school shirts. Offending students
will be asked to remove them.
(v) Jumpers are to be worn or kept in lockers or bags. They are not to be
carried or tied around student's waist or shoulders.
(vi) No jewellery is allowed except wrist watches and (for girls) sleepers
or plain studs for ears. One stud per ear. Coloured studs are banned.
Boys may not wear sleepers or studs in ears.

Prohibited are rings, necklaces of any nature, anklets, make-up and
nail polish.
   Any jewellery worn by students will be confiscated and made
available to that person at the end of the year.

(Sacred Heart College 1993: 55A–B)

Clearly it is moral to follow these rules, but is it ethical? The rules offer
a clear example of the juridification tendencies mentioned by Habermas
(1987) who suggests that some of the consequences of juridification are
dysfunctional, since they undermine life-world conditions necessary for
welfare and education. Compare (iii) (d) above about hairstyles with this
policy from another Catholic boys' school (Curtis 1995: 1). This next one
is a little more flexible, allowing some independent judgement as to what
counts as neat or clean, and what counts as 'inappropriately short'. They
are expectations, rather than rules, closer to a code than a law.

HAIR STYLES

As parents and students know, we have been campaigning this year
and last year to engender a strong sense of personal pride in each
student's appearance. Most students have responded well and are
looking smart and well-groomed. Most parents have supported this
policy strongly. We still, however, have a minority of students who
definitely see it as 'uncool' to appear neat and tidy and need strong
urging to have their hair cut or reasonably styled.
   To assist parents and students, I list the following expectations:

• Hair should be well-styled, neat and clean.

- Hair should be cut so that it clears the collar at the back and so that it does not fall in front of the face.
- If the fringe is able to be tucked behind the ears it is too long.
- Hair styles should be of a conservative nature and not inappropriately short or shaven.
- Hair cuts with a no 1 blade are not acceptable.
- Portions of the scalp must not be shaven (eg undercuts).
- Artificial colours or highlights are not allowed.

These sort of restrictions are not new. In 1929 an Arkansas court upheld the expulsion of a girl from school for wearing talcum powder (quoted in Strike and Egan 1978: 139). It reasoned that although such an infringement of personal choice would be objectionable in any other public institution except a school, the school is different from other institutions since it has among its legitimate tasks instruction in citizenship which includes obedience to authority. Since enforcement of rules *per se* may teach obedience to authority, the enforcement of rules, regardless of their content, can be viewed as serving the legitimate educational goals of the school.

Another primary school in Western Australia survives with no more than three simple rules for students, namely 'Be neat, be punctual and show respect for others.' In this latter school there are, it is true, some difficulties in enforcing appropriate dress, but then there is little need to enforce it. The school has a 97 per cent use of the non-compulsory school uniform and the students are as tidy as school children can be. While the ends of the three schools might be similar, they use different means to reach that end, the latter school placing more emphasis on ethics than morality. At the first Catholic school, a great deal of time is spent monitoring the dress code, a duty handed over to prefects rather than teaching staff, with punitory visits made by 'offenders' to the principal. If the efforts to prop up the basic rules with further prohibitions are anything to go by, there has been a great deal of resistance by students to the dress code, which takes the form of defying the dress code as far as possible, requiring its constant modification and elaboration.

THE ETHICS OF DRESS CODE

What is the point of dress codes? It seems partly a matter of creating an identity for a school to which it is hoped that students will conform, although the level of resistance may well mark a conflict between the students' perception of their identity and that being imposed by the school.

These rules relating to dress and appearance have been created to establish a level of which everyone can be proud. At all times student dress should be of a high standard. Parents are asked to ensure that the correct uniform is worn at all times.

(Sacred Heart College 1993: 55B)

Ensuring that the dress code is adhered to makes it reasonable to apply some form of sanction to those who do not conform. Are the rules formulated as regulations or recommendations? Can they be implemented without coercion? Regardless of whether they are practices or regulations, what freedom is there not to conform? What do these codes have to do with social justice or equity? The matter lies partly in the way that they are formulated, and whether students and parents had input into their formulation. The ethical perspective raises questions about the contribution that school uniform makes to the well-being of students or to the good life.

The issue of conformity to school codes in the matter of dress became both ethical and legal in Victoria two years ago when a 15-year-old Victorian school boy was suspended from class for refusing to cut his hair (Hawes 1995). The school uniform policy had said that students must keep their hair in a 'neat, appropriate and conventional style'. Girls must tie it back if worn longer, while boys must wear it to 'collar length at a maximum'. The boy, Samuel Copes, had tied his hair back and, after having been asked to cut it, had even worn a 'short back and sides style wig' to school to comply with the rules. But the school then issued him with a uniform defect notice ordering him to cut his hair or face suspension. He refused and was suspended. He complained to the Equal Opportunity Commission, alleging discrimination on sexual grounds. If girls could tie their hair back, why couldn't he? The school's legal representative argued that its policy was aimed at neatness and only in that context did it differentiate between the sexes. But the student argued that he had been neat, and that the school's case rested on different interpretations of what was 'conventional' for boys and girls. Gender was an irrelevant difference that should not have been taken into consideration when deciding how neat he was. The Board agreed, ruling that there was *prima facie* evidence to show that he had been discriminated against and that he should be permitted to return to school. The school appealed against the decision, unsuccessfully. Certainly the school could not argue that it was safe for girls to wear their hair in a pony-tail but not boys, or even that a girl's hair tied back was neater than a boy's.

The issue is not resolved simply by referring it to law. As Lyotard (1988) reminds us, instances of dispute conventionally determined as political or legal are seen to be more justly considered as sites for indeterminate judgement in which the criteria for reaching a judgement have yet to be decided. Nor is it simply a textual matter. It is a matter, as I suggested, of an a-rational care, a holistic responsiveness to existing practices which is necessary to provoke change in structures of language and law.

A similar question which also confronts our structural expectations of boys not wearing long hair could arise from the requirement that girls are required to wear a different uniform from boys. It arises from the normal social custom of gender-differentiated dressing, but maybe with more cross-gender clothes being worn in the streets, the notion of gender-differentiated uniforms may change. The relationship between the moral norms and ethical aims is being tested at such a point and in many others. If we are aiming at developing creative and critical thought, why do we not extend this to the wearing of the school uniform? A similar theme will run through the body of this chapter. In which sense is it ethical or equitable to maintain difference, even where that difference has been constructed for moral purposes?

There are many differences enshrined in school practice that embed conventional understandings so deeply that we are often unaware of them. Why, in those few Western schools where corporal punishment is allowed, is it restricted only to boys? The principle of social justice requires us to treat unequally those who are unequal in relevant respects. But the principle is problematic. Religious, gender, ethnic and socioeconomic differences abound. When are certain ones relevant to certain other issues, especially dress code? Is gender relevant to the mainstreaming of the intellectually disabled? Could religious difference be a good reason for excluding someone from a social studies weekend camp? A social justice policy tries to overcome educational disadvantage by trying to act consistently with the policy to treat unequally those who are unequal in relevant respects.

WHEN DO ANTI-DISCRIMINATION POLICIES IN EDUCATION DISCRIMINATE?

Samuel Copes demanded that he be treated equally with girls in respect to hairstyle. He won his argument that he had undergone sex discrimination, because his gender was not considered by the courts to be a difference relevant to his appearance in the school. However, there are differences considered to be more relevant to a person's chance of success in schools. When those background differences likely to affect a young person's education intersect with school-based factors – such as inappropriate and exclusive curriculum, an unsupportive or discriminatory environment, ineffective teaching and inequitable resourcing – a social difference is translated into educational disadvantage.

Social justice policies in educational institutions aim at ensuring that students are placed in the most educationally enhancing environment, or what used to be known as the least restrictive environment, so that for instance Aboriginal students may be given additional homework classes after school at government expense, so that their education will come closer to those of upper middle-class white children with parental help, home computer access and library resources. The question of relevance is apposite here too. While there is evidence to demonstrate that many Aboriginal students need and benefit from additional support, one might ask whether subsidized homework classes ought to be available to all socioeconomically deprived children, regardless of skin colour or race. It has been suggested by some Aboriginal groups that it is racist to make race the criteria for any differentiation, and that other criteria can usually be found for taking action that may benefit disadvantaged Aboriginal groups. Ironically, in the Copes case, the ethical issue of what is to count as a relevant difference was raised in the matter of hair styles, and the implication of the court's decision was that gender did not count as an appropriate difference for mandating length of hair.

What do educational institutions believe constitutes a difference relevant to educational justice? The Education Department of Western Australia (EDWA) divides its social justice policy and guidelines (October 1991, supp. 1993) into four distinct groups for those students whom they perceive as having different types of social disadvantage: students with disabilities, Aboriginal and Torres Strait Islanders, non-English-speaking background (NESB) students and gender equity. The national policy (MCEETYA 1994: 4) does not recognize gender as a group requiring social justice but in its six priority groups it adds the non-exclusive groups of students at risk, students from low socioeconomic backgrounds or living in poverty and students who are geographically isolated.

Should we be trying to ensure that all families have an equal income so that no children are disadvantaged by relative poverty? Should we force all families to move away from remote areas to the advantages of the metropolitan area to remove the disadvantage of distance? No, because the differences exist for good reasons, and the agenda is an equitable rather than an equalizing one. The nonsense of trying to give each student an equal background in relevant respects exposes some of the normalizing aspects of many social justice policies.

Each of these lists discriminates in a neutral sense, that is, it differentiates some groups more in need of social justice than others. It is not ethically wrong to discriminate; our language requires us to do it all the time. It is important to make sure that the discrimination between groups is ethically based, and that it is appropriate to the situation that marks the difference.

Are there any areas of disadvantage that cover all of these differentiated groups? More importantly, are there any groups left out? The national policy (MCEETYA 1994: 2) lists the background factors most likely to influence a young person's education as poverty, low socioeconomic background, poor literacy, family breakdown, violence, abuse and isolation/rurality, but it is difficult for legislation to equalize opportunities in many of these areas without appearing to cater to a deficit model. The whole issue of constructing difference, that is defining minority groups as being different from the dominant group in order to exclude them somehow or require them to change if they are to be included in a certain community, is ongoing and contentious.

Australia's Equal Opportunity Act 1984 provided remedies in respect of discrimination on the grounds of sex, marital status, pregnancy, race, religious conviction, impairment or involving sexual harassment. Existing policies made some provision for academically talented students, isolated students and poor students. Is there a policy to cater for religious disadvantage, sexual preference, age discrimination, unfit wimps, intellectual dissidents, artists? The department's social justice policy does not yet provide for discrimination against those who are obese, or those who have blue eyes.

We are concerned with equity here as well as discrimination. In both national and state policies there has been a shift from equal opportunity to social justice outcomes. This is partly an acknowledgement of a pluralistic society in which there is seen to be no one cultural standard or attainment. The policy no longer aims at equal outcomes but at equitable and appropriate outcomes. While one can support equity as a concept, what its conception is or how the ethical principle is to be transformed into moral practices continues to engage debate. The problem of an equitable reconciliation between Aborigines and Western education has not yet been resolved satisfactorily. The principles of the national Aboriginal and Torres Strait Islander educational policy of 1989 in the Department of Western Australia's social justice policy document included the following:

• involvement of minority groups in educational decision-making
• equity of access to educational services
• equity of educational participation
• equitable and appropriate educational outcomes.

I raise the earlier question about the relevance of race as a criterion for any of these policies again, as these principles of Aboriginality would apply equally to Asians, Jews, homosexuals. Yet, if we look at the practices in schools since the social justice policy was released, we do not see boomerang-throwing as a sport replacing football or netball as the predominant sport in schools, nor any discussion as to whether it should have a priority over soccer or badminton. We do not see the static rows of desks rearranged to accommodate the learning needs of Aboriginal children, perhaps because there is no one learning style that suits all

Aboriginals, or for that matter all non-Aboriginals. The offering of more informal discussions in classrooms is a concession to learning theory rather than cultural or racial difference, and the increasing use of oral as opposed to written language is a gesture towards multiple intelligences rather than racial accommodation. Does the difficulty in defining cultural difference make it an impossible base for educational policy?

We are left with the question of what counts as a relevant difference. Multiculturalism incorporates the three dimensions of cultural identity, social justice and economic efficiency. Aborigines themselves have protested that they are not a homogeneous group and that there are significant differences, say, between Koori and Nyungar groups, in different regions of Australia. Do we include all Asian students in the same group, from wealthy Singaporeans to Vietnamese boat people? Do we push Thai and Chinese together, or keep them as culturally separate sub-groups, along with Korean, Indian, Indonesian? Do we need further sub-groups of Chinese, such as those from Sichuan? While it is difficult to see how British students come under the umbrella of NESB students, some people of British nationality have very solid cultural roots from Jamaica and Pakistan. Do we give them equal consideration in Australian schools with New Zealanders and Americans (and here I do not mean only American Hispanics or New Zealand Maoris)? Within the English-speaking background there is also cultural difference that is profound, if we consider Jewish citizens and surfies (a hedonistic Australian youth cult which worships the sun and sea more than work) as inhabiting totally different life-worlds. The issue of multi-literacies is with us, and the notion of a standard English considerably under threat.

From another area, equity of access to services and participation for NESB groups includes funding for ESL (English as a Second Language) and literacy programmes. What concept of an English-speaking nation or of literacy underpin these moves? If the government allows anyone's standards to be equally valued, what happens to the concept of standards? It might be that they become less visible, couched in apparently flexible terms, allowing a free range of processes, as long as the students attain the desired end or outcome. The move from opportunity to outcomes allows one to measure more specifically the attainment or otherwise of the objectives, which are spelt out in each section, but this can lead to a rigidity in the requirements which could well be discriminatory to minority groups, unless there is set in place separate sets of objectives for each of the multi-literacies.

Why are these differences considered irrelevant to educational disadvantage? We could make a point about discrimination by saying that neither state nor national policy currently considers epicenes, that group of people who could comprise up to one out of every 500 of our population (the same proportion as Down's syndrome children) and who are neither male nor female. Social justice policies, even those for dress code, are premissed on a female/male distinction. What differences are we encouraged to respect and what differences might we ignore as inconsequential? Postmodern theories would argue that our social institutions play a larger part than we realize in the formation of what we perceive to be unalterable differences (Burbules 1996). What part does political correctness have to play in all the differences you see marked by your school practices? Can you detect any examples of social injustices in your school that are not covered by the school's social justice policies? In our educational decision-making, how do we decide what is a relevant difference? These large questions are continually raised by deconstructionists who place existing systems under such close scrutiny that the systems often seem under threat of collapse.

We construct difference, and we do so for different purposes. The whole question of cultural difference is an expression of a political trend, a framework within which groups can argue their separateness and distinctiveness, against conceptions of community, solidarity or liberal consensus that tend to stress common needs and interests. Burbules (1996: 1) notes that difference

is an expression of social and psychological models of identity and subjectivity that highlight the internally fragmented and performative aspects of human personality and action; as the identities and positions of cyborgs, hybrids, and creoles become more a topic of reflection, difference comes to be seen as a profound feature of inner life and not only a matter of encounters among diverse groups. Overall, these trends have sought to shift the focus away from a presumption of sameness to a recognition of difference; to highlight issues of fragmentation and hybridity; and to shift the burden of proof off the shoulders of those who have often had to justify their nonconformity with conventional, dominant norms or identities.

Even the commonplace difference of gender is contentious, especially in regard to social justice. The Education Department of Western Australia says confidently that 'Gender is no longer a variable affecting patterns of student participation, achievement and post-school options', that 'the curriculum is enriched for all students through the inclusion of perspectives, values and contributions to society of women and girls'. It is debatable whether that last 'is' is a descriptive or a prescriptive one – that is, whether it is a statement of fact that the curriculum is enriched, or whether it means that it *ought* to be. We could ask whether there is an equal move to have more boys in arts and nursing as well as more girls in science and maths. The social justice policy (EDWA 1993: 16) claims that any move to make the girls more like the boys is sexist. Is it sexist to make the boys more like the girls? Is it sexist to have single-sex classes?

Some boys feel that now they are being disadvantaged by the additional attention paid to girls in schools.

Does this make us as modernist as Saussure who believed that matters of gender or race, for instance, were significant only insofar as they were inscribed within the system of differences that makes up the *langue* of a culture? No, because both Merleau Ponty (1962: 164) and Lyotard remind us that seeing a person as one gender or another, as one race or another, is not merely a matter of passive object and distanced subject. The subject and object come together in an act of perception.

We could ask to what extent the difference between girls and boys is one that is relevant to education. Do they need separate toilet facilities? Is it a difference that we could remove from educational practices? The question becomes pertinent if we consider what schools do about other genders, especially those that are chromosomally based, where children who are epicenes, that is neither male nor female, are forced to identify, often with massive doses of oestrogen or testosterone, with one sex or the other. Is it right that a 16-year-old epicene should feel pressured to have a double mastectomy because his/her budding breasts interfere with his/her rugby playing, and cause merciless teasing in the shower-room? This hidden gender throws all sorts of doubt upon many existing social and school practices, not only the difficulty of male and female toilets from which they are technically excluded, but also including the use of differentiated pronouns and prizes, participation in sports, sexual partnerships, socially acculturated expectations of behaviour and vocation. More particularly it raises the bigger question of whether we could do away with gender distinction altogether. Some epicenes feel strongly that this would be unfair. After all, they claim that their identity as epicenes is possible only in distinction to males and females. Their unease is similarly felt by feminists who believe that removal of gender stereotyping will leave power in the hands of the prevailing dominant gender.

THE CONSTRUCTION OF SELF

Derrida asserts through a concept of *différance* that the modernist subject is constituted through the binary opposition of the subject and object. 'The movement of *différance* is not something that happens to a transcendental subject. It is what produces it' (Derrida 1973: 82). Kohlberg's model shows growth of the autonomous self through a process of distancing one's decisions from the immediate experience, usually through the categorization of linguistic concepts which become increasingly abstract. Gilligan's criticism of the Kohlbergian model was that the abstracted demands of Kantian moral principle – to be fair, honest, keep promises – moved too far away from the experienced reality as though the impersonal perspective from which actions are understood were not part of an acting self. In his effort to deconstruct this subject or self, Derrida argues that the binary opposition between subject and object should be displaced not by an appeal to yet another opposition but to a non-oppositional metaphor, that of the trace or the other, which means that, for instance, males/females is not a binary opposition, but that males are different from all other genders, females are different from all other genders, epicenes are different from all other genders.

The discussion of social justice makes difference relevant. The subject is constituted by the play of meanings within language. What Derrida and Lacan (1975) ignore is that this play is a serious business, whose end product has nothing to do with fictions and vacillations between difference of text but constructs social beings seeking to make meaning out of their perceived differences and similarities. The play of meanings within language produces real subjects with coherent subjectivities that constitute their identities. Subjects do not choose or change their identities as they do their lives; rather, a particular definition of subjectivity provides the ground for meaning and value in a subject's life (Hekman 1995: 79).

Many principals would claim that the main benefits of a school uniform are to construct a community identity, a feeling of belonging to a group and therefore with identification of certain values, which society in its turn values. Adults who interact with the child do not teach identity, but they present and create behaviours within the child which eventually form what one would call a 'person' or, in Foucauldian terms, a subject. The external shaping of behaviour sits oddly with the notion that there is an autonomous self which decides to act in the world. The notion of individual responsibility for one's action lies at the basis of existentialist thought, especially Heidegger.

Only when a newborn has become sufficiently formed by its environment does it become what Heidegger calls a *Dasein*. These behaviours – moving, thinking, speaking – which make up our existence are so basic that we never realize their significance. Heidegger called one's particular culture, the social environment into which one is thrown, one's 'world', and the idea has been echoed in Habermas's life-world and Kuhn's large paradigms or frames. The different social practices of a specific culture make up the 'world' of that culture. The shared public 'worlds' constitute the standards by which the *Dasein* of a culture act. In turn each of these larger worlds can be broken down into smaller ones that more specifically define a *Dasein*, which could be a church group, the world of experimental physicists at a university, the theatre world, or a school.

To stress the importance of the 'world', Heidegger called *Dasein*'s activity of existing 'being-in-the-world'. The use of the hyphens emphasizes that there is no distance between ourselves and the world. We are as much a part of the world as it is of us. The ideal community where people unconsciously share mutual agreement and similarities approaches the concept of *Dasein*. The 'in' from 'being-in-the world' indicates involvement or care rather than a spatial indicator. *Dasein*, this particular way of existing, is different from the ordinary existence of things in the world around us. The difference is that things are determinate and have their distinctive properties. That is their kind of being. But the sort of being that people manifest is not that of a thing-with-properties, it is a range of possible things to be. We define the individual we become by projecting ourselves into those possibilities which we choose or which we allow to be chosen for us. Who we become is a matter of how we act in the contexts in which we find ourselves (Campbell and Christensen 1996: 184).

Maybe it is not important to understand Heidegger's notion of *Dasein* to practise ethics. Yet Heidegger is one of the few philosophers, along with Buber (1961), Arendt (1958) and Noddings (1984), to write about interpersonal caring and the consequences for living together communally. A school community represents a group *Dasein* for many people, especially those living in boarding schools. Students are immersed in the school and deal with the things in it, not as required by traditional epistemology, by bridging an unbridgeable gap between a self-enclosed consciousness and an external object, but by relating objects to their practical concerns: as tools, as something at hand, or missing. It is existential rather than intellectual.

For many people there are conflicting worlds through which they move daily, changing practices as they move – for instance, the different rituals and practices of the classroom, the playground and the home, noted by McLaren (1993). If we are going to understand our lives, our average 'everydayness' in which I have located the care aspects of ethics, we have to invert the Cartesian view of ourselves as a thinking thing which sees structures of the world as they are. We have to invert 'I think, therefore I am', to the more Heideggerian 'I care, therefore I think'. *Dasein*, the quality of being-there, makes sense of itself out of the world into which it is thrown, and a group *Dasein* has a normative function in the sense that it shapes behaviour.

Language and education help us to develop our theoretical concepts and regard things with their essential and accidental properties as objects of theoretical knowledge, and this in turn makes it possible for us to think of our existence as if it is of the same kind as that of objects in a reflective mode. It is by revealing the fundamental features of *Dasein* – of the kind of existence we have – that we can come to understand other kinds of existence, i.e. other senses of being.

What has *Dasein* to do with equity? If we return to the issue of school uniforms once again, it will be apparent that one of the main functions of school uniforms is to define identity in terms of various concepts, to help students to see themselves as a student at a school, and even as a male or female student at that school. At the same time that that gives identity to the majority, it excludes others. How fairly does it exclude those who do not fit in easily with the defining categories? As a young girl I was always the character who, if I did not have a ladder in my black stockings, would have been hatless or without a glove. Such misdemeanours were not deliberate contraventions of the rules on my part, but my insistence that I was something over and above those rules – an artist perhaps, or a free spirit. No matter how I saw myself, there were always social criteria to guide me to define myself in certain ways. We see the same trend today, especially in high schools where there are sub-groups or communities who will adapt the uniform to create a sub-identity – it could be through a common hairstyle which is within the regulations but which binds the sub-group together as being different from the rest. The self needs a concept to hang itself upon, and this is agreed upon by convention and those shared practices that define a community. Difference is constructed and without it identity has no meaning.

COMMUNITY AND THE EXPANDING CIRCLE

Superficially similar ideas about self were espoused by the American social behaviourist George Mead (1934). Mead (1934: 200) said:

> The self appears in experience essentially as a 'me' with the organiza-
> tion of the community to which it belongs. This organization is, of
> course, expressed in the particular endowment and particular social
> situation of the individual. He is a member of the community, but he
> is a particular part of the community with a particular heredity and
> position which distinguishes him from anybody else. He is what he is
> in so far as he is a member of this community, and the raw materials
> out of which this particular individual is born would not be a self but
> for his relationship to others in the community of which he is a part.

However, Mead speaks of the development of the self from the 'me' to the 'I' in language strongly reminiscent of Kohlberg's rational developmental scale and he has a greater belief than Heidegger on the power of rationality and thought to lift one's self out of the 'world' into which one was thrown.

Some people have never questioned the values that are presented in their home and school, have never questioned the meaning of their life, have never recognized the fact that they have been thrown into such a place in the world. Heidegger would say that their existence is *undifferentiated*. It is not dissimilar to a Piagetian pre-conventional stage, where the child is unable to distinguish the way that they view the world from that of other people and indeed cannot distinguish the world as separate from their own experience of them. Faced with alternative ways of living, some people suddenly realize that their world is a result of sheer coincidence. They may decide to change their life and assume a completely different career or role. At this point they enter what Heidegger called an inauthentic mode of existence, simply substituting one life made possible by circumstance for another. One day, faced with the realization that her existence as a teacher is a result of sheer coincidence, a person might decide to change her life, her world, and become an actress. At this point she has entered the inauthentic mode of existence, inauthentic because she cannot change the form of her life, which her past existence has shaped, by changing the context of her daily living. The realization of the coincidence of life may result in anxiety, the realization that anything that they might possibly do has already been defined for them in advance by their environment and their reaction to it. Anxiety appears when they face the possibility of never being able to escape from their presented form. At this point any of these people can either refuse to recognize the situation at hand and immerse themselves back into their arbitrarily chosen world, once again becoming inauthentic, or they can face up to the existential present and say, if I am like this, I might as well take responsibility for the life I am going to live. No one else is accountable for me except me. I will do what I decide is best even if it is a way of life created by others. At this point this person becomes what Heidegger called a 'being-toward-death'. Heidegger calls this transformation 'care'. In caring for its world, *Dasein* makes the most of its own possibilities – even if these possibilities were originally defined by the world into which a person was born. A person who exhibits care towards its world exists in an authentic mode of existence and is an experiential version of the rational autonomy required by Kant and Kohlberg. They *exist*, not simply living as a teacher, administrator, student, Aboriginal, non-Australian, non-scientist, mother or a socially distinguishable concept.

The Kohlbergian mode ran the risk of abstracting people into 'thinking things' for which we often provide the metaphors of a 'subject', a 'self', an 'agent', an 'individual'. For this thinking thing, the world exists because they exist. In the end everything refers back to himself, as the ultimate reference point. That ego cannot think of a tree without seeing the tree as existing for it, as a giver of oxygen so that it can breathe, as a supplier of its building materials, paper or shade. From this point of view nature is outside ego and exists for ego's use. The egocentric human frames the world and turns it into an object in order to make it more accessible. Rather than recognizing their place in the world, a status as one being among all other beings, the egocentric turns the world into something that exists for and because of the thinking thing. In refusing to consider the outward-turning responsibility of care, the 'self' becomes a 'selfish' one, which does not truly fit in with the needs of the community and try to foster those needs. The authentic being, however, chooses to belong to a community and constantly reflects on the ethical value of that with other possibilities. There is a necessary commitment to reflective participation in a community. So the ethical self responds to one community by choice, and tries where possible to accommodate itself to an expanding community which includes rather than excludes others.

The inability of a person to move consciously and authentically outside their own world was noted by Marilyn French when she analysed feminist attempts to move beyond power in a dominantly paternalistic society:

If we decide actively to oppose patriarchal values, and try to create a new system, we find no clear direction. For our system incorporates patriarchal values; our institutions are invariably hierarchical. Hierarchy is a structure designed to retain and transmit power, thus as long as our institutions are hierarchical, power remains supreme. Yet because power is indeed supreme, no alternative structure is as successful in our world.

(French 1986: 215)

The move outside one's lived world is not impossible, as Heidegger implied, but it has to be gradual and dialectic, one in which there are equal possibilities of moving in either direction.

EQUALITY AND EQUITY

The relationship between an 'authentic being-in-the-world' and an intellectual awareness of the world through categories can best be analysed by exploring the assumed categories implied in any claim for equity. The notion of equity fits most easily inside the consistency frame because it is guided by the central principle of justice – that of equal respect for persons.

Secada (1989) claims that even though one of the most powerful constructs at the disposal of equity is inequality, the fundamental difference between equity and equality is that equity is a qualitative property, while equality is quantitative. Sometimes equity concerns coincide with those of equality and sometimes not. How can we tell?

Let us assume that a minister for education is concerned with equity for all disadvantaged bodies. He says, 'Women now account for more than half the total enrolments in higher education, but they remain heavily concentrated in a narrow range of courses and disciplines. This high degree of concentration is not only a significant barrier to women's full and equal participation in subsequent employment but it is also a major source of structural rigidity and inefficiency.' The same minister later says, 'Structural rigidities have been an important factor in the perpetuation of these inequities.' His words exemplify the vicious cyclical effect of prevailing structures of belief, the experienced world which it is difficult to evade. The means by which he could try to remove inequities (national accountability, women in non-traditional courses, special entry and childcare) seem in many ways to perpetuate them in the light of existing inflexible ideological structures. But these are institutionalized structures and just as they gradually came into existence, so they can be gradually and subtly transformed

By bolstering childcare and subsidizing the entry of more women and girls into maths and science, a minister might be convinced that he was removing gender stereotypes, and giving women the right and the training to enter maths and science. One of the underlying flaws in his policy is that he equates equity simplistically with equality. There are fewer women than men in maths and science. So he tries to even up the numbers by campaigning to get women to enrol in maths and science. Because he inhabits a 'masculine world' he is blind to the possibility of numerically equalizing the sides of an equation or balancing it by adjusting either side. He could have funded the increased entry of more males into the arts, teaching and nursing. Inequity always implies injustice, inequality does not. By balancing the equation in the 'non-normal' direction, we can make transparent the values that decide what rights are to be extended to women – male values, not necessarily female ones.

EQUITY FOR THE INTELLECTUALLY DISADVANTAGED

Social justice policy requires that all students, irrespective of the degree of sensory, physical or intellectual disability, should have the opportunity to be educated in the least restrictive environment consistent with the provision of a quality education which best meets the needs of the individual student. Students with disabilities will be educated as close as possible to their homes and alongside their age-appropriate peer group. It is recognized that all students, regardless of their disabilities, are entitled to a quality education and can benefit from schooling. It is also increasingly recognized that students with disabilities should be educated alongside their peers. Since 1984 more services have been provided in regular schools, despite the need for differential provision in resources and facilities.

The following general equity principles apply equally to children with learning disabilities, even where those disabilities are so severe that they have been removed to special schools which are designed to meet their particular needs. It is desirable that

- all students fully develop their abilities, talents and interests and assume responsibility for their lives
- all students participate in a relevant and enriching curriculum within a supportive environment that is free from harassment
- all students understand the nature of the society in which they live and are empowered to redress inequities (EDWA 1993: 1).

4.1 Mainstreaming

Jane is principal at an education support centre which is on-site with two large primary schools in a remote mining area on the edge of the Great Victoria Desert in Western Australia. Education support centres are small schools, with less than forty students, specifically catering for students with intellectual disabilities, and this one has students with mild to severe and/or multiple disabilities. In metropolitan areas, students with severe or multiple disabilities are placed in education support schools that have greater physical and human resources to cater for those with high dependency needs. With Jane are two full-time teachers, one part-time teacher and two full-time assistants. All teaching staff are trained special educators and the teacher assistants have been working in the centre for some time.

One day, one of the teachers at the support centre received a note from a parent of a 10-year-old girl, Julie, with a severe intel-lectual disability, requesting a parent–teacher interview at the parent's home after school. Although the request to have the interview at the parent's home was not unorthodox, it was unusual, and Jane suggested to the teacher that they go together. The parent was informed that the principal would also like to be present and the two were met by the parent and her friend.

Both the parent and her friend were known to be keen advo-cates for the rights of people with disabilities. The parent was requesting inclusion of her child in a Year 5 class for at least 50 per cent time in a regular class, with a view to full inclusion by the time she left primary school. The teacher felt very threatened by the parent's position, feeling that the parent was implying that Julie was not receiving a good education in her class and would be advantaged educationally by being mainstreamed. The interaction between the teacher and parent became slightly tense. The teacher said that she saw potential problems arising from including the child in a regular class. The student was so dependent on others that she could be integrated only with support from a teacher or teacher assistant. It was therefore unlikely that the level of integration that the student was currently receiving, twice a week, could be increased the following year. The teacher, however, had no right to refuse or allow Julie entry to a regular school. The parent has the right to do what she believes is best for her child.

Jane reiterated that the ideal educational environment did not exist for many students and that these remote schools were not generously funded. Students could receive greater integration opportunities if staff numbers were increased. In the current situation support time for students who are integrated must be shared equitably. She believed that the child would not make the academic gains that she was currently achieving in her class at the centre, as she would be in a much larger class with greater distractions and would not be receiving the expertise of a trained special education teacher. Nor did the school have the staff to support such a programme. She did not use the maximizing benefits argument that other children in the regular class had an equal right to a good education too, and that their rights would be minimized by the additional attention that the teacher would have to give Julie.

The parent repeated that children with disabilities learn vicariously in a regular classroom and that Julie would learn to behave more appropriately by observing students without disabilities. She claimed that she could receive funding to provide a special teacher assistant for Julie and that Julie would not be disadvantaged in any way by being included. This is partly an appeal to a consistency principle which argues that any teacher would want to maximize the learning potential of any student if they could. Jane explained that it was her responsibility as a principal to ensure that each child at the centre was receiving the best education possible, that she would approach the principal of the upper primary school to begin increased inclusion, but that if she believed at any stage that Julie was not receiving the best education for her, she had a moral obligation to call a halt to the inclusion programme.

The above decision is an ethical one of balancing interests. But the whole burden need not fall on Jane's shoulders. Even on the issue of deciding placement and services there are regulative guidelines for a placement review meeting which will include the district superintendent, parents and guide, principal, teachers and 'relevant officers'. When the placement review is unable to agree on the strategies for resolution, the formal procedures in Section 20 of the Education Act are invoked. How ethical is it to use the legal process to make the decision? Did the discussion make any difference? What happens when the negotiating parties are (a) at different Kohlbergian stages or (b) operating from different frames of consistency, consequences or care? Should the cost of placing the child in the normal classroom be a consideration when the ethics are being considered, or does this make the decision merely a prudential one? If a school can only place a few such children in the normal classroom, on what ethical basis can the decision to include or not include best be made? First come, first served? Educational potential? Compatibility with the rest of the class?

THE ARGUMENT BY RIGHTS

It is the principal's professional responsibility to ensure that her school operates within the physical and human resource boundaries set by her employer. As a person she is obliged to do what she can to change inequities that she believes to exist in the system, she is obliged to provide support to the families of students at her school and, as we saw in the last chapter, she is obliged to make the well-being of any student central to any decision that she makes as an administrator.

At the beginning of this chapter we showed that social justice policies require students to be placed in the most educationally enhancing environment. How are we to do this and at the same time assist students to develop their abilities, talents and interests fully and assume responsibility for their lives? Is there a practical way, as opposed to an ideal way, to allow them to participate in a relevant and enriching curriculum within a supportive school environment that is free from harassment?

As many primary teachers will tell you, the consequences of placing a child with a severe intellectual disability in a mainstream class may be 'disastrous'. A relevant or enriching learning programme could not be provided for this student in the mainstream programme. If Jane is to be fair, she must consider the stress and anxiety of the primary school teacher who would have Julie in the class. The decision will rest on the provision of any evidence as to whether or not it is possible for Julie to reach her potential outside an education support classroom. But how does one tell when Julie is reaching her potential? And how would the regular system cope if all parents wanted their children mainstreamed?

Conversely the parent perceived the situation from a sense of duty or rights. Her child was being discriminated against by being denied the right to be educated alongside her own age peers. As a result of the discussion the principal became less concerned with the consequences and more concerned to do what she perceived to be the right thing by the parent or child. She was reminded of the care framework by the parent talking of Julie's needs. Ethical decision-making is indeed situational and complex. All parties were concerned that any detrimental effects on the student be minimized. All were consistent with their past actions and beliefs. The need to focus on the well-being of the student beyond the regulations requires care.

The issue of inclusion brings us full circle to the question of difference and equity with which this chapter began. If social justice consists of treating equals equally and unequals unequally, then should Julie be treated equally with others in the regular classroom by respect of her being an equal person with equal social needs? Or should the difference in her learning ability be made the salient feature in her treatment, as it was when she was first placed in the centre?

The factor that helps us to act one way or another is not equity itself but the relevant difference that drives it. This is where we turn to the need for conceptual categories to decide who is equal to what. Do we see Julie as deprived of social interaction, or a child who cannot benefit from primary classroom learning? Do we see her first of all as a person, or as a student, and of the latter is she a student in the same way that the others in the class are students?

For reasons like this, Mary Warnock (1979) argued that the whole question of equity would always be problematic, that it was probably a term that could be done away with, because it was not itself the basis on which decisions were made, and there will be other principles deciding which differences are the salient ones. I would argue, on the contrary, that equity is one of the central ethical principles which cannot be removed. It underpins social justice and it underpins distributive justice. Charles Handy in *Understanding Organisations* (1986) says that many union arguments are not about money as such but about equity. The absolute levels of pay are not as often an issue as the equitable level, in relation to others, to one's own pay curve. As an example, union unrest in schools in Western Australia in 1995 resulted in union members receiving a lower rate of salary than those who signed a negotiated agreement. This meant that teachers were working under the same conditions, with the same workload for different salaries. There has to be some moral notion or concept of equity that drives any action to redress this wrong, some ethical notion that says this is unfair.

Equity usually means paying a rate for the job rather than paying the man for his results. Under conditions of liquidity, the rate for the job should be assessed as objectively as possible, for equity must be seen to be equitable. Job definition and evaluation systems, competitors' rates for similar jobs, job grade levels related to salary grade – these are some of the methods used in the pursuit of equity.

(Handy 1986: 272)

The identification of pertinent differences gives something to act upon. What count as pertinent differences, and the most important ones to consider, could well depend on the ethical frame from which we are looking at the ethical issue. On the idealistic consistency frame, all persons have equal rights as persons; in the consequences frame their real and perceived differences have practical consequences which must be considered. We create categories, such as those of the gifted and talented, because we perceive that there is a group that has a different set of needs. The social justice policies tend to operate at an ideal level of concept, which fades into a fuzzy background in the experienced level of conception in classroom practices. When care comes into being the totality of a person is experienced, not the logical abstraction of a conceptual category of race, gender, culture or disability. In the next chapter we will look more closely at the origins of the concepts of justice and rights which have informed our construction of social justice policies.

Chapter 5

What is a right?

We hold these truths to be sacred and undeniable; that all men are created equal and independent, that from equal creation they derive rights inherent and unalienable, among which are the preservation of life, and liberty and the pursuit of happiness.

Thomas Jefferson, original draft for the American Declaration of Independence

I believe that withholding rights from students is worse than extending them. But . . . liberal societies generate educational dilemmas to which solutions in public institutions are unlikely.

Kenneth Strike (1982: 129)

Justice faces in two directions: towards the right moral action, insofar as it marks the extension of interpersonal relationships to institutions; and towards legal rights, the judicial system conferring upon the law coherence and the right of constraint. This whole book is concerned to discuss why we have a notion of right and wrong actions in ethics, but rights, though related to right action, seem to be more closely related to the law. The word *droit* in French has the same two aspects; in French we can speak of *un homme droit* (a righteous man) and also of *le droit* (law school, the discipline of law). When we looked at the differences between ethical and legal decisions in Chapter 1, we should not forget that they are also linked very closely conceptually.

FAIRNESS AND JUSTICE

When, in Chapter 2, I asked readers to think of an educational situation that they considered unfair, few would have had trouble finding an example. It often seems easier to think in the negative, to think of unfair situations than fair ones. Ricoeur (1992: 198) gives two reasons for this:

- justice is more often lacking and injustice prevails
- people have a clearer vision of what is missing in human relations than of the right way to organize them.

Let us go back to a real situation and pull out the abstracted issues so that we can think of the 'right way' to organize our thoughts about justice and how we can best promote it. In many schools, arts teachers feel frustrated by what they see as an unfair distributive formula that consistently allocates more money to science departments than to arts classes. While science has traditionally been the prestige discipline, arts teachers say that they too have safety requirements to meet, and with the increase in technology needed for photography, musical instruments, airbrushes, jewellery-making, ceramics, sculpture and stage equipment, they believe that they have a claim for a more equitable distribution of the school budget. Can you think of a fair reason to reduce the relatively high funding to science?

There are related arguments regarding the maximum number of students allowed in a science laboratory compared with the maximum number of arts students, and the scaling of school results used in tertiary entrance requirements which arts teachers claim discriminates against their less precise grading methods. In all of this debate, issues of justice and rights emerge. A major feature of justice is that it is often concerned with equitable distribution, although the distribution can be of roles, tasks or advantages as well as of goods. Distributive justice is concerned to allocate benefits and burdens fairly and thus is of major concern to school administrators, who not only have to ensure that the budget is ethically used, but also that workloads are distributed as fairly as possible.

Unfairness is one of the motivating forces underlying any affirmative action. It seems unfair, for example, that Aboriginal students should have to compete on academic grounds with affluent middle-class white Australians, when their educational background has been so different. Feminists too have argued for affirmative action on the grounds that they have been deprived of equal rights in the past, and some kickstart is needed to put things back on an equitable basis. However, such further discrimination to overcome past discrimination leaves the initial aggrieved parties with no consistent position from which to argue. It is rumoured that for entry into a conservative law school, if you are male or Caucasian, your application will immediately be put on a 'seconds' pile, creating a further need for affirmative action to redress this new inequity. Affirmative action such as this is actually illegal in Canada, because it is treating unequals unequally in what are seen to be irrelevant respects. Race and gender are and should be irrelevant to academic entry. Legalities aside, it is clearly a violation of human rights and could there- fore be investigated by one of several international bodies. Affirmative action uses a consequentialist position to equalize numbers, for instance by insisting that each committee should have either proportional repre- sentation or equal numbers of each of the two genders. Such a position is incompatible with a consistency position. Affirmative action is actually contradictory because it discriminates in order to overcome discrimination.

In the opening two chapters, much was made of overriding principles and moral laws where the moral law could override a regulation or rule if that regulation or rule was in itself immoral. One of the criteria of a moral law was that it had to be universalizable, that you could act only in such a way that you would allow any other person to act in a similar way. Remember Kant's categorical imperative, that one should act only according to that maxim by which you can at the same time will that it should become a universal law. Kohlberg's developmental model of ethics partly relied on Kant's principle of respect for persons but it also owed a great deal to the classic work of John Rawls, who argued that in an ahistorical situation men would logically and pragmatically agree to be just, because it was in their best interests to do so. There have been numerous papers on the limitations of Rawls's notion of justice, but for the purpose of this chapter we will follow out the implications of promoting a just school along Rawlsian lines.

DISTRIBUTION OF GOODS

Rawls's notion of justice covered a broad ethical base even if it did not deal with honesty or empathy. In the dominant male community of values, a notion of inclusive or responsible community discussed in the last chapter is defined in terms of personal rights, those that vest in individuals the power to enter into social relationships on the basis of simple membership in the social collectivity, i.e. non-hierarchical. Michael Apple (1986: 171) says that this notion of personal rights contrasts with a recent shift towards a more egoistic rights which invest in individuals the power to enter into social relationships on the basis and extent of their property, a sort of identification of social good with consumer goods, which he deplores.

5.1 Distribution of goods

A person with a right has grounds for grievance when it is denied. A group of postgraduate students go to their head of department complaining that they are crowded, that it is impractical for them to share the computers and that the telephone in their room has been taken away. Some of them are in windowless rooms and demand that they have access to the same standard of accommodation as other students. They insist on their right to a private room, computers, free printing and

---

photocopying and a book subsidy equivalent to that given to academic staff, saying that their research contributes to the welfare of the department on an equal basis with academic staff.

The students are well aware that the overall budget is tight and that academic staff have had to forgo book subsidies and assisted travel for conferences. The head explains that telephones and photocopying are a historical privilege, that as there happened to be staff absent and some spare computers and telephones lying around, students have been allowed access to them on the ethical principle of maximizing benefit, the greatest good for the greatest possible number. The department at that stage could afford to pay for them and if students felt contented they might work better and more efficiently. That was ethical decision-making based on a consequentialist approach. However, the photocopying bill has tripled, the allure of studies has increased the number of students enrolling so that there is insufficient room space, the department could not afford to upgrade the computers for students on a decreasing budget and students had been spending a great deal of time making personal calls on the telephones and disrupting other students in the room. The money saved by the head's decisions could probably be more productively spent on research grants to staff.

Trying to persuade the students that they have to face a responsible sharing of the burden of cuts★ to finances in the department did not work. It seemed that what was a privilege had become a right. The principle of distributive justice requires that equals should be treated equally and unequals be treated unequally. Some PhD students have rooms with windows and a telephone, others not. They demanded equal consideration.★ That would be an ethical decision based on consistency, or at least rational principle. The head had originally acted on the principle of extending to others the considerations that she would like extended to her, namely the best working conditions possible. But the consistency frame is the ideal one, and there are just not enough resources to give the students what they want.

The head had been appointed on a policy of equity which sought to distribute power equally and rationally. She had hoped to persuade rational postgraduate students that they should voluntarily share scarcer resources and cut down on the use of the telephone and photocopying and just use the rooms to get on quietly with their work when necessary, vacating them if they were needed for other reasons.★ But the squabbling

> continued and the head was forced to step in and dictate a
> policy that equalized resources by giving less to everybody. It
> was an exercise of brute power which honoured the principle of
> distributive justice but also reflected a hierarchical authority
> which the head had not wished to exercise.

In the last chapter we distinguished between equity and equality.
Similarly, Aristotle claimed that justice was not the same as equal distribution, that it could not be confused with arithmetical equality because
of the nature of the persons and things being shared. Justification of
unequal distribution of goods on the basis of different merits presumes
that the merits assigned to different persons are right or correct. That was
precisely what was in contention in the students' grievances. The head
could dismiss their case to be treated similarly with staff by saying that
they did not have equal responsibility with staff, and therefore were not
entitled to equal rights to equal goods.

Gilligan says (1982: 164) that the masculine and feminine ideologies
present themselves in adolescence particularly as a conflict between
integrity and care arising from the recognition of opposite truths,
including those of rights and responsibility:

> The morality of rights is predicated on equality and centered on the
> understanding of fairness, while the ethic of responsibility relies on
> the concept of equity, the recognition of difference in need. While the
> ethic of rights is a manifestation of equal respect, balancing on the
> claims of other and self, the ethic of responsibility rests on an under-
> standing that gives rise to compassion and care.

Her defence of the priority of care or identification with the other rests
on her Aristotelian presumption that ethical decision-making cannot be
based on calculations or reason alone, nor on the property notion to
which Apple referred. So postgraduates could argue that they deserve
the right to use the telephones and photocopiers if they do it responsibly,
that is, with an eye to the equal rights of future students and staff – they
are bound in a web of responsibility that responds to the needs of others.

Right is tied to social responsibility in much the same reciprocal way
that justice is tied to care. Lawyers would claim that every right rests on
a relative duty lying on a party or parties other than the party in whom
the right rests. To say that everyone as a member of society has a right to
social security (and to a standard of living adequate to the health and
well-being of them and their family, including food, clothing and
housing) is not to say that the government has a duty to provide these
things. Instead they rather provide a common standard of achievement

for all peoples – i.e. canons of social economic and political arrangements which can be criticized.

CHILDREN AND RIGHTS

The students in the above case study were asking for the same rights as academic staff and each other. Considerations of difference were as relevant here as they were to issues in the previous chapter. But a more pertinent issue for schools is the extent to which children have the same rights as adults. Kleinig (1981: 195) argues that while children are frequently recipients of great tenderness and affection, their powerlessness and dependence has been highlighted in demands for children's rights because they are seen to be vulnerable to oppressive treatment and compulsion. But he concludes that children are different and should not be accorded most of the rights, freedoms, privileges and immunities considered essential by most adults.

J.S. Mill (1975: 10–11) argues that this is ethically appropriate:

The only purpose for which power can be rightfully exercised over any member of a civilised society, against his will, is to prevent harm to others. He cannot rightfully be compelled to do or forbear because it will be better for him to do so, because it will make him happier, because, in the opinion of others, to do so would be wise or even right . . . This doctrine is meant to apply only to human beings in the maturity of their faculties. We are not speaking of children or of young persons below the age which the law may fix as that of manhood or womanhood. Those who are still in a state to require being taken care of by others, must be protected against their own actions as well as against external injury.

Mill's position justifies those laws that deny children the right to vote, drink in pubs, smoke or drive a car. Children are compulsorily schooled and must do as they are told. 'Within fairly broad limits such choice as they have in the matter of what they eat, wear, say and with whom they associate is dependent on the discretion of parents, teachers and others deemed (without consultation) *in loco parentis*' (Kleinig 1981: 195). Yet the mother of a 7-year-old girl who crashed a plane that she was flying in an attempt to break a record for the youngest person to fly across America reconfirmed her belief that her daughter had a legal and moral right to do as she wanted, and that she should be treated as an adult.

Strike (1982: 135) argues that children can be presumed to have, or have the potential for, those capacities that distinguish persons from things.

They are moral rational agents. Therefore it is immoral to treat children as though they were conceptually indistinguishable from tables, cats and rocks. As persons, children have rights. They must be treated as ends, not means. Their wants and needs must be taken as having prima facie validity.

Do children have the same rights as adults? The primary fact is that children do not fully possess many of those characteristics which define being a person. Children are rational agents in the same sense that an acorn is an oak tree . . .

He uses Mill's argument to provide the paternalistic case that the immaturity of children does provide grounds for the view that the rights of the immature should differ from those of adults, just as the rights of the insane or senile equally differ from the common person. This is a similar argument to those that we had in Chapter 4 where equity consisted in treating equals equally and unequals unequally in relevant respects.

We showed how one of the main aims of justice is the equitable distribution of goods. Referring back to the support for the intellectually disadvantaged implied by the social justice policies, consider an equal distribution of government funds to the intellectually advantaged student, that is the gifted and talented. An ethical argument could be mounted using the consistency frame that the intellectually disadvantaged need more support both in funding and staff to help maximize their educational opportunities and to bring them as close to the norm as possible. Gifted students, on the other hand, do not need additional support, because they have been given the advantage of natural talent. But if we look at the distribution of goods through the consequentialist line of maximizing benefits, one can see that the money spent on the gifted leads to a much higher return and benefit to all, including the valuing and nurturing of the world's finest minds and an incentive for those who consider themselves normal to try to aim to join the elite. On the argument of just desert, the gifted student has a greater right to increased resources than the intellectually disabled.

But Strike (1982: 136) insists that the arguments for distinguishing the rights of minors from those of adults do not diminish the fact that children are persons and that as such their wants and beliefs are objects of respect and should not be gratuitously overruled. They have basic rights as persons. There are many consequences flowing on from the acceptance of rights as an integral part of the ethical school. The extension of rights to children means that they must be allowed due process in the administration of penalties or low grades, and that penalties and rewards should in principle at least be justifiable to an external body, not given arbitrarily, hastily or without good reason.

The professional code of ethics for educational administrators exhorted administrators to avoid using positions for personal gain through political, social, religious, economic or other influence. For medieval philosophers the problems of political ethics were problems not of rights but of duties, the duties that a man owed to his lord, his king, his church or his God. In the seventeenth and eighteenth centuries such considerations gave way to notions like 'an Englishman's birthright' or, still more personal and universal, 'natural rights'. In France and America revolutions were waged and won for the right to 'liberté, égalité, fraternité' and 'life, liberty and happiness' respectively. Yet these too have become somewhat dated. Spinoza had claimed that a man's natural right amounted to the power that he could exercise over another, and this was certainly true in the 1980s when a manager of a large company seemed to have a right to secure his own fortune at the expense of his shareholders, and a right to declare himself bankrupt to escape financial commitments.

Would a school principal, given increased budget autonomy, be considered ethical if they spent an unreasonably large proportion of the budget on additional secretarial support for the principal, or on lavish entertainment expenses? Does the status of principal bestow that right? Politicians seem to consider that they have a God-given right to determine their own salary, but there would be a considerable outcry if principals awarded themselves an increase in salary at the expense of others in the school. Yet there is considerable evidence of a belief in a right to personal gain in many schools. Some use school stationery without permission. Others borrow the sporting equipment for family use or use telephones and photocopiers for personal use.

In the Western Mining Corporation *Code of Conduct* booklet (1995: 22), workers asked if they could provide a load of sand or a front-end loader from the company to build a BMX track at the local school. The answer given is that company assets should not be used for private gain. If these assets are used with the approval of the resident manager for local community projects that are supported by WMC, there is no conflict of interest. The issue of the right to use school property for personal gain features in case study 9.3 where a teacher borrows the school CD player for after-hours dancing lessons.

Where do rights come from? Does everyone have equal rights? I believe that no school teacher deserves more holidays than others, but some of higher status may feel that they have a legitimate right, for instance to have conference fees paid, because their professional development will benefit more people. A teacher has a right to annual leave, but not at the moment free professional development, medical treatment, a decent standard of living. It is all open not so much to awards but to negotiated agreements with the employer. Questions that we have raised in other chapters re-emerge here under a slightly different guise. Do we provide education for the learning disabled or to those who can benefit most, the gifted? When we look at the property rights, does a teacher have a right to use school stationery, to have the best offices, to take food from home economics classes? Do science labs have more of a right to funding than arts classrooms? Who has the right to receive a prize – only those with academic or sporting excellence?

5.2 Rights in schools

What rights, if any, do or should those in schools have? Consider the following rights:

- of a teacher to smoke where a student may not
- of a deputy to administer corporal punishment where no one else may
- of a principal to have a personal secretary
- of a principal to give themselves an additional responsibility allowance
- of Year 12 students to have a common room
- of a government school to levy charges on parents for the use of special equipment for optional classes
- of a principal to recommend dismissal where no one else may
- of a principal to swear where no one else may
- of a principal to enforce standards of dress where no one else may
- of an 18-year-old student to have an affair with a teacher
- of a teacher to have an extramarital affair which does not intrude on school grounds
- of a male teacher to have a child
- of an unmarried female teacher to be obviously pregnant while teaching
- of a teacher to receive two years' salary package when dismissed for unsatisfactory conduct
- of a teacher to continue teaching after they reach 65 years of age.

What is this thing called a right? Benn (in Benn and Peters 1959) claims that human rights are statements of basic needs or interests, as grounds of protest and justification for reforming policies. As we have seen, they differ from appeals to benevolence and charity in that they invoke ideals like justice and equality. Benn says that a right is commonly held to be a claim upheld by the law, but, as we have seen, the law is not necessarily ethical. Perhaps we need to keep in mind the distinction between a legal right and an ethical right. He also says that a right is an interest protected by the law.

WHERE DO RIGHTS COME FROM?

Traditionally rights were supposedly derived from and guaranteed by natural law or the Roman *ius naturale* which corresponds to that which is always good and equitable, a sort of pre-Kohlbergian belief in universal principles. Kohlberg's empirical investigations into a universal concept of justice were part of trying to demonstrate that justice was not a human or social artefact, that it existed over and above convention. The American Constitution presumes an eternal and immutable justice when it uses the term 'inalienable rights'. Common to all notions of natural rights is the idea that there are certain rights that all people simply have, whatever the laws of the land in which they live, regardless of the circumstances of their birth or life, and even if somebody is effectively denying them enjoyment of those rights. This seems to bestow on every-body some entitlement, whether it is a right to education, to life, liberty and happiness, or even, the catchcry of the French revolutionaries who died defending their natural rights, to 'Liberté, égalité, fraternité'!

I believe, however, that much talk of rights, natural or otherwise, is little more than a rhetorical trick. Naturalizing the concept of 'rights' is one way of legitimizing any position – naturalism has worked in many other areas such as intelligence, sexuality, male privilege. Where does the justification for those rights that we currently have come from? It would seem to be a self-referential tautology: certain rights are measurable as institutional constructs, therefore they are justifiable rights. These certain rights are institutionalized since they are justified. Likewise, rights become rights when those possessing the most social and institutional power dictate this. It is hard to see how someone can sensibly make claims about rights that are not institutionalized interests.

Barrow (1975: 143) says that when we appeal to rights, we are appealing to a presupposed moral schema or set of rules. We assume and implicitly demand that others share our assumption, that there is a particular system of moral rules binding on persons, such that it is true that a person ought to be free, ought to be self-governing, ought to be educated and so on. This has its parallel, as Barrow notes, to what is happening when a person says that they have a legal right and are thereby saying that there *is* a system of rules, embodied in our law, such that they are entitled to a free and compulsory education, the right to vote, the right to do pretty much as they like in their own house. But there is a significant difference. The laws *are* there, enshrined in yards of library space, verifiable and existing. We can agree on whether people have particular moral rights only if we share a particular moral view-point. The air of finality with which one claims an ethical right is misleading and dangerously so. Ethical rights, it seems, appear only when the existing laws conflict with prevailing ethical conventions and are espoused when one wishes, on acceptable ethical grounds, to change the law. So in states where abortion is illegal, there is a strong appeal to the right for a woman to decide what she should do with her own body. In states where abortion is legal, the right that is produced as a natural one is the right to life. Similarly in Australia, where the euthanasia laws are currently in question, there are unresolvable debates between those who believe in the right to life and those who believe in the right to die with dignity. Rights emerge in situations in which it is considered ethi-cally desirable to change an existing law.

5.3 Right to due process

A parent whose child was being taught to swim in the school holidays by a teacher reported to the principal of the school that the teacher had molested her son.★ The principal called the teacher in ★ and the teacher hotly denied any such molestation. The principal believed his story ★ and did not report the matter to the police. However, the teacher demanded to know who had made the complaint ★ as he considered that he had a legal right to sue that person for defamation of character. The principal refused to give the accused teacher the name of the parent. ★ The teacher does, on the face of it, have a right to due process, that is to present his side of the story to the principal. He was accorded that right and to that extent justice was seen to be done. The consequences of the false accusation are, however, that his reputation may be ruined by the parent spreading false rumours about him, and unless he knows who it is, he can do nothing to prevent it. He would argue that he has the right to defend himself in court, so that the truth can be publicly known. If you had been the principal, would you have released the parent's name? Would you have used an argument of rights to justify your decision, or would you have used other arguments of consequences or care?

Our question about the source of rights is answered tentatively by saying that they seem to emerge from a social and political manipulation of existing legal codes and common-law moral conventions. Can you think of issues in your school where rights might become an issue? Do you think that teachers have a right to take paid time off during school hours for professional development, especially where it becomes necessary because of mandated changes in the curriculum? And how would you justify that right? To what extent do your justifications take into account consistency, consequences and care? When Gilligan calls the 'masculine ethic' the ethic of principle, she refers to it as the ethic of rights, while the ethic of care she considers the ethic of responsibility.

Gilligan's point was that the ethic of principle usually acted in the interest of those who believed in the abstractions that language had currently made dominant. The idealized abstractions do not take into account existing differences in power. This means that law-makers actually can have more of a chance to act in their own interests. The consequentialist position of maximizing benefit gave those in power a strategy for distributing wealth and powers, which could be said to be just. However, maximizing benefits and distributing equally to equals are both notions of equitable distribution of goods which are incompatible with a notion of merit or just desert which says that certain people have special rights to an unequal distribution of goods because of their special needs or merits or position. 'Justice' and 'rights' are concepts that are becoming less visible in common discourse in education these days, because they are seen to operate in favour of existing hegemonies. It might be more useful to see them as markers of contestation, where those holding less power are enabled to argue for change in norms.

Chapter 6

Maximizing good

That grounded maxim
So rife and celebrated in the mouths
Of wisest men; that to the public good
Private respects must yield.
     Milton, *Samson Agonistes*, 1.865

In nature there are neither rewards nor punishments – there are consequences.
     R.G. Ingersoll, *Lectures and Essays*

Teachers can sometimes become impatient with lengthy discussions about justice or virtue. The aim of reflecting on ethics is neither scientific nor philosophical, but practical. Somehow we want to understand ethics better to make people and their actions better. Aristotle (1969) speaks of eudamonia as contributing to the commonwealth, the good society, and of ethics as the only way to lead to creating that good society. While self-sufficiency was to be aimed at as far as it is attainable, Aristotle warns us that 'by self-sufficient we do not mean that which is sufficient for a single man leading a solitary life. We include parents, children, wife, and in general friends and fellow-citizens, since man is born for citizenship.' We might not agree with Aristotle's teleology, but ethics has in common with citizenship a concern for the Other, being responsive to the needs of other people. The current federal interest in promoting citizenship arises from a practical concern to make people get on better together, to make them civil, participatory members of a commonwealth. The consequentialist view encourages us to anticipate results when considering a moral action. The practical results of taking any action must be considered alongside the practical consequences of not taking it. We call this being rational. Rationality is the ability to go beyond the present and take into account the relationship of what one is presently doing to the past and to the future. Any individual considering what to do in a moral situation has to take into account the good and harm that would result from a contemplated action, and particularly the good and harm that would come to other people, and not merely to oneself. Good to others, good to oneself, harm to others and harm to oneself are four of the considerations that a moral individual must entertain. None alone is absolute, but none can be omitted when considering what to do.

I mentioned the felicific calculus in which one tries to do a calculation of the benefits and costs of any action in terms of the benefit that it brings both to self and others. Consider the hypothetical situation presented in a novel used as a school text, Ursula le Guin's novel *The One Who Walked from Omelas* where one child is sacrificed each year to keep the large community in a state of well-being. One child's death could make a thousand lives happier. How about ten thousand? Does that make the situation more ethical? The more usual philosophical example is of allowing one hostage to be killed in order to save ten other hostages' lives. Now change the number of hostages saved from ten to one hundred. Or a thousand. Does it make a difference to your decision? Someone might object that these examples are pure fantasy and not likely to occur, but, like the situations described throughout this book, they are to be seen as thought experiments that help us to reflect on our own ethical assumptions.

THE SINKING-BOAT DILEMMA

As we saw in the last chapter, in educational administration, principals often face the problem of distributing a limited set of resources in either the fairest or the most effective way. This issue has been dramatized in the classic sinking-boat dilemma. If there are ten people drowning and room in the lifeboat for only six, what do you do? Try to save the greatest number and risk drowning everybody? Select according to your own values of who is worth saving, justifying it on the grounds of the greatest good for the future of society? Save your friend? Your father? Save the lawyer and the doctor and leave the old alcoholic pensioner behind? How does one maximize benefit in this situation where either some or all will be harmed as a consequence of your decision?

In education, administrators are often faced with a similar problem in the distribution of goods, even in making the budget decisions we discussed in the previous chapter. There is a limited amount of money to share around. How best to distribute it to maximize benefit? Do they give larger amounts to those who will use it most productively and have shown that they can do so, or do they give the same minimum amount of funding to everyone, regardless of quality, to enable those who have not had a fair chance before to do something positive? Consider the consequences of both. Take into account what might happen in the school if either recommendation was to take place.

You can see that the problem is a problem only in the light of maximizing benefit or considering consequences. The caring perspective cannot answer the question. To save the person in the sinking boat about whom you feel most positively does not seem an equitable answer to the question, just as a principal could not allocate scarce resources only to those for whom he or she cares. Note that here caring does not simply mean maximizing benefits for those you like. The benefits could be distributed to the most unfortunate, on the grounds that they need care most, as Sister Teresa offers care first and foremost not to those whom she likes, but to those who need care most. The principled answer requires that you give equal respect to everybody and do unto them as you would they would do unto you. Few people would be willing to be sacrificed for others, so, as Rawls suggests, in an even power game, the option of doing your best to save everybody will be the only fair solution from the consistency framework.

Another difficulty with the principle of the greatest good for the greatest number of people that is raised by the sinking-boat dilemma is that it appears to justify taking steps that may harm some people, on the grounds that more people benefit than are harmed. The difficulty arises from the inherent problem of trying to quantify benefit as if it were a commodity or good.

Considering the policy of maximizing good, how would you decide if you were the principal in the following situation, and to what extent would you consider it necessary or desirable to act by making your priority the greatest good for the greatest possible number?

GREATEST GOOD FOR THE GREATEST POSSIBLE NUMBER

The Plymouth Brethren form the majority in a small country town and therefore have a majority of students in the local school. They will not allow their children to use electronic technology, believing that these are the instruments of the Devil.

6.1 Religious majorities

A country school principal, Bruce, is faced with the problem of having a majority of his students belong to a religious group, the Plymouth Brethren, which holds that any technology, including videotapes, computers, radio and television, is the work of the Devil. The same religious group is the major cultural group in the small town as well, with its elders influential in town politics.★ If he believes that the education of his students is hindered by them not having access to a richer world through information technology, what will be the consequences of his

---

belief for the children belonging to that religious group, and for those children in his school who have a reasonable expectation that they will receive the educational benefits of technology? If he tells the Plymouth Brethren to provide their own private school so that they can follow their religious beliefs,★ the number of children remaining in his non-religious state-funded school will be so small as to face a distinct possibility of closure and, at best, a diminishment of resources and facilities, including the technology that the Plymouth Brethren wish excluded from the school. But he has not the resources available to offer split classes, with technology★ and without,★ nor is he allowed to place in charge of classes non-trained teachers.★ What action of his will minimize harm? Is there any way in which he can turn this potential conflict into a win–win situation?

How large is the frame within which the greatest number is to be counted? A principal who was involved in this situation resolved the issue by simply considering the needs of the immediate community and negotiating to have virtually two schools within a school, one with technology and the other without. On the Kohlbergian framework of principle, i.e. consistency, all people are equal and the most ethical decision will be made only for the greatest good of the whole of humanity. The further ethical issues that are raised by this case study include the involvement of any multicultural community within school timetabling and equipment considerations, to say nothing of the curriculum content. To what extent can/should one incorporate different community values within the community within the school and still retain an identifiable educational ethos? A high Aboriginal population in the town or community might raise different issues again.

The problem of depriving some children of electronic aids to education to preserve the perceived greater good of tolerance of difference does not seem, on the face of it, to be a serious ethical problem, but if the teacher really believes that she is harming the children's future growth as informed individuals by denying them access to a broader vision, then she is grappling with the issue of double effect.

THE DOCTRINE OF DOUBLE EFFECT

Two doctrines, the Doctrine of Double Effect and the Doctrine of Doing and Allowing, are sometimes used as guidelines to measure the morality of an action when the consequences are complex. The Australian Medical Association uses them as guidelines from time to time in medical ethics, and it guides legal debate at the moment in euthanasia. The easiest way to explain the Doctrine of Double Effect is to appeal to an example from medical literature. Consider these two cases:

Case 1   There is a woman in labour who will die during childbirth unless the head of the foetus is crushed. (This procedure is called a craniotomy.) The doctor performs the craniotomy and saves the woman.

Case 2   A woman has uterine cancer and will die unless a hysterectomy is performed. She is nine months' pregnant. The doctor performs the hysterectomy and saves the woman.

Are case 1 and case 2 morally on par with one another? Not according to the defenders of the Doctrine of Double Effect. They claim that case 2 is justified, while case 1 is not. Why the asymmetry? In case 1, the doctor committed a restriction violation because his direct intention, his aim, was to crush the foetus's skull and thus kill it, whereas in case 2, his intention was to remove the mother's uterus. The foetus's death was merely a secondary effect. He foreseeably produced the result that the foetus died, but the foetus's death was not his aim.

The defenders of the Doctrine of Double Effect claim that if your actions cause or fail to prevent some morally objectionable thing, but you were not aiming at that outcome, then you have not necessarily committed a restriction violation. Sometimes you are permitted to fore-seeably produce a result that you would not normally be allowed to aim at. Let us suppose someone comes up with an argument from a stronger consequentialist position and claims the opposite, that in case 1 the doctor is certainly acting in good faith because he is not only preserving a life, but offsetting the loss of a single child by enabling the woman to have ten more children. Therefore, the sacrifice of one in order to preserve the possibility of many defines this act as not 'evil'. In the second instance, the doctor not only aborts a baby, but denies the mother the capability of bearing children in the future – a truly negative (in terms of production) act, and therefore 'evil'.

Only a consequentialist would be willing to say that it is all right to kill one baby so that ten other babies may be born. A person operating from the consistency frame would strongly resist this idea. The point of the craniotomy versus the hysterectomy case is that the baby in both cases is a moral patient to which the doctor has a moral responsibility. As with the sinking-boat dilemma, we have equal moral responsibility to the baby and the mother. Once the decision has been made to save the mother first, how the doctor goes about doing it has moral weight according to defenders of the Doctrine of Double Effect. In one case, the doctor can kill the baby, and in the other case, he can foreseeably produce the result that the baby dies but not, strictly speaking, kill the baby.

The introduction of the Doctrine of Double Effect is to illustrate the logic of cause and effect that underpins the consequential position and how a notion of intention is still bound up with it. To show that any action is problematic, one would have to show not only the consequences of the action but that it is irrational or self-contradictory. A simplistic consequentialist line cannot admit the doctrine of double effect – it provides a link between the consistency and the consequences positions.

Let us place the dilemma of the principal in our earlier example in this frame. Again there are two cases. In each case, we have a dedicated teacher who believes devoutly that education is about opening doors of opportunity for all children and that in a country town the best resources are electronic. In the first case, he will promote the use of them in class, even if it happens to result in ideological damage to the Plymouth Brethren in his class. In the second case, the teacher is aware of the conviction of most of his students but believes that they are operating within a narrow set of beliefs which it is his duty to challenge by presenting them with a broader set of alternatives, especially through information technology. He insists that they access the Internet and discuss alternative points of view, despite protests by local parents and elders, with a view to having the children change to what he believes is a better world-view.

In the first case, the teacher is justified because he did not aim at damaging the children's religious beliefs. He merely foreseeably produced the result that they received instruction in school that was inconsistent with their home instruction. What he aimed at was the education of the children. On the other hand, in the second case, the teacher has done something wrong. He was aiming at the destruction of the religious beliefs of the children. The main difference between the two is their intention. If the teacher could have somehow educated the children without destroying their beliefs, he would have been satisfied, and even relieved to have such a choice. However, in the second case, if the teacher were presented with an option that did not change the beliefs of the children, he would not take it. His very purpose is to move them beyond their beliefs, using information technology to do it. That is his direct intention, his very aim.

In *The View From Nowhere*, Thomas Nagel supports this Doctrine of Double Effect, saying that aiming at an evil result is somehow worse than foreseeably producing an evil result. He offers an explanation for this assertion in the following passage:

> to aim at evil, even as a means, is to have one's action guided by evil. One must be prepared to adjust it to insure the production of evil . . . But the essence of evil is that it should repel us. If something is evil, our actions should be guided, if they are guided by it at all, toward its

elimination rather than toward its maintenance. That is what evil means. So when we aim at evil we are swimming head-on against the normative current ... What feels peculiarly wrong about doing evil intentionally even that good may come of it is the head-long striving against value that is internal to one's aim.

(Nagel 1986: 181–2)

The purpose of the Doctrine of Double Effect was not to pass a judgement of good or evil on every action. It is more of a 'moral map' that guides those wanting to look at a person's intentions as well as the consequences. The doctrine is supposed to help you determine whether what you are doing is right or wrong. If *you* are aiming at something evil, then you are doing something wrong in violating restriction of your particular ethical principles, because you are being inconsistent. But if you are aiming at something perfectly innocent (and probably necessary), with the regrettable result that something bad comes of it, then you are not really violating a restriction in the same sense. Thus, the principal who tries to replace a religious belief with his own doctrines aims at evil, while the principal who tries to persuade the Plymouth Brethren of the educational value of his beliefs does not. Seeking to find a joint compromise between educational values and incompatible religious beliefs is not in and of itself an evil thing to do; unfortunately, it may have a result of weakening the religious beliefs.

CONSEQUENTIALISM AND UTILITARIANISM

That showed again how the consistency position overlaps with the consequentialist one. Barrow (1975: 91–115) is thorough in detailing the strengths and weaknesses of consequentialism, which he calls utilitarianism. He states that there are two principal objections to any consequentialist theory, a shift from 'is' to 'ought', and a confusion of utility with justice, each involving a confusion between fact and values, a lack of discrimination between a scientific and an ethical point of view.

First, there is too sudden a shift from the naturalistic assumption that everyone *does* seek pleasure, to the normative judgement that it is rational or right to regard all happiness, whether one's own or that of other people, in the same light. This commits the naturalistic fallacy of deriving an 'ought' from an 'is', a fallacy to those who believe that logically one cannot derive a value statement from a statement of fact. That position has come under considerable attack since factual statements have been shown to be value-laden (Kovesi 1978; Kuhn 1972). It would be preferable to make explicit the values that underpin your description of those facts that many take for granted as neutral and show how those values are consistent with the ethical position you wish to defend. This is consistent with postmodernism and poststructuralism which hold that our facts and values are tightly bound together within cultural frames and proto-theories and that examination and exposure to public scrutiny of presumptions can make decisions easier.

The inability of a consequentialist theory to tell us what we ought to be doing can be illustrated by the administrative problem of a limited budget. If an education system has only $200 million to spread around 800 schools, should it give $1,000,000 to twenty élite schools, perhaps enabling them to become maximally efficient for their pupils and more productive for the commonwealth, and distribute the other $230,000 to each of the remaining schools or give just $250,000 to each school? This is a principle of utility rather than a principle of justice. Ivan Illich spoke of the tendency of any large institution, medical, educational or religious, to make decisions on a number count as if that decided the ethical issue with the graphic illustration of using a body count to determine the victor in war. The principle of utility has been appealed to in such cases as the bombing of Hiroshima, where it was argued that despite the killing of millions of innocent people, far more people would have died if the war had not been stopped by the dropping of the bomb. It is measuring the consequences as if they were things, as if a felicific calculus were in fact possible. The current agenda to reward schools financially for the improvement in standardized test results builds in similarly a principle of utility with a whole set of assumptions about cause and effect, and no principle of justice or human intentionality apparent.

The consequences of the first action add up to a greater total of happiness, but of course fewer people are positively affected, as against the thousands that would benefit from the second action. The second action follows the principle of egalitarian justice: in Bentham's words, 'everybody to count for one, nobody for more than one'.

THE CONSEQUENCES OF PUNISHMENT

A utilitarian/consequentialist argument has been used in schools to justify punishment that causes harm to a student, which seems to go against the first code of ethics that the welfare of the student should be paramount at all times. We saw in Chapter 3 that punishment is often painful, even humiliating for the one student suffering it, and that it is deliberately unpleasant if not harmful, but that this is usually justified on the grounds of preventing possible harmful long-term consequences of not punishing. In that chapter I talked about means and ends and some problems arising from confusing the two. Here I want briefly to look at a rights-based argument concerning the right to punish.

Anyone who believes that persons have natural rights to liberty, life and property will tend to oppose any restrictions, confinements and deprivations of property and life that make up standard civic punishments imposed in non-penal contexts. A person subjected to them could object to their treatment in ways that would have serious moral weight unless they were justified by an argument from the principle of justice.

Act consequentialism justifies an individual act of punishment by direct reference to its results. Among the most useful of these is strengthening the deterrent effect on others of the ongoing threat.

In rule consequentialism, which is sliding on our developmental scale towards principled action, the kind of benefit that is maximized enters into a general justification of punishment. For a practice, insofar as it can be consequentially justified, includes those events that help constitute its existence and these constituents must, in the present case, include the particular acts of punishment that would not otherwise occur. These acts are therefore a large part of what is justified when the practice as a whole is justified, and their deterrence effects on others are a large part of what does the justifying. If we apply a consequentialist theory of justification to the question of rights, we seem driven to the following result. Punished persons have no rights that stand against their punishment because, in part, punishing them is so often helpful in helping to deter others from committing crimes.

There are problems of universalizability arising from this justification. Do we want to make a generalizable rule that properly punished people lack the relevant rights because, in large part, they make useful object lessons for others? We might move outside a frame of principle in certain situations to appeal to circumstance, in which pragmatism would override moral rights.

The consistency frame usually argues that retribution is the main reason for punishment and that it is just or ethical to harm someone else's moral interests simply because they have harmed someone else's interests. This is the moral principle of just desert. But we have no way of grounding a moral principle in any other way than by referring it to a felicific calculus or the principle of universalizability and we have to remain aware that one of the consequences of being consistent might well be to set in place a kind of vendetta theory that all punishers are equally entitled to punishment.

Quinn argues in detail (1993: 60–133) that consequentialists face the problem of punishment from the wrong end. Using what appears to be a modification of Rawls's argument for distributive justice, he (Quinn 1993: 60, 61) says that we need to have the threat of punishment in order to protect ourselves, and that we should be focusing on the harmful consequences of not having such a threat. It is morally legitimate to create these threats because it is morally legitimate to try to protect ourselves in this way against violations of our moral rights. My personal view is that he is too committed to the existence of moral rights, and does not see them from a postmodern point of view as the point of inter-section between code law and common law, between conventional law and the need for ethical modification of those laws.

If I have sounded a little negative about the value of consequentialism, it is really because I tend to operate from a framework in which responsi-bility and care are paramount. But the consequentialist framework is necessary to remind us that we live in a real world in which our actions and even our words can have certain consequences. It requires us to take these into account, and consider before acting whether the possible outcomes of those actions are likely to be damaging or beneficial. Ruth Groenhout, from the Philosophy Department, Southwest Missouri State University, wrote by email:

> in the real world we can never know what all the results of our actions will be (in fact much of the time we end up surprised). If we begin to think that we *should* be willing to sacrifice individual others for the greater good, we have taken a step toward repeating the Third Reich.
>
> Under conditions of uncertainty, when there's no Great Philosopher in the sky to guarantee that the story ends properly, we never can be even somewhat sure that this evil action (for which I am responsible) will prevent those other evil actions (for which I am not responsible) from happening. Given the uncertainty, utilitarian reasoning seems little more than an invitation to evade responsibility for the evil one does.

You might want to turn this into an exercise where you as administra-tors consider situations in which you have had to sacrifice individuals for the greater good. Has reading this chapter made any difference to the way that you would act? What would be your reasons for changing your mind? Is it one of the other two frames?

THE RELATIVISM OF CONSEQUENCES

I am aware that often I conclude by insisting on responsibility and care. But the preceding discussion of the interconnections between consistency and consequences only makes sense in the total frame of a holistic concern for others, a frame that has care at the beginning and end. In the introduction I included consequences at the lower end of the consistency table and then showed how the consistency table is simply a part of a holistic theoretical framework with care at the beginning and end. If we view ethical concerns as arising in a spiral of growing care for others, then any one of the three faces of ethics may become of prior importance in the decision-making process at any one time.

This may appear to throw us into a sort of relativism – those who claim that what we need is a division of moral labour, employing different moral approaches in different domains (Flanagan and Jackson 1987). Kohlberg himself advances this thesis – it allows him to incorporate the care voice as another (albeit implicitly inferior) moral realm without altering his original theory. But he still presumes that the ethic of justice is the all-embracing one within which the other domains are adjudicated. Gilligan's declaration that the moral realm is equal to the masculine justice realm aroused some misgivings from feminists on the grounds that such a position perpetuated female inferiority and promoted a revival of traditional middle-class conceptions of femininity (Tronto 1987; Card 1991:17). Other feminists argue for the superiority of the female voice (Ruddick 1989; Noddings 1984), saying that the justice voice has produced continual war, class, race and gender oppression. The conclusion that a care orientation rooted in traditional feminine virtues would result in a more human world is similarly appealing.

But no one voice is adequate; each must make constant deferral to the other. It is difficult to say whether the movement is that of a spiral, which presumes evolutionary progress, or an ongoing dialectic up and down, a hierarchy of progress. It is difficult to imagine a moral debate that does not contain a notion of a better argument at the conclusion. Maybe we are misguided in asking which ethical frame is the best. They are not themselves arranged on a hierarchy of development. Each of them is best for certain ethical purposes. Ethical growth or moral maturity comes about by considering all factors and by having considered each of them, perhaps more than once, and by making connections between them all, transcending each of them.

Does this inability to find a foundation for ethics in any of the approaches make the whole case for moral maturity relativistic? The postpositivist followers of W.V.O. Quine, including Evers and Lakomski (1991), might well argue that ethics, like science, is a communal activity wedded to both values and metaphysical commitments on the one hand and yet constrained by the world and resting on a theory of evidence rooted in sensory experience. Ethics as much as science needs to be 'tested' continually against touchstones of shared sensory experiences. To a certain extent, the consequentialist position presents the 'scientific' face of morality. It is embedded in generalizations arising from our physical and sensory experiences, even as basic as a slap. Yet evidence, whether in ethical or scientific matters, no matter how firmly anchored by a touchstone, is still bound by theory, which is humanly constructed. Theories are as much idealistic and metaphysical as 'physical', and, as Foucault (1980) reminds us, are intimately connected to institutionalized power relations.

A poststructuralist position allows us to read any mention of consequences ironically, with only one foot in the theoretical assumptions that lead us to describe one thing as being causally related to another. For example, Jungwirth (1991) gave student teachers the task of evaluating gender interactions in the primary school. Jungwirth was concerned to discover whether there were gender-specific methods of managing classroom situations and gender-related patterns of interaction. She found that in the main there were not.

In the 'concealing of failure' and in the 'argumentative insistence' boys seem to be judicious students who can realize the correctness of the teacher's statements . . . the boys manage the discourse in the mathematics classroom more successfully than girls. Generally speaking to say nothing is considered as a failure . . . The mathematical incompetence on the part of girls is constituted in the interaction. All participants, in particular the girls, themselves contributed to it.

(Jungwirth 1991: 279)

An anonymous science student in E421 class on Gender in Education at Murdoch University wrote the following summary of the description:

Competence is seen as a male trait and incompetence as a female trait. This is achieved by the boy's immediate response following a teacher's feedback – the boys accept the criticisms and pretend to understand it or see their error. The girls do not and appear not to be as bright as the boys.

To this summary, he added the following comment:

Wow! This is a startling revelation. This explains an enormous range of behaviours and perceptions of Mathematics abilities. Why this disruptive behaviour that is so normally displayed by boys? This is almost a reversal of behaviour traits. More research is warranted on this one.

(Anonymous 1996)

It is as if he has suddenly seen the effect of presumptions, in this case gender stereotypes, on descriptions of behaviour in the classroom, an effect of which neither he nor many teachers are usually aware. The assumption may well free him from the control of his own embedded theories about the world which have in the past led him to engage in certain practices.

Ethics tries to move beyond the power relations embedded in our tacit assumptions and it can do so more easily in the care frame than in the consequentialist one. If we just focus on the perceived or anticipated consequences of action, we are stuck in existing descriptions of cause and effect which are essentially conservative, based on our scientific assumptions about the 'real' world. We need to articulate the basis for our generalizations on which we predict consequences, and also step outside a rational theory to question it. What is right about the consequentialist position of maximizing benefit is that it does tie us to sensory experiences and that is important in grounding our moral agendas in a world where there are causes and effects. But we might have got the causes and effects wrong by acting under certain assumptions about them, assumptions that have been shaped by our culture and our history.

Looking at longer-term consequences rather than the short-term helps to make any decision moral, but also seeing where the frame that picks out certain salient features of long-term effects is consistent with other moral values is equally a move towards moral growth. If the student teacher could have at any time said, 'What if I were a girl in that maths class who was being treated as incompetent? Would it have made a difference to my identity? Could I allow any teacher to treat any person as incompetent on similar grounds?', he would be acting in the consistency frame, as well as the consequences frame. If, looking at the face of a mute child in a maths class, he feels unable to make the judgement, he is responding as a human being in whom the consequences and consistency frame have been assimilated.

Most analytic philosophers (Strike 1982; Scheffler 1970) argue that ethics must always aim at consistency, but that consistency is intimately bound up with the consequences. If you accept a goal, you must choose whatever action best promotes that goal. This implies that one could not rationally decide to do something that would maximize evil. Very crudely: if we do not like something, then we want as little of it as possible. If we do not like the idea of people being killed, then the idea of more people being killed should be more disturbing to us than the idea of less people being killed. If we are repelled by one instance of something, then we should be proportionately more repelled by many instances of it. This is only reasonable, whether you are a consequentialist or not.

We might feel that there is something wrong about this argument, but we cannot refute it rationally, that is, on a consistency base. It seems to me that we do attempt to maximize rationality and on these occasions the consistency framework and consequences framework are working together productively.

Let us go back to the sinking-boat dilemma with which we opened this chapter. Running a school will involve many principals in similar situations where they must make a decision that will impact on some individuals differently. They can begin to argue on the basis of maximizing beneficial effects but that cannot be their only argument. They must also consider the well-being of each student as a person, and if they want to treat some differently, they have to be able to justify it publicly showing that there is a difference relevant to their decision. In other words, they must be able to defend their actions rationally.

Chapter 7

Community and loyalty

The notion of diversity is a mainstream liberal one that speaks to the importance of plural, democratic societies. But with diversity comes a 'transparent norm' constructed by the host society that creates a consensus. A normative grid locates cultural diversity while at the same time *contains* cultural difference . . . In order to ascertain better what a politics of difference might look like, it is productive to follow Bhabha (1990, p. 293) in recognising the 'metaphoricity of the peoples of imagined communities'.

McLaren (1993: 283)

UNION PRACTICES

The code of ethics of a teachers' union usually contains a clause about loyalty to the union. The 1993 code of ethics of State School Teachers' Union of Western Australia stated:

Members shall abide by the following Union code of ethics.

(a) Members shall acknowledge the authority and responsibility of the Union.

(b) Members shall support and assist in raising the standard of the teaching profession.

(c) Members shall be loyal to other members and refrain from discussing other members in the hearing of the public.

(c) Members should not seek to compare themselves publicly with other teachers to their own advantage.

(e) Members shall not falsely, maliciously or recklessly injure or attempt to injure, whether directly or indirectly, the professional reputation or prospects of another member.

(f) Members shall issue public statements only in an objective and truthful manner and shall not issue anonymous public statements.

(g) Members shall show due consideration for their successors.

(h) Members shall zealously guard their civil rights and those of the students in their schools.

(i) Members shall guide their students to attain the highest possible level of academic, social, moral and physical achievement.
(j) Members shall deal justly, respectfully and reasonably with students.
(k) Members shall exercise discretion in dealing with confidential matters relating to students and their parents.
(l) Executive members shall act as exemplars for all members in their adherence to the Code of Ethics.

Compare this with the general code of ethics for teachers in Chapter 2. What significance can you find in the different wording? Has either code left out any moral value that is in the other? What significance, if any, do you find in the different ordering of codes?

The union code of ethics seems at first glance to offer a different view of professional integrity, defining it in terms of loyalty to the union rather than exercising independent judgement. One could develop a scenario in which a principal has to decide between loyalty to the union and caring about the current and future welfare of his teachers. The code of ethics, which enjoins the educational administrator to 'implement the governing board of education's policies and administrative rules and regulations and/or pursue appropriate measures to correct those laws, policies and regulations that are not consistent with sound educational goals, ensuring that where possible no person shall be disadvantaged by a change in regulations', conflicts with the union's requirement for loyalty to the union.

7.1 Informing

The union is seeking an across-the-board salary increase of 25 per cent. Industrial action endorsed a variety of strike actions and bans. A letter has been sent to all principals from the chief executive officer of the state employing body to clarify their responsibility as principals to their chief employer. The letter states in part: 'Teachers who fail to comply with the order will have Section 7D of the Education Act invoked (i.e. no work as ordered – no pay) in respect to Section 7D, which will be invoked in respect to bans. Pursuant to Section 7D94, teachers have a right to appeal to the Government School Teachers' Tribunal within fourteen days of service of a declaration, but only on the grounds that they did not refuse or fail to comply with any order, and on no other grounds.' A copy of Section 7D which was invoked several times in the letter was attached.

Principals were formally ordered to inform the Education Department immediately of all staff who did not turn up to work or who took part in any industrial action. Teachers who went on strike were to have their pay deducted for the duration of the strike. The letter pointed out that even if the principals decided to participate in industrial action themselves,★ they resumed full responsibility to the ministry as soon as they resumed duty, and were they to participate in industrial action, they were to provide advice concerning teachers involved in strike action without delay on their return to duty.★ Multiple copies of the Teachers' Industrial Action forms were forwarded to each school with the instruction that ID number and names of all staff were to be printed on each form, and the exact times that the teachers refused to carry out any duty, including marking, report writing, yard duty, teaching relief and bus duty, were to be noted on the form.

Should the principal list the names of teachers who do not report for duty? Should the principal refrain from giving any orders? Is caring about the union the same as being loyal to it? Is caring about teachers/friends the same as being loyal to them? To what extent could the principal be described as 'whistle-blowing' if they inform the employing body? 'Whistle-blowing' would seem to sit uncomfortably between the codes (c) of not speaking publicly about other members and (e) and (f) about being truthful, even where truth might be damaging to others or the organization. The matter of honesty, and particularly when to speak out and not to speak out, will be examined in Chapter 9.

There will be very different responses to this particular case of reporting apparent dereliction of duty. A decision will be made partly on the basis of the extent to which the principal sees themselves *as* a union member, or *as* an employee, or *as* an autonomous person, in the metaphoric way mentioned in the epigraph. The decision may be made on the basis of loyalty to one group or the other. All the issues of acting authentically as opposed to acting within a role which were raised in Chapter 4 re-emerge.

The decision will also depend on what other features of the situation are considered most important. Some will see the quoting of Section 7D94 as the most important detail, others their loyalty to the union. There will be others who have no concept of whistle-blowing to inform their actions. It is not just the set of values that will inform different responses to this situation; it is a holistic bundle of cognitions, values, emotions, knowledge and past experiences that determine what features of the situation are relevant and which not. That bundle of responses is what constitutes personal integrity or character.

> Each man has his own peculiar character. It enters into all he does; but as it enters into all his cognition, it is a cognition of things in general. It is therefore the man's philosophy, his way of regarding things – that constitutes his individuality.
>
> (Peirce 1931–58: 1.501)

David Bricker (Strike and Ternasky 1993: 13–26) criticizes the Kohlbergian model for treating moral reasoning as if it was unaffected by character. Like Heidegger, he believes that character can affect moral rationality through the perceptual preoccupations that persons bring to reasoning. He draws upon the Aristotelian notion of habit, which says that we cannot reason about anything unless we have some ability to pick out salient or defining features of any situation. What do we make of a person who sees good in virtually everyone, or someone else who sees sexual innuendo in most small talk? How do we account for the fact that reasonable people can come to different conclusions? There is something that binds these together to form personality or, in a more enduring form, character. Yet we do not, as Peirce and Bricker tend to do, see character as some fixed or innate trait. It is a way that an individual adapts to circumstances, and while it is stable enough to be able to detect style or consistency, it can change gradually in response to those circumstances.

We are back at the topic of the necessary interdependence of the subjective and objective worlds with which Chapter 1 opened. Moral reasoning is not a disembodied activity, disconnected from people's habits of seeing. It is not just a mental artefact communicated through language. Thought is no internal thing and does not exist independently of the world and of words. Likewise character does not exist independently of language, social structures, physical events. Character, like language, is not just an objective thing. Nor is it just as an intellectual process or an invented system of signs, but a fact of consciousness, a mode of being, an intentional structuring of human reality. Merleau Ponty (1962) in *Phenomenology of Perception* said that his language was not the clothing of his thought, but its body. This is like Sartre's famous saying that language is the condition of my being. Sartre, in common with the phenomenologists, held that he was what he said and what he saw himself as being. A character is someone who is loyal to a set of values that has been partly conditioned by the practices of their social community.

We see here how what is a subjective understanding of any concept has been formed by practices and experiences in a social group which provided the language. Loyalty is important in the union code of ethics because members are defined not only by their payment of dues, but by an assumption of shared values which become really shared by being regularly assumed. Similarly professional loyalties to a body of members are often not defined, but arise from shared practices with a historical growth and are rarely questioned until they are confronted with opposing loyalties.

COMPETING LOYALTIES

Some educators in their studies of the moral climate of schools have indicated the influence of what they have called 'aggregate norms'. Aggregate norms arise within student peer groups without the reflection of discussion. People follow them not because they believe that they are necessarily right, or even self-serving, but partly out of habit, because that is the life-world they inhabit, and partly out of a desire to 'fit in' or conform on a behavioural level with their peers.

In the first scenario above, a principal was in conflict only to the extent to which loyalty to the employer has equal value with loyalty to the ·union. Power (in Strike and Ternasky 1993: 148) cites a legal case in 1986 in which employers were jointly found responsible for one person's acts of sexual harassment because, while they did not sanction the sexual harassment, they failed to establish procedures to check such outrageous conduct or to bring it to their attention. The individual was seen to be acting within a microcosm of a wide culture which portrayed women as sex objects. A social justice policy which requires employees to take affirmative action to redress past wrongs to women will meet with resistance in a school in which sexual harassment is not seen to be an issue.

Power also cites a discussion (in Strike and Ternasky 1993: 150) with a group of high school students about an incident where a student had stolen a tape recorder from an unlocked locker and later bragged about it to his friends. While they admitted that stealing was wrong, they did not feel it their responsibility to report it, or to persuade their friend that stealing was wrong. One said, 'If somebody is going to be dumb enough to bring something like that into the school, they deserve to get it stolen.' Another, when the group was asked if it had a responsibility to try to talk the thief into returning the stolen goods, replied, 'The school is responsible for enforcing rules. We're teenagers. We have our own responsibility, but we can't be responsible for everything. It's totally ridiculous to put it on the students . . . the teachers are grown up. They're the big people. They're supposed to control the people in the school. We're here to learn.' In this one the students did not feel any ethical loyalty to the school. They saw it as an institution which enforced sanctions, rather than enabling them to make ethical decisions.

As we have seen, often student norms run counter to the rules of the school or to the expectations of administrators of teachers. Power *et al.* call these aggregate counternorms, but they make their own moral appeal to a protective sense of in-group loyalty. To report a peer for cheating, using drugs or alcohol, for instance, would be seen as betraying these counternorms. In the above case, there may not be conflicting values over the rights and wrongs of stealing; there is just no connection made between the values of the school and the values of the students. One way of describing this would be to say that the students felt no loyalty to the school. Very often counternorms are established as a deliberate attempt to resist collective responsibility for the school, what McLaren (1993: 146, 229) called 'resistance'. It could arise from a counter-productive reliance on external measures of control. The student aggregate norms do not include opposing stealing – they take it for granted as a way of life that others should control. In many cases teachers and administrators reinforce this by providing harsher penalties, more secure locks and surveillance. They do not enlist students as partners in the disciplinary process but resort to largely ineffective external controls. What this can do is to dissociate students from the school community, setting them apart from the habit of practising those moral virtues that the whole school community has decided are appropriate ones. The moral dissociation need not be caused by neglecting the moral quality of institutions, as McLaren shows, but it can be exacerbated by a lack of openness and negotiation to try to engage student values and to allow students to take responsibility for their own actions.

PERSONA AND PERSONAE

One of the deepest difficulties in understanding ethics is to understand how societies can make persons act ethically and autonomously. The problem is not unrelated to the issue of free will and determinism, or even the existence of an all-powerful god who knows everything, and therefore what will happen, but still wants to hold us responsible for our actions. To what extent are we pawns in an evolving fatalistic evolution of ideas, in which to take responsibility for our decisions is seen as empty rhetoric? Are we just objects as passively tossed around in society as billiard balls on a table, determined by laws of cause and effect, or are we persons, able to modify the pathways of objects and ideas through our capacity to become rational persons? If we inhabit a world where law-like events occur, to what extent can we apply the laws of cause and effect to our own actions with any plausibility or predictability?

Philosophers promoting the ethic of care protested against the abstraction of the consistency position's move towards universal principle or moral law. Practical wisdom, or what Aristotle called 'phronesis', cannot just be concerned with universals only. Aristotle proposed that practising the ideal of 'doing well' has much to do with particulars, that is with recognizing the features of a situation that are salient to a way of living that give witness, action after action, to one's commitment to the ideal of doing well. The challenge that people face is not to identify those actions that might lead to some future goal, be means to an ideal end; rather the challenge is, situation after situation, to act consistently with those over-arching ideals by looking at the situation in order to see what would best embody that ideal at that moment. Seeing the salient features of a situation as relevant or appropriate to that ideal or end involves perceptual ability, an intuitive reason. So in some circumstances, joining a picket line might well just appear to be the right thing to do, intuitively, because it is consistent with the ideal of loyalty which has become embodied in a person's normal practices.

Aristotle's emphasis on becoming habituated in daily practice to meet certain goals raises interesting issues about the reflective quality or even the self-consciousness needed to be an ethical person. A more modern philosopher, Michael Oakeshott, elaborates. The intuitive aspects need not be conscious, but they are not thereby passive. Oakeshott (1962: 60) said:

> The moral life is human affection and behaviour determined not by nature but by art. It is conduct to which there is an alternative. This alternative need not be consciously before the mind; moral conduct doesn't necessarily involve the reflective choice of a particular action.

Oakeshott (1962: 62) echoes Heidegger in saying that because we are all born into societies, we are not given a choice as to the form of moral life that we will adopt. Habermas, too, would say that our life-world is shaped for us at the start, as it is with animals. Oakeshott describes the following two contrasting definitions of morality, though from our perspective they represent opposite poles of the consequences/consistency dualism, with a continuum in between.

The first is through what we have represented as situated care – the morality we receive through education as a habit of affection and behaviour. It is not based on reflective thought but on conduct, as at the earliest stages of the Kohlbergian hierarchy. Moral education does not involve memorizing rules and precepts; rather 'by living with people who habitually behave in a certain manner we acquire habits of conduct in the same way we acquire our native language' (Oakeshott 1962: 62). So moral education is not a distinct aspect of education, one of the subjects to be covered, but is part of all activities. The result of moral education is the ability to act in certain ways, not the ability to explain our behaviour in abstract terms. Change therefore cannot be dramatic or revolutionary, it has to be evolutionary and gradual. 'The sort of change which belongs to this moral life is analogous to the change to which a living language is subject; nothing is more habitual and customary than our ways of speech and nothing is more continuously invaded by change' (Oakeshott 1962: 65).

The second form of moral life corresponds to Kohlberg's stage six, the reflective application of moral criteria. Moral ideas are more important than moral action in this form of moral life; education in it requires moral training, and thus only philosophers will do it well. They do it by argument and the revolutionary imposition of justified rules rather than by evolution, privileging a morality of rules over the morality of habit. By subordinating the morality of habit to the morality of rules, we have built what Oakeshott calls a tower of Babel – 'we exaggerate the significance of our moral ideals to fill the hollowness of our moral life . . . what should be subordinated has come to rule, and its rule is a misrule' (Oakeshott 1962: 74–5). Morality is a practice, and we can call habitual morality rational if we define rationality as 'the certificate we give to any conduct which can maintain a place in the flow of sympathy, the coherence of activity, which composes a way of living' (Oakeshott 1962: 109). A practice is, for Oakeshott, a language of self-disclosure. It comes to the speaker as 'various invitations to understand, to choose to respond . . . it is an instrument to be played on, not a tune to be played' (1975: 58).

While it seems obvious that a certain command of language is needed for the second form of ethics, the first is more ambiguous. Just as the feminist ethical philosophers largely rejected the consistency/consequences models because these models separate themselves from daily experiences, Oakeshott (1975: 78) insists that

> a morality then, is neither a system of general principles nor a code, but a vernacular language. General principles and rules may be elicited from it, but (like other languages) it is not the creation of grammarians; it is made by the speakers.

What we ought to do is connected to who we are, because what we are is what we believe ourselves to be (Oakeshott 1962: 248). The question arises as to how explicit these vernacular languages must be. Does the signalling of birds, which ornithologists say is socially acquired, count as a vernacular language? Humans are told stories about who they are and what they ought to do. Their belief in these narratives provides them with both an identity and a moral practice. In reacting to narratives as well as to situations they can continue to construct themselves, into *personae*, the *personae* of teachers, clever people, parents, citizens, males, which we noted in Chapter 4. The ability to stand outside one's *persona* and reflect, perhaps modify it through self-awareness and self-reflection, is the mark of a form of morality that is the defining characteristic of a rational person.

I propose that part of what it means to be a person includes at least three awarenesses:

- an intra-personal awareness that one is different from and yet part of a social community of shared understandings and practices
- a personal awareness that those shared social practices arise out of an individual concern for what other people do and are made meaningful through abstracted language that constructs shared knowledge and values
- an impersonal awareness that one's actions have an effect on other events and things in a real world regardless of how one individual perceives them.

It can be seen that these relate, roughly speaking, to our three ethical domains of care, consistency and consequences.

CAN ANIMALS BE LOYAL?

If this is what it means to be a person, to what extent can animals be persons? At the beginning of this book I limited the discussion of ethical conduct to rational human beings. If it is the case that ethics is restricted to rational persons, what sense, if any, does it make to apply ethical concepts such as loyalty to animals? Singer's *Expanding Circle* (1983) and the Green movement have made us much more aware of our responsibilities towards animals, but our assumptions about the dominance of humankind because of its rationality or self-consciousness or personhood seem to have changed little since the 1940s when the following was written:

> A voluntary action is an action that a man could have done differently if he had so chosen. Voluntary actions include all willed or volitional actions in which there is a conscious process of willing.
>
> ... It must be admitted that there is something like goodness about a dog's loyalty to its master, but psychologists are so far from agreeing as to whether any of the actions of the lower animals are voluntary in the sense given to this word in the last paragraph, that it would be unwise to add to our complications by including animal activities within the limits of our subject.
>
> (Lillie 1948: 4)

While there is much in Lillie's book that would now be recognized as politically incorrect (especially his exclusion of women from consideration), what assumptions do we as educators still make about higher animals and lower animals? Descartes believed that only humans were rational and that animals, possessing neither souls nor minds, were simply automata, behaving on a sort of automatic stimulus–response mechanism. That appears to be true of amoeba, but, as Popper (1972) would argue, there are many different levels of intelligence in the animal world and he would plump for the potentiality of any animal species to be as intelligent as a human. The animal/human distinction is beginning to break down for many purposes, including that of rights (Singer 1983). Does it also disappear in relation to moral responsibility?

Recognizing that there are many different levels of intelligence in humans also, do we deny personhood to some animals and some humans? What are the criteria that determine whether an animal or a person could be morally responsible for their actions? Do we allow children the same rights as adults? Do we consider the severely mentally retarded to have forfeited their rights to personhood, by dint of the fact that, like many animals, they appear to be incapable of voluntary actions or free choice? All the writing of social justice documents does not immediately change our cultural attitudes, our conceptions, of what it is to be a person. We simply behave differently towards different people, often by imitation of the others around us. While Oakeshott insists that morality in its vernacular form is intuitive and unreflective, he also has to include the impact of language and rules in helping us to confront our own assumptions.

LOGIC AND ETHICS

I present below a classical logical puzzle familiar to most philosophers, which would certainly be beyond the capacity of non-human animals to understand, let alone solve. Mackie (1977: 16) uses a traditional ethical conundrum called the prisoner's dilemma to show the limits of using formal logic to arrive at an ethical decision. Mackie prefers a game theory approach, a sort of minimax or felicific calculation of consequences. I have adapted his comments to a more appropriate example. You could ask whether the proposed solution to the unionist's dilemma is ethical or merely prudential.

7.2 The unionist's dilemma

Two teachers believe that signing negotiated workplace agreements with the major employing body will destroy the power of the teachers' union. Despite considerable pay incentives, they refuse to sign the workplace agreement★ and continue to pursue the work bans imposed by the union.★ If they both continue,★ they have a fairly good chance of resisting pressure by the minister and succeeding in contributing for overall pay increases to all teachers in the state. If they both sign the workplace agreement,★ the minister will have won and the chance of the union winning an overall deal is markedly less. But if one refuses to sign while the other signs it,★ the one who signs will immediately have a 7.5 per cent pay rise, while the one who refuses to sign may well lose the support of a weakened union and lose their job. The one who signs will have an even better chance of improvement in conditions than each will have if both refuse to sign, while the one who does not sign will have an even worse chance than each if they both sign.

Suppose that these facts are known to each person and each calculates it in a perfectly rational way with a view simply to their own betterment. Mary reasons: if Tom does not sign, I shall have a better chance of a pay rise if I sign than if I refuse; but also if Tom signs, I shall have a better chance if I sign than if I do not sign; so whatever Tom is going to do, I will be well advised to sign. Since the situation is symmetrical, Tom's reasoning is exactly the same. So both will sign. And yet they would each have had a better chance of long-term betterment, that is, of achieving the very end they are, by hypothesis, aiming at, if both had continued to refuse to sign.

At first sight this may appear a paradox, but Mackie believes that there is nothing paradoxical about it. Why should it be surprising if two people, making separate, uncoordinated choices of action aimed, however rationally, at separate private goals, should fail to achieve them, or that they would have a better chance of each achieving their own interests if only they could coordinate their choices of action?

The best symmetrical result, and therefore the best that could be achieved by any device that both could freely accept, is that both would abstain from signing the workplace agreement. But how could this be achieved? What they need is something that will literally or metaphorically connect their actions. If they both know that the only options open are that both should sign or both should not sign, then, calculating traditionally but selfishly as before, both will sign. But what will serve to tie their actions together? Suppose they make a bargain; each says, 'I will follow the union directive if you do.' If they are rational egoists, that is, they are consistently acting out of their own interests, each will have the same motive for breaking the agreement between them that they had originally for disobeying the union directive, so we seem to have made no progress.

If Tom and Mary have a general tradition of keeping agreements, then they will be able to achieve much the same result as agreeing to respect the conditions of union membership. They will then be able to make a bargain that each will be a loyal union member and the agreement-keeping tradition will then prevent each from signing the negotiated workplace agreement. Moreover since it is a bargain, each will feel bound to keep it only as long as the other does, and each will know that the other feels this, and then if each can see whether the other is remaining loyal to the union, each will have a further motive for doing so themselves, namely the knowledge that, by remaining, they encourage their comrade to remain. The general agreement-keeping tradition is likely to be less effective than the more traditional agreement of honour and loyalty, but it has the advantage of being more flexible; it can be applied to support the making and keeping of all sorts of useful bargains.

> One moral that we might be inclined to draw from the game theory analysis is that prudence is not enough, that the rational calculation of long-term self-interest is not sufficient in itself to lead men to make mutually beneficial agreements, or, once made, to keep them.
>
> (Mackie 1977: 119)

There are further complicating issues raised here that were not present in the original prisoner's dilemma. The major one is that both Tom and Mary have opted into the teaching profession and have signed a contract with the employing body that is as binding as their becoming members of the union. Deciding to which body their loyalties should be stronger will depend on their ideological commitment to the teaching profession or to union membership, as much as to their self-interest. At least it will involve a definition of 'self-interest' that goes beyond the acquisition of material benefit, a definition that defines themselves as either loyal members of the teaching profession or loyal members of the union. The codes of ethics of each body are in conflict.

AGAINST EXTREME ACTION

Codes of ethics, like any system of beliefs or values, often conflict, and their various incompatibilities act as a brake on extreme action. You cannot follow any one code too zealously because it is held in check by all the others. Many teachers in the 1995 industrial action refused to take extreme action on the grounds that the consequences of extreme industrial action were far more detrimental to current students, for whom teachers had an ethical responsibility, than current conditions were for teachers. So there is a caring and a consequentialist basis for their refusing to engage in strike action. Milder forms of industrial action, like not working out of school hours or taking on any duties that were not specifically stated in the conditions of employment, such as orchestra practice or youth camps, were favoured. This was consonant with what

Aristotle took to be the highest form of ethical behaviour, to be moderate in one's actions, partly on the grounds of the consequences stance, for moderate action was likely to have the least effect on anyone or anything.

If it does have minimal consequences either way, then from a union point of view it negates the point of industrial action. Not to participate in any industrial action sanctioned by the union, but to carry on one's duties as usual, would have minimal bad consequences for the running of the school, and therefore on those grounds teachers ought not to participate in any industrial action. In Chapter 9, we shall look more specifically at the ethics of failing to act, merely noting here that Aristotle saw deficiency of action as a vice equivalent to that of taking extreme measures or excess of disposition.

Loyalty has been one of the sub-themes of this chapter, but other themes have included the need for rationality or language to determine ethical responsibility, the inclusion of animals to the social sphere, the issue of professionalism over unthinking 'intuition' for moral decisions. Loyalty to one's professional community is not a legal requirement but an ethical notion, as is being a professional.

Chapter 8

Censorship and curriculum

Teachers, like mothers, want to produce acceptable persons – persons who will support worthy institutions, live compassionately, work productively but not obsessively, care for older and younger generations, be admired, trusted, and respected. To shape such persons, teachers need not only intellectual capabilities, but also a fund of knowledge about the particular persons with whom they are working.

Noddings (1988: 221)

If you don't like the images of sex the pornographers offer, the appropriate response is not to suppress them but to overwhelm them with healthier, more realistic ones.

Bloch et al.('Cyberporn', 1995: 55)

It makes little difference whether loyalty is called upon to justify behaviours within a union or within a school, if the key appeal is to shared values and conventions. Phenix (1964: 290) distinguishes between two intimately connected moralities in education. One is the morality of the educator in choosing among alternative teaching procedures. The other is the morality of the person being educated. Phenix argues that because education is essentially a moral enterprise, the concept of sanctions within society confirms the moral insight that the right is not right because people approve of it, but that what is right ought to be approved of, whether or not persons actually do so. The moral standards of the developing person are fashioned in the context of the educator's moral choices about educational aims, teaching methods and curriculum. We have not yet spoken much about curriculum in schools, but educational decisions about what, how, when and to whom instruction should be given inevitably have their effect upon the moral nature of the persons taught. We see that not only with the arrival of the internet, but with the rivalry of the mass media as a basis of information for children, the teacher and school have far less control over what can be presented to children.

Nozick says:

We want our individual lives to express our conceptions of reality

(and of responsiveness to that); so too we want the institutions demar-
cating our lives together to express and saliently symbolize our
desired mutual relations. Democratic institutions and the liberties
coordinate with them are not simply effective means toward controlling the powers of government and directing these toward matters of
joint concern; they themselves express and symbolize in a pointed and
official way, our equal human dignity, our autonomy and powers of
self-direction.

(Nozick 1989: 286)

We have seen how difficult it is to keep our regulations symbolizing
our corporate values and maintaining individual dignity and autonomy.
Nozick additionally raises the issue of determining what those desired
mutual relations are, and how one maintains them.

CONTROLLING INFORMATION IN SCHOOLS

Many Christian schools in Australia currently will not allow standard
texts to be used in schools because they believe that students should not
be exposed to, among other things, the heresy of evolutionary theory.
This is obviously a protective device, designed to ensure Christian values
and it is consistent with the expressed wishes of the parent-based school
council. Over twenty years ago the classic *Catcher in the Rye* was banned
as a Year 11 English syllabus text because it contained the word 'fuck',
a word still taboo in most schools. And yet it could have been argued that
the book itself was a celebration of human connection and caring. The
banning occurred at a time when a replica of Michelangelo's statue of
David was removed from a Melbourne city store window because it did
not have the necessary superimposed figleaf. Few now would express
horror at the exposure of a marble penis on a work of art, but there is still
a lot of uncertainty as to how much the question of sexual expression
should be open in the schools.

A local Catholic school was recently rehearsing the play *Home Is Where
Your Clothes Are* by Anthony Marriott and Bob Grant. The play had been
advertised and was to be presented to the public on Friday. The play was
censored and cancelled on Tuesday afternoon by the high school principal under questionable circumstances. The principal was horrified that
reference was made on stage by the young actors to sexual acts and
homosexuality. From an administrative point of view, one wonders at the
drastic nature of the sanction and whether there could have been a less
dramatic 'chain of command', i.e. school board, play adviser, teaching
staff, principals, parents. But here lack of communication about the
content of the play seems to have been the main sin. The teacher
directing the play had not intended to be provocative or to offend and it

is doubtful whether set policies and procedures in the school would have assisted him to consider the ethics of producing such a play, although in many Catholic schools there is explicit instruction to avoid discussion of HIV. Many schools have written policies for the suitability of library and instructional materials, but it is not clear whether they apply to extra-curricular activities.

PORNOGRAPHY ON THE NET

Current debate on censorship of the erotic on the Internet is a general instance of the particular issue of deciding what information should be made available in schools and whether some information ought not be allowed. In the United States and Asia, tough anti-pornography laws have been recently passed to try to keep a wave of erotica out of cyberspace (Elmer-Dewitt 1995: 48). While policy-makers and parents have a shared vision of superhighway access giving open access to all information, there is a feeling that flooding the Internet with freely available pornography will affect desired mutual relations and respect for persons. How can policy-makers best ensure that pornography will not negatively affect those in their care? Policy-makers must balance public moral safety with essential civil liberties, the right to freedom of self-expression enshrined in the first Amendment of the American Constitution.

8.1 Pornography on the Net

In March 1995 Paul Kim, a 17-year-old senior at Newport High School in Bellevue, a suburb in Seattle, Washington, created an 'Unofficial Newport High School Home Page'. The home page included, under a category about students' likes, links to three other servers that had a Playboy centrefold, an article about masturbation and another about oral sex. As a joke, Kim made the document available to on-line computer users by locating it on a public directory on the Internet.★

Paul Kim was an exceptional student with an overall grade point average of 3.88. He achieved a near-perfect score on the Scholastic Aptitude Test. He had been endorsed by the school for a $2,000 national merit scholarship and his index of 216 placed him ahead of students who obtained national merit scholarships in the past year. Paul was also involved in many extra-curricular activities, e.g. knowledge bowl, maths team, literary magazine, school choir, jazz vocals and student government. He had applied to Columbia University, Stanford University, the University of Washington, the University of Chicago, Swarthmore College, Princeton University and Harvard University.

Paul's home page was noticed by a staff member at another Bellevue school, who reported it to Newport High officials. He was summoned to a meeting with his assistant principal, Ms Kay Whelan, and his guidance counsellor.★ He agreed to take his home page off the Yahoo directory and the administration promised him he would suffer no disciplinary action.★ Shortly afterwards, he completely eliminated the home page from the Web.★ He was possibly the first person ever to have his own home page on the World Wide Web censored.

The Newport High School principal, Karin Cathey, however, was angered by Paul's behaviour and ordered the school to withdraw their endorsement of Kim's national merit scholarship,★ having first determined by phone call that this action would make Paul ineligible for the scholarship.★ The school then sent faxes to the seven colleges to which Paul had applied, notifying them that the school's national merit endorsement had been withdrawn, without detailing the reasons for the school's sudden withdrawal of support,★ thereby leaving the reasons to the readers' imagination.

Five days after informing the National Merit Scholarship Corporation of this decision, the principal called a meeting with Paul and his sister, to inform them that the school had withdrawn its endorsement.★ Paul's mother was out of the country on business, but Paul's guardian had not been notified.★ Paul was extremely distraught by this news. Without notice or a chance to defend himself, Ms Cathey had unilaterally stripped him of the opportunity to receive a $2,000 scholarship and all of the associated rewards that come with that honour. Paul rightfully assumed that the school might seek further discipline against him, and asked repeatedly whether any further punishment would be forthcoming. Ms Cathey told him that this was the only step she had taken and that the matter was now closed.★

The day after her meeting with Paul, Ms Cathey sent a half-hearted retraction letter to the colleges.★ Although she noted that 'Paul has exceptional intelligence' and 'has been an excellent student, actively and productively engaged in school activities during his entire four years', she also said that 'he is going through a difficult time right now'. The lawyers said that this letter did further damage to his college applications and could scarcely make up for the damage she had already caused. Soon afterwards, Harvard rejected his application.★

On 6 April, after Paul had endured the worst weeks of his high school career, Ms Cathey asked Paul to suggest an 'alternative punishment'★ in exchange for her agreement to contact the National Merit Scholarship Corporation and re-endorse his application. Paul telephoned the National Merit Scholarship Corporation and learned that the scholarship decisions had already been made. Accordingly, it was too late for him to be considered. He refused Ms Cathey's offer.

In an out-of-court settlement in December, the school district apologized to the student, promised to have him reinstated as a National Merit finalist, and agreed to pay him $2,000 for a potentially lost scholarship (*The New York Times* on 24 December 1995: 9). Kim became a freshman at Columbia University in New York, majoring in Chemistry and triumphantly creating a new home page at <http: / /www.cc.columbia.edu/~pkk11>.

The lawyers defending Kim used legal rights arising from the First Amendment entitling him to freedom of expression and the Fourteenth Amendment entitling him to substantive and procedural due process of law. But if he had written his home page in Australia, he would have had no such constitutional rights. Would that have denied him the ethical rights to publish on the Internet? World Wide Web authors were quick to emphasize a global right of freedom of speech. Paul had not written the pornographic literature, he had merely provided a link to it. The student should not be charged for freely expressing his own thoughts about his schoolmates: he has a right like everyone else to express himself through speech or press without being penalized for his statements. That was what the school board finally decided, that 'the district has no right to punish students who, on their own time and with their own resources exercise their right of free speech on the Internet'.

Freedom of speech on the Internet, however, is a contentious issue and is not always guaranteed. In February 1996, both houses of Congress passed a telecommunications bill that made it illegal to discuss abortion anywhere on the Internet. This includes newsgroups, Web pages, ftp sites, gopher sites and emails of any kind. The law is now in effect, so that if an American posted this chapter on email, the very mention of the law itself exposes that person to the possibility of a prison sentence or heavy fines.

As always, though, there are other considerations to be made. Under obscenity laws, if a satirical poster pasted on a city wall causes public offence, the person putting it up can be fined even though he or she did not intend to offend. Paul's schoolmates could counter-claim damages for having been publicly offended. If, moreover, Paul's classmates manage to show that what Paul has so publicly spread is totally or partially false, or at least doubtful, they could accuse him of slander. If the judge manages to demonstrate that the Web links were above all intended to be particularly addressed to (and read by) his own under-age classmates, Paul's posting could be considered a public attempt to induce young boys less than 18 years old to commit obscene acts. Within the frame of justice, or rights, if one prosecutes Paul for distributing the pornography of others freely on the Internet, is one also obliged to prosecute those shops that not only openly display similar material but sell it for profit? Notice that this is the law of universalizability in a slightly different guise. The law must be universalizable, that is it must apply to similar people in similar circumstances, in the frame of consistency.

More ethical issues for educational administrators were raised by the lawyers themselves. Does it make a difference that the student was publishing from his own home? In this case, Kim developed a parody of his high school on his own time away from school. Even if he had expressed his opinions in the school, American law has found that students may express their opinions, even on controversial subjects, if they do so 'without materially and substantially interfering with appropriate discipline in the operation of the school'. In the Tinker v. Des Moines Independent Community School District, 393 U.S. 503 (1969) case, the US Supreme Court recognized that students do not shed their constitutional rights when they enter the high school campus. In order for the state in the person of school officials to justify prohibition of a particular expression of opinion, it must be able to show that its action was caused by something more than a mere desire to avoid the discomfort and unpleasantness that always accompany an unpopular viewpoint.

In the case of underground publications (i.e. student papers published off campus and without school funds), the American law has a precedent in the Papish v. U of Missouri Curators case where the university expelled a graduate student on grounds of indecency for publishing her own paper showing a political cartoon of the Statue of Liberty being raped. The Supreme Court decided in the student's favour, on the grounds that

- the picture was not obscene by legal standards and 'indecent' was too vague a charge to be decided
- the publishing of the paper and the picture did not interfere with the university's educational mission

- students have the right to publish their views without impedance as long as it is truly an 'underground' publication and not officially sanctioned.

Paul Kim had placed the 'Unofficial Newport High School Home Page' onto a specific Web directory called 'Yahoo'. Besides the 'unofficial' in the title, he also placed various disclaimers on the home page that alerted any reader who might retrieve it that the home page was 'unofficial' and intended only for amusement. Several teachers at his school noticed it and commented on it to Paul, indeed discussing it within the school's technology committee. The school did not take action until it received criticism from an outside school.

Educators believed that the principal had no authority to discipline a student for expressing his opinions in his own time on a home computer, and some asked whether the principal was punished for her over-reaction.

Ms Cathey's action in Paul's case is described as unlawful, not unethical. What are the ethics involved? Apparently no one at Paul's school felt that there was anything to get excited about until a colleague at another school reported it to the principal. One can imagine the reaction of a self-righteous principal who believes that the school's taboos are not only being openly flouted, but ridiculed. Discrimination is a strong word to use in this situation, but there is no doubt that Paul was not only different from the regular American student, but openly different. His obvious intelligence made him a potential leader into deviance. He openly criticized 'the system' and he was openly gay in school. He is Korean, a permanent resident, born on 27 August 1977 in Seoul. His father was a Catholic priest and his mother fled the devastation of the Korean War. Paul's grandmother ran away from home at the age of 16 to get herself an education, because her parents did not support the education of women. He was disenfranchised not by his age but his permanent resident status. One could ask whether his rights as a Korean were different from his rights as a homosexual or as a student.

FREEDOM TO EXPRESS DISCRIMINATION

The tension between freedom of expression and a distaste for public racist remarks has been evidenced in recent national elections in Australia where several politicians have been requested to stand down for public remarks that many people have found offensive and racist. On the Stanford campus in 1991, students who had been ostracized in the student newspaper for speaking publicly about immigrants who had been taking up 'American' places in class and also were succeeding, reacted by appealing to the First Amendment and their right to free speech. Their argument was that they were not doing the Asian students who were their main target any physical harm, and that to impose censorship on them was to deny them freedom of expression.

Because censorship in the Kim case is partially a legal issue and certainly one of control, talk has been largely in terms of individual rights. The principal has a right to protect those in her care. Kim has a right to express his own views in and outside school. The librarian has a right to exclude from the library any material that he or she considers harmful. The teacher has a right to decide what information will maximally benefit the students. Even if Paul Kim's case was settled to his own satisfaction, the central question about censorship is not resolved, and probably will not be finally settled, by the courts. We also see that in Paul Kim's case when the issue is made a legal one, in which rights are addressed to the exclusion of consequences, the battle over definitions and rights is one of almost infinite regress, as it was in the case of Tony's punishment in Chapter 1.

I do not know any way out of this impasse other than an idealistically educational one. Any top-down restriction on what can be read or said can be distorted into a manipulation of thought which is unethical, if it involves power to the end of social control. Orwell's novels *Animal Farm* and *1984* presented in narrative fiction the dangers of thought control, terrifying in both cases because of the helplessness of the citizens to fight back against the manipulation of their language. Freedom of information is essential to freedom of thought. We need freedom of speech not simply to emphasize the importance of but to ensure free access to different ways of describing the world. If we destroy the possibility of personhood and autonomy, we preclude the possibility of free choice on which knowledge is dependent.

We have already seen in the last chapter that the issue of rights seems to take arguments down an insoluble impasse. One needs to have a further argument beyond rights themselves to decide which rights should prevail. If we are to retain an interest in the ethical side rather than the legal side, we should, I believe, tend to favour those ideas that make us more, not less, human. The censorship of the school play with which this chapter began may have been to prevent the presentation of damaging values, and used as its justification the greatest good for the greatest number of people, but perhaps the damage done by closing it down so dramatically was greater.

We should consider whether censorship or even the notion of political correctness has at its root a mistrust of ideas and people. It certainly represents a mistrust of one's ability to think for oneself at a Kohlbergian level five, and perhaps it also indicates a lack of trust in ideas themselves.

WHO SHOULD CONTROL THE CURRICULUM?

Schools generally promote the proliferation of ideas and alternatives, up to a point. But the pragmatics of schooling require us to make choices filtering the information to be presented to students. In some cases the filter may not be chosen. Remember Nozick's point made at the beginning of this chapter that democratic institutions are not simply effective means towards controlling the powers of government and directing these towards matters of joint concern; they themselves express and symbolize, in a pointed and official way, the autonomy and powers of self-direction.

One could argue that patterns of control, even in schools, are not a matter for decision, that they evolve through a culture and history of practices, often unrealized. Using their theory of 'interests, rights and power', Ury *et al.* (1988) use two databases, field interviews and simulation transcripts to indicate that American business managers favour interests-based behaviours (pragmatic consequentialism), German managers favour rights-based behaviours (principled interests) and Japanese managers favour power-based behaviours. The Catholic school that intervened to prevent a school play being offered was operating through a power base, at least at that point, although it may have been parents who were driving the intervention as much as the principal. If a national picture can be accurate, one would expect that the Australian stereotype would support a curriculum of resistance to power, with some independence of spirit and antagonism to the imposition of inflexible structures of control. The same national cultural biases might well influence the curriculum structure. In a devolved educational system, who decides what frame the curriculum should be presented through, and what values it should represent?

In Australia, despite the attempt of a recent federal minister of education to impose a unified national system of education at all levels, there has been a resistance from many sides to the traditional bureaucratic model, with its focus on centralized authority, clear chains of commands, defined roles and the rational pursuit of quantifiable goals. Lynn Beck (1994: 72–3) quotes many (including Murphy 1990; Sizer 1984; Chubb 1988) who claim that a bureaucratic top-down model is neither appropriate, nor effective, nor efficient. There are others who argue on ethical grounds that traditional structures are oppressive, especially to women, to racial minorities and the poor (Ferguson 1984; Clark and Meloy 1989). The bureaucratic model largely uses efficiency as its main criterion of success, and is therefore basing its argument largely on the greatest good for the greatest number of people, even where that often results in treating people, both students and teachers, as means to an end.

Ferguson (1984) and Beck (1994), both women, propose, in effect, that the 'impersonal' bureaucracy has become anachronistic because it ignores the responsive aspects of ethics of responsibility. This goes beyond a redistribution of goods within a justice or consistency frame, where both power and resources are taken from those who have more and redistributed to those who have less (Strike 1982). It incorporates a responsiveness to difference which is not measurable but human. It is more like a community of inquiry in which negotiation and conversation are the main agents of attitude change. Homosexuality, for instance, will be better understood in a school if it is raised as an item for discussion in an appropriate context rather than removed from discussion to emerge only as a tacit motive for punishing pornography.

We are faced here with an issue similar to that in many religions – the problem that the good life must be freely chosen. How can we expose the vulnerable and strong-minded equally to all possible choice, without damaging the vulnerable?

To establish a community of inquiry requires knowing individual students (and teachers) and knowing how far their systems of belief can be challenged. If this seems impossible in multiple classes of thirty-five students each, then perhaps all we are doing here is triggering a deep and devastating critique of the present structures of schooling. Perhaps individual autonomy is an impossibility with things the way they are. It might allow a teacher to stay with the same group of students for three or more years (with mutual consent, of course). One teacher might teach two or more subjects to thirty students instead of one subject to sixty students (Sizer 1984) or a team of teachers might work together with a group of students for several years, a process that has already been trialled successfully in some private schools. We must not convert caring into a manageable formal professional set of behaviours (Noddings 1993: 51). But the point still applies here. The idea of moving beyond the shared conventions of one's immediate group has implications of distance, of making an 'independent judgement' divorced from one's life-world, and it is that sort of autonomy that needs to be the goal.

THE FEMININE DIFFERENCE

Many modern principals seek to organize their schools as a devolved community. Instead of a hierarchy of power, decisions are made through dialogue at all levels, without any clear centre. It is done through negotiation of difference rather than by rule or edict.

Before Beck and her colleagues, Carol Gilligan had claimed that Kohlberg's hierarchical scale was actually a scale of power and therefore measured the dominant masculine morality as opposed to a feminine one. In the early stages the person must defer to others to gain a sense of rightness and identity; in the late stages the person transcends other people entirely and guides their own behaviour by moral or legal codes. At the very highest level, achieved by only few humans, according to Kohlberg, the moral relation between the person and the world is characterized by distance, formality and judgement. She defines traditional male values as those of independence, formality and judgement. Gilligan (1982) argues that Kohlberg's six stages of moral development assume an impersonal masculine 'justice perspective', thereby ensuring that women are seen as morally deficient because of their tendency to understand moral issues in emotional and personal ways. She claims that the developmental ideal that emphasizes a 'rights perspective' over a 'care perspective' is biased against women not because women are less rational, but because men and women depend on different notions of self, one built on separation from the other, the other built on relations.

Sheila Ruth (quoted in Spender 1990: 203) claims that three particular characterizations of a feminine ethic are as follows:

- a critique of abstraction, and a belief that female thinking *is* (and moral thinking in general *should be*) more contextualized, less bound to abstract rules, more concrete
- a stress on the values of empathy, nurturance or caring, which again are seen as qualities that women both value and tend more commonly to display
- a critique of the idea that notions of choice or will are central to morality and of a sharp distinction between fact and value; a stress, instead, on the idea of the demands of a situation, which are discovered through a process of attention to it and require an appropriate response.

Many female philosophers who have contributed to recent discussion on ethics have picked up similar common themes. Phillippa Foot (1967, 1978) places more emphasis on the descriptive elements of morality than the prescriptive idealism offered by Hare (1952), that is, she is more situated in the world of action than rules. Mary Midgley (1981) offers an account of human behaviour that emphasizes humans' similarities with animals as well as their differences of rationality and autonomy. Annette C. Baier (1985a) and Amelie Rorty (1991, 1992) give a Humean account of the passions that dominate moral decisions rather than the reasons offered. Iris Murdoch (1970) speaks of the sovereignty of the Good; Marilyn Frye (1983) and Hannah Arendt (1970) offer their idiosyncratic views on active contemplation and the daily situations that require resolution.

I think, however, that it can be misleading to focus on building a community as a gender issue. It is consistent with the 'care' focus, but there are many males writing in this mode such as Alasdair MacIntyre (1981, 1990) and Ian Hacking (1995). As Noddings reminds us (in Strike and Ternasky 1993: 43), if caring is a desirable moral orientation, both females and males should engage in the sort of work that induces it – work that Sara Ruddick (1980, 1989) calls 'the work of attentive love'. Attention, or engrossment, is central to an ethics of caring, because it is 'taking care' in both senses, and therefore according to Murdoch (1970) is essential to moral life.

Is a feminist 'caring' related to the consequentialist position? This sort of 'taking care' or 'paying attention' by considering the consequences of action for others is in this sense outward-looking, linking the subjective feelings and the outward experiential consequences. But it is debatable whether it is just a feminist view. You can imagine the possibility of an infinite number of incommensurable ethical 'theories'– for Africans, both male and female, or Aborigines, as opposed to a Western ethic. The possibility of an endless regress into competing abstract theories of ethics would be anathema to most of these philosophers – it would simply throw them back into the abstraction of argument about competing theories that they were criticizing. They usually wish to include competing theories within their compass rather than set themselves up in opposition to them. Gilligan (1982: 174) concludes her book: 'To understand how the tension between responsibilities and rights sustains the dialectic of human development is to see the integrity of two disparate modes of experience that are in the end connected.'

Chapter 9

Omissions and commissions

Truth telling is not always good, but it's a good thing, morally and practically, that most people tell the truth, as they see it, at least when there is nothing important to gain by not telling the truth. The greater good of the community needs looking after by the individuals who benefit from it. Non-truth telling is a deviation from this simple and direct way, and it requires a self-conscious effort.

David Nyberg (1993: 43–4)

HONESTY AND CONFIDENTIALITY

We are often enjoined to 'be good' as if being good involved doing something. This chapter asks in what sense it could be ethical or not to refrain from action. For any practice to be reasonably construed as a profession, then honesty and candour at least would seem to be obligations from the professional to the client. The recently revised code of ethics for doctors requires them to reveal truths uttered if keeping patient confidence could threaten or place another person in danger, either because of a potential life threat to a family through psychiatric problems or through HIV transmission. One can think of some professions, for instance chess-playing and politics, where veracity and candour may not be core virtues, but these are regarded as marginal professions, perhaps because of that. Honesty seems to be a fairly central criterion for educators, especially if they are to serve as moral models for growing citizens.

Yet two of the codes of ethics for educational administrators appear to contradict one another: an administrator is expected to fulfil professional responsibilities with honesty and integrity but is expected to maintain professional confidentiality at all times. Legal requirements to report crime or possible crime also confuse the ease with which we can require teachers always to be honest. Consider the following scenario.

9.1 Reporting abuse

It is a shared reading session in a junior primary school in a remote country area. The children are sitting on a mat at Catherine's feet. Sally put her hand up and asked if she could sit on a chair as her bruises were hurting. Catherine assumed that the child had hurt herself at a physical education lesson. Rather than interrupt the flow of her lesson, she asked Sally to move to a comfortable position and continued with the lesson. The child again raised her hand and said she was still uncomfortable because of her bruises. Catherine asked her to come and show where it was hurting. Rolling up her track-suit trousers, Sally revealed dark bruises and red marks criss-crossing her legs and large welts on the back of her thighs. In front of the class, Catherine immediately called the teacher next door to look after her class so that she could investigate the situation further. She took Sally outside and asked how she had received the bruises. The child replied that her mother had hit her with a stick because she had thrown a ball across the room and broken some plates on a shelf. Sally went on to say that she had bruises on her arm and chest from the same stick.

Catherine had been involved in a disclosure case during the previous year and was aware of the State Education Department's policy towards children disclosing physical abuse. She was required to inform a member of administration as soon as possible. The male deputy principal arrived quickly, but out of concern for the child asked the female deputy to inspect Sally's bruises. The female deputy noted the criss-crossed bruises along Sally's right arm. The bruises were in bands of three centimetres thickness and were both black and white in coloration. There were no visible bruises on the child's chest. The two deputies consulted the principal, who knew that Sally's mother was working as a classroom aide in the school. Sally volunteered the information that her mother had said she was sorry for hitting her but she had not done what she was told and had deserved the punishment. Sally appeared to have little fear for her safety or well-being and accepted the beating without complaint. She related her story as though her injuries were annoying but not of any significance to her, beyond preventing her from reading the story with the rest of her class.

In any instance of disclosure the school should not make any judgement as to the nature of the injuries nor investigate the issue further.★ Once a disclosure is reported by a child, the school must call in officers from the Department of Family and Children's Services (DFCS). The local department was telephoned and said that it no longer handled situations of this nature. The principal would have to contact the Esperance Office 200 kilometres away. The telephone call to Esperance was a lengthy one as the principal was required to give all the available details that the school had on the child and the family, including relatives in the town and grandparents and siblings of the injured girl. The field officer constantly put the principal on hold as she had to pass on the information to her supervisor and ensure that she was completing the appropriate forms.★

The field officer required a great deal more information on the nature of the bruising and requested that the principal carry out some of the tasks that she would normally do had she been on site. DFCS required a detailed description of the girl's injuries and asked the principal to view the bruises again, requiring measurements, drawings, coloration, descriptions and, if possible, photographs of the affected areas. The principal was required to estimate how recent the bruises were and whether there were any other marks on the child that indicated other possible forms of abuse. The principal was serving in effect as surrogate field officer and could have refused to undertake these duties,★ but felt obliged to do so to justify her actions, should this be required. She is permitted and indeed encouraged to take actions that she believes are in the best interests of the child. But it is not in her best interests as manager of the school, particularly where Sally's mother is an employee and she is moving outside the boundaries of appropriate procedure. The teacher once again removed the child from the classroom and asked the female deputy to assist rather than the school nurse to try to limit the number of staff who knew about this.★ During further investigation the child again openly stated that she was used to this sort of bruising and that both her mother and father usually hit her like this when she was naughty. She showed Catherine a number of very faint bruises on her arms and legs and said that her father had hit her with a stick a long time ago because she had not done what he had asked. She showed the female deputy her chest but there was no sign of bruising.

Sally returned to the class and the principal telephoned the field officer again. The field officer asked if the child would be safe going home with her parents that afternoon. If the principal had said no, the field officer would have to drive the 200 kilometres to organize a shelter for the child until an interview with the parents could be arranged. The principal had known the family for some time and had had no idea that the child was being disciplined in this manner. She felt that the child was not frightened at the prospect of going home so decided that the child was not in imminent danger.★

The field officer asked the principal to send the child home as usual and not enter into any discussions with the family, although this was really a matter of convenience, given the distance he would have had to travel, rather than considering the best interests of the child. He also required both parents to attend a meeting with two officers from DFCS in the school the following morning.★ The principal refused to have the parent interview in school, because she wanted to protect the mother as a staff member. Instead she called a meeting of the staff members involved and asked them to maintain confidentiality and the next morning spoke privately to the parents about their behaviour, warning them that they would be reported to the police if there was any further evidence of such abuse.

PRUDENTIAL/ETHICAL CHOICES

What should the teacher do? There is no ambiguity about the legal situation. The 'should' here is ambiguous, being both a practical and an ethical question. The revelation of truth here is more a legal requirement than an ethical one. We profess and demand honesty in our professional code of ethics while hardly beginning to understand it. There is a pragmatic reason for being honest. Speech must presume credibility. If we cannot presume truth-telling as a basic condition of speech, then our speech will not get us very far. That is why Geach (1976) makes it one of his conversational postulates, one of those requirements without which human communication cannot get off the ground. It is prudent. But there is also the ethical dimension of moral reprobation. The dishonest person becomes by his or her actions a deceiver. Are there any circumstances under which it is appropriate not to reveal the truth? And is refusing to say anything as morally reprehensible as uttering a deliberate falsehood? Catherine's decision seems as much based on prudence as on ethics. But as long as she is considering the consequences of her action for the child and the school, and the consistency of her actions with the basic concern for the welfare of the child and the parents, she is being ethical in her actions as well.

Before moving on to another case where honesty and confidentiality conflict, I should like to direct the reader's attention to the powerful and individual position of Hannah Arendt (1958). In an essay called 'The banality of evil' she describes the Gestapo as evil not because they intended harm to their Jewish prisoners, but because they did not think about the consequences of their actions, nor did they care. It was prudent for them to follow their orders. She says that evil arises from passivity, the unthinking acting according to rules because they are imposed from above, because it is easier to do that than think about them. We can think of instances where simply following the rules may be prudent and may be unethical. An example of this may be the principal in a publicly funded school with a high proportion of Aboriginal students who are constantly going walkabout with their tribe. Should he declare that they are present, being enrolled in his school, even where they are not anywhere in sight? If he does, he benefits the school because he will get additional resources. It is not really untrue to record them as students in the school in his reports to the State Education Department, but this is certainly a prudent interpretation of the rules to the school's advantage. In this case, he must make a decision to record something that he knows is not quite accurate, but may be justifiable. My concern is the ethics of *not* taking action to reveal the truth and the following example moves closer to that end while raising another issue related to honesty, that of confidentiality.

9.2 Professional confidentiality

The teacher notices that Susan is looking puffy and grey and has left the room rapidly on several occasions in early morning classes. She asks her if there is anything the matter and if she can help.★ Susan looks surprised that a teacher would take any notice of her as an individual and confesses that, after using a home pregnancy kit, she has discovered that she is pregnant. She does not know who the father is, and she has not yet told her parents anything of her troubles.★

She suspects that the father is one of a group of boys with whom she and a number of girls were sharing heroin just before a school dance. It is probably Tim, who has been sitting next to her at lunchtimes and has expressed his interest in her through various inarticulate body languages. She rather likes Tim. He is good-looking, gentle but shy, and finds any expression of emotions difficult. She thinks he is a little immature, and she is aware that if she made any overtures to him he would probably be afraid of an aggressive female. So she has let things ride, waiting for him to make the first move, to invite her out. But it may not be Tim, who needed drugs to gain enough courage to have sex with her. She had earlier rejected the advances of one of the other boys, Larry, because he had been heavily drinking. It was not impossible that he had taken advantage of her. She does not remember clearly anything that happened after the school dance. The boys had smuggled some vodka into the cloakrooms, pouring it into Coke bottles and buying the girls what the girls had thought were innocuous soft drinks.★ She can remember raucous laughter, but when she asked her girlfriend what happened Mary would only look embarrassed and say that Susan had been making a fool of herself and falling all over Tim. She remembers waking up on the morning after the school dance on her home front lawn. All she can vaguely remember is Larry taunting Tim that he could never succeed in having a girl.

The teacher remembers the table at which Susan was sitting and that Lisa and Terry were also present. She wonders whether to go and ask them to give their account of what happened at the ball and afterwards.★ She is aware that even on the verbal evidence given by Susan she is required to tell the police about the presence of drugs on school grounds, and aware that the consequent investigation may well reveal the truth about Susan's pregnancy to others. Yet she should also respect the confidentiality of Susan's condition.★ What should she do? Anything?

What makes the principal's actions more moral may well rest on an ethic of care, but the care should not be centred simply on Susan. It extends to the boys who were at the dance, and requires attention to the whole context in which Susan may have become pregnant. Critics of caring often make the mistake of supposing that caring is inherently soft and sweet. In reality caring requires heightened moral sensitivity (Noddings 1993: 349). It requires attention not only to Susan's welfare, but to the consequences of making an unjustifiable accusation of rape and to the consistency that what she is doing may well be construed by others as interfering rather than caring.

Is the teacher's first inquiry viewed as a legitimate concern, or as interfering? To what extent is it the responsibility of any teacher to show concern for a student's private circumstances? Or to take on the role of sleuth to try to uncover the truth of something that occurs outside school hours or outside school grounds? What sort of parallels are there with the instance of child abuse outlined above, and what dissimilarities? Is the age of the student a relevant difference here? You could well imagine similar situations with different details, for instance if a student discovered that they had tested positively for HIV on the basis of sharing needles for drugs.

HOW IMMORAL IS IT NOT TO ACT?

Let us move on to the ethics of failing to act, beginning with a non-educational example. In his book on *Moral Reasoning*, Grassian (1981: 23) asks the reader to judge the relative morality of Tom and Joe in the following circumstances:

> Tom hates his wife and, wanting her dead, puts poison in her coffee, thereby killing her. Joe also hates his wife and would like her dead. One day, Joe's wife accidentally puts poison in her coffee, thinking it's cream. Joe, who happens to be a chemist, has the antidote, but he does not give it to her. Knowing that he is the only one who can save her, he lets her die. Is Joe's failure to act as bad as Tom's action?

The difficult task is not only to justify one's answer to oneself but persuade someone who has a different stance, and possibly a different answer. There are similar unresolved disputes over the relative merit of non-intervention over euthanasia for the terminally ill, where the justification for inaction is presented in the form of Pope's verse 'thou shalt not kill, but needst not strive/officiously to keep alive'. But to quote Pope is an argument by assertion, not reason. Joe's failure to act is a conscious one and therefore he must be held as accountable as Tom for the consequent death, even if it was caused by inaction. But it is more contentious as to whether one can be held to be immoral for failing to act when one is simply not aware of possible consequences or has not even considered the possiblility of acting otherwise. Is there an onus on every human being to be aware of all possible consequences of action or non-action? The ethic of care would, it seems, require us to be positively responsive at all times towards all living creatures, but this would place an almost impossible burden of responsibility on us. Was Arendt right to imply that any unthinking following of the rules is 'evil'?

Imagine comparable examples in education where it would be considered immoral not to take action. The Head boy at a school made public homophobic remarks about another homosexual student at a school assembly. The whole assembly, including the teachers, laughed at the remarks and the homosexual student successfully sued, not the Head boy, but the principal for discrimination because he failed to take action either at the assembly or later to reprimand the speaker for his discriminatory remarks. The ethical situation here, rather than the legal one, should be your focus. Should lack of action be discriminatory, for instance when a student is being harassed for their differences and no teacher steps in to support them?

Does silence mean consent? A separate issue which may be worked into this case study might well be mainstreaming the intellectually disadvantaged where, for example, to take action to provide special education may be viewed as discriminatory but to fail to take special action may equally be discriminatory. We looked earlier at the question as to whether concealing the truth was as bad as telling a deliberate falsehood. Now we look at the broader question as to whether it is morally defensible not to take any action in a situation we know to be morally wrong. The same question arises again: is intention a necessary component of the ethical judgement or is it enough to simply look at the consequences? Contrast this with the examples of the Doctrine of Double Effect in Chapter 6 where it was the intention rather than the consequences that defined the difference between what was considered professionally ethical and unethical.

If silence is often taken for consent, the converse may also be true. Speaking up does not necessarily mean that one thinks that the action is wrong. One day after a football training session at a private Catholic College, John noticed that Peter had a tattoo on his upper arm. It was professionally done, a small cross, with 'I love you mum' underneath. Peter explained that he had done it as a birthday gift for his mother, his father having died about a year before. Later that day, John mentioned the tattoo in the course of conversation with one of the PE teachers who then informed the head of faculty. There was nothing in the school rules to prevent students having tattoos but the head was a little worried that John would tell other students and teachers and start a new craze. The year coordinator was requested to ask Peter to see him. When he asked Peter to show him his new tattoo, Peter refused, saying that it was none of his business. The coordinator called in the male deputy but to no avail. Peter was asked to come back to see the principal with his mother. The principal explained that he did not wish the practice to proliferate in the school and wanted Peter to get rid of the tattoo. His mother explained that this would require an operation which she could not afford, and besides both she and Peter liked the tattoo. The principal explained that having a tattoo is contrary to the school ethos and school code of conduct and unless his request for removal was satisfied, he would have no option but to remove Peter from a situation that may influence students to do the same.

How ethical was it of John to mention it to the PE teacher? Does the Doctrine of Double Effect apply here? If John did not intend by his action to do any harm, then by the Doctrine of Double Effect he is not being unethical. But the Doctrine of Double Effect presumes the ethical primacy of intentionality. If we think about the ethical principle of doing unto others as you would they should do unto you, we may be less willing to do something that might have harmful consequences. Thinking about the consequences in this situation seems more important here than being consistent. If John had thought about the consequences of his telling anyone, even Peter's friends, Peter might not have got into trouble.

Should the PE teacher have reported John's information to the head? Think of a more serious case of whistle-blowing where, for instance, a staff member is aware that senior administrators have claimed credentials that are false. Should the staff member report this to central administration or just keep quiet? What obligation is there on a director-general, having been given information about unethical behaviour? In any of these cases, would silence have indicated either consent or collusion? Are we honour-bound to always tell the truth?

Following from the decision to take action or not is, of course, what kind of action should be taken. In this case, as with the haircut discrimination case, the action taken seems a little extreme. Rather than a discriminatory case, it seems a bit like a conflict between authority and authoritarianism. But it can be justified using a 'slippery slope' argument, a consequentialist one. Let this boy get away with it and who knows what other body adornments might follow that we do not want to see? The principal is looking at possible consequences, and he is also applying the rules of ethical consistency, in that he treats this as he would any tattoo as contributing to the destruction of the ethos of the school and therefore needing to be removed. The response to Peter as a person or Peter's intention is not considered to be relevant. How common do you think the principal's reaction would be? What sort of argument could you use to persuade the principal to take a more lenient line of action? How much of your argument will involve argument over concepts and conceptions like ethos and body mutilation and expressions of love? To what extent is this similar to the haircut discrimination case in Chapter 4? It seemed there that there could have been, and was, considerable discussion as to what counted as conventional neatness, and whether the criteria were the same for boys as for girls.

Our main focus was, however, on the circumstances in which it could be unethical/ethical to refrain from acting. In the more serious case of whistle-blowing, of someone reporting an unethical action, there have been instances where a person in power, having had unpleasant truths revealed, has been so unwilling to take action that might have further damaging consequences that the ensuing cover-up has required distinctly unethical action, such as placing considerable pressure on the whistle-blower to remain silent or resign.

We noted in Chapter 2 that teachers may sometimes be compelled to ignore the rules, on moral grounds. But they will have to exercise moral judgement as to whether it is more appropriate to apply the rule or ignore it. If disobeying the rule might lead to chaos or harm, carers would probably do better to follow the rule. But from the perspective of care, the following questions must always be asked: 'What is best for the person concerned? Will doing what is best for them hurt other students? What effect will the decision have on the network of relations on which all depend?' Asking such questions, we are sometimes led to follow the given rule, and sometimes to fight it publicly, even at the risk of considerable personal sacrifice. Often, however, we simply ignore it.

CAN WE BE BLAMED FOR WHAT WE DO NOT KNOW?

Lack of knowledge could potentially be an excuse for some actions, in that the agent can only consider the consequences if they are reasonably well informed. In law, however, ignorance does not remove blame. The following presents a case where a teacher might be excused for not knowing the consequences of her act. Would she be open to Arendt's charge of not thinking enough about what she was doing? Consider some situations where, in hindsight, you would have acted differently.

9.3 Trust

The Parent and Citizen's Association (PCA) at Lavenderdale Primary School had recently purchased a portable CD player. A young female teacher, Sue, in her first few months of teaching, started weekly dancing classes with students outside school hours in the shire hall, charging several dollars for her dancing tuition. An irate parent complained at an informal parents meeting at which Sue and the principal were present that Sue was using the school's CD player for personal gain.★ The use of government property for private purposes is strictly forbidden. If school resources are removed from the school grounds there is a borrowing process – the borrower must ask permission from one of the three administrators and sign their name and date in the book and the administrator must sign out the property. This process is clearly detailed in the teachers' notes and was referred to in the first day of the school year. When the principal looked at the record book, there was no record of the CD player being borrowed. What are the consequences of reporting Sue?★ The district superintendent, also present, said that Sue should be reported at once to the local police for stealing the CD player. The atmosphere was emotionally charged.

'Moonlighting' without permission from the State Education

Department also carries a severe penalty. To prevent prosecution and possible dismissal, the teacher must write a 'please explain' letter through the district superintendent to the director-general of education, explaining why she is earning money other than from teaching.★

The consequences go beyond the legal ones. Even if the charges of stealing and moonlighting are dismissed, the public accusation is serious enough to start gossip in a small town, which can do irreparable damage to Sue's career. She naturally was alarmed and accused the principal of being non-supportive, lacking trust and understanding.★ She had seen herself as being professional in providing students with lessons that they would not normally get. She had had no intention of keeping the money for personal gain but was using it to fund a trip for the children to Perth. Moreover, she had not known that she was required to sign the equipment out.

Once the situation has been publicly brought to his attention, the principal is required to take action.★ How ignorant had Sue been of the rules? Was ignorance an excuse? Some parents defended her by saying how much the children were enjoying the dancing lessons. Two other teachers, defending Sue, confessed that they too had taken school equipment home without following correct procedures even though they knew of the borrowing book. If Sue was to be charged for 'stealing' then they were at least equally culpable. Consistency does matter.★ Sue apologized to the PCA for not asking permission for her use of the CD player.★ The principal said that he would more clearly define rules and regulations governing borrowing school equipment to try to prevent the situation happening again.★

Although the confrontation between parents and the teacher was unpleasant, the consequences were fairly positive. The PCA decided to make a submission to the local sports club for the purchase of a CD player specifically for dancing lessons and recommended that the dancing lessons be made part of an after-hours school service for which no additional payment would be made. Sue was required to offer her services after hours for no fee, so that she was not moonlighting. Any recompense she received was on a voluntary basis only.★ Parents were asked to provide money for those children who participated in the dance club for a dance club trip to Perth with a certain percentage of their monies paid going to support Sue's fares. The borrowing

> book is now routinely used by all staff members on the under-
> standing that the equipment is legitimately being used for
> educational purposes.

In the case above it was clear that Sue had not acted as she should
have, that is, she had not signed the necessary borrowing book, although
that in itself is not adequate evidence that she had not sought permission
to use the record player. Issues of responsibility for what is not done as
much as what is done also arise in issues of work efficiency. It is always
easier to document wrongs effected than things not done. Can you
imagine a principal being sacked who has done nothing wrong, except
that he has done nothing? How do you measure lack of action?
Principals who apply for promotion are sometimes asked as a test question what they would do in the case of an incompetent and inactive clerk
typist, who appears to have the will to try hard but is unable to do the
work, so much so that work tends to be directed to other members of
staff who can carry it out more efficiently.

What would you do about it? Or not do? How would you use the
answers to decide whether the principals merited promotion or not? One
can see that the most common course of action is failure to act. But the
consequences of ignoring incompetence of any staff member and taking
no action would lead to inevitable psychological or physical exclusion
from the school team. Is there a win–win situation here that could allow
the staff member to build up confidence and be a productive part of the
working team? It might be that the person is encouraged to take unpaid
leave to develop professional competence, but that the school offers to
pay the cost of courses and re-employ them if improvement is noted.
Perhaps, however, the situation cannot be judged in the abstract. We
need to find out more about the staff member – find out what strengths
they have to build on, find out whether there are not private difficulties
affecting their work for which support can be given, find out to what
extent other staff are placing them under such stress that they become
incompetent through pressure. Caring about the staff member means
placing the principal empathetically in their situation, by talking with
them as an equal person to find out what they think might best resolve
the difficulty. It is action, but not action according to principles of
management formula or consequences alone. What sort of place does
ethics play in your decision, and to what extent is your judgement based
on prudential or industrial considerations rather than ethical ones?

If we have had more rapid examples for you to consider in this
chapter, that is partly because by now you should be aware that the principle of universalizability always requires us to consider similar

situations to see whether they are different in crucial respects. Examining why you would act in one way in one situation and another in a similar situation will reveal to you your rational ethical frame. This is not to say that you are required always to be logically consistent, but that the rationality of ethics requires you to justify those cases in which you do act differently by giving a relevant difference, just as Maria did for treating the boys differently in the example in Chapter 2.

Chapter 10

Making progress in ethical judgement

We are not merely empty buckets to be stuffed with happiness or pleasure; the self's nature and character matter too . . . Just as a nation is in part constituted by its constitutional processes of change, including the means of amending that constitution, so the self is in part constituted by its processes of change. The self does not simply undergo these processes, it shapes and chooses them, it initiates and runs them.

Nozick (1989: 128)

Is postmodernity the pastime of an old man who scrounges in the rubbish heap of finality looking for leftovers, who brandishes unconsciousness, lapses, limits, confines, goulags, paratoxes, non-senses, or paradoxes, and who turns this into the glory of his novelty, into his promise of change?

Lyotard (1988: 136)

HOW DO WE KNOW WE ARE ETHICAL?

I originally headed this concluding chapter 'What underpins ethical judgement?' because I wanted to go back to the central question about how we know we are making ethical progress. But such a question presumes that if academics or researchers thought about ethics or searched diligently enough, they could construct or find a foundation that would explain or ultimately justify our ethical judgements. Such an agenda seems impossibly out of touch with the postmodern brief that foundations will always be epistemologically suspect. Equally, it seems naive for Nozick in the epigraph above to talk of 'self's nature' as if it existed over and above a human idea of it.

Recent philosophers of epistemology argue quite persuasively that all of our theories about the world, while they are about something, are simply constructed representations of that world. That does not mean that they are just a game with concepts that philosophers are particularly clever at, divorced from a real world. It means that while the self is real, it does not have an existence outside our understanding of it. Ethics is about the construction of a self or person in relation to other social beings or persons.

It was not entirely irrelevant to begin this concluding chapter with an epigraph about the controlling aspects of self. Charles Taylor (1989) has written a fascinating philosophical history of the formation of a modern conception of the self, arguing that our understanding of the evolution of self is intimately connected with the evolution of ideas of the human good. Much of what he says provides a history of ethical assumptions and I would recommend the interested reader to read what he has to say about the relation of traditional philosophers such as Aristotle, Plato, Descartes, Kant and Heidegger to modern poststructuralist and feminist philosophers. He describes Plato and Kant in terms of what he calls the idealist inward gaze, what I have presented in Chapter 1 as a subjective introspection. The rational inward looking which I have termed the 'subjective stance' and which Taylor (1989: 115) calls 'internalization' presumes that the order involved in the paramountcy of reason is constructed by individuals, not found. It is not immediately sensed but is mediated by language and conceptual structures. To grasp by reason is to be able 'to give reasons, or give an account of one's actions'. Kohlberg (in Sizer and Sizer 1970: 54) described his theory as a modern statement of the Platonic view. The highest moral condition for Plato and for the Kantian Kohlbergian self is one in which we are reflective and self-collected. It is a tendency to reason.

Aristotle believed that Plato placed too much emphasis on reason. He believed that moral character was grounded in good practices and evolved from practising the habits of temperance, liberality, pride, good temper, truthfulness and justice, especially temperance, which meant an absence of extremes. The practically wise person has a knowledge of how to behave in each particular circumstance which can never be equated with or reduced to a knowledge of general truths. Yet even for Aristotle, this practical wisdom was a kind of awareness of order, where all the goals and desires were integrated into a unified whole which was the correct order of ends in one's life. It is not incompatible with a func-tionalist or 'scientific' ethics which allows treatment of a person as a means to an end.

The slogan of the later utilitarians – 'the greatest happiness for the greatest possible number' – emphasized the wide distribution of human pleasure as well as its maximization, and, as Aristotle did, tended to define 'good' in terms of human goods. For instance, utilitarians regard punishment as a matter of deterrence, that is in terms of its consequences, rather than in terms of merit which places actions in a conceptual frame of good or bad. Their doctrine is comprehensive and simple, and is forward-looking in placing the emphasis on consequences rather than ideas.

Major objections to utilitarianism have been discussed in some detail in Chapter 6 but they can be summed up by saying that there is an illogical move from the truth that everyone *does* seek pleasure to the judgement that everyone *ought* to seek maximum pleasure for as many as possible. It has an underlying principle of utility which can become pragmatic and prudential rather than ethical when it considers consequences to the exclusion of universalizability or care for others.

At the turn of the twentieth century, G.E. Moore claimed that ethics was neither rational nor utilitarian, but that it was intuitive. The contemporary author William Gass (1957: 195) uses a striking example to show what Moore regarded as the concrete, intuitive nature of moral knowledge and the limited usefulness of moral principles in 'The case of the obliging stranger':

> Imagine I approach a stranger on the street and say to him, 'If you please sir, I desire to perform an experiment with your aid.' The stranger is obliging and I lead him away. In a dark place conveniently by, I strike his head with the broad of an axe and cart him home. I place him, buttered and trussed, in an ample electric oven. The thermometer reads 450°F. Thereupon I go off to play poker with friends and forget all about the obliging stranger in the stove. When I return, I realize I have overbaked my specimen, and the experiment, alas, is ruined. Something has been done wrong, or something wrong has been done.
>
> Any ethic that does not roundly condemn my action is vicious.

Gass makes the point that no moralist's principle will help in the least to explain why this act should be condemned. The moral certainty we feel in this case we feel directly; we do not derive it from grander or generalizable certainties in the shape of principles. The example is extreme but similarly in the case studies I have presented to you in this book I have presumed that readers will respond with reasonably similar feelings and beliefs, particulars and principles, responsiveness and impartiality, clarity and simplicity, about the right thing to do. It is a morality that has room for natural impulse and intuitions as well as rationality. With postmodern insight, however, we become aware that many of those things that we believe are immediately intuitive have been shaped by past social practices, even non-verbal ones.

Nussbaum (1990: 27, 95), on the other hand, says that ethics is founded not so much on reason, scientific investigation of consequences or even intuition, as on a literary imagination. She advocates the attentive and loving reading of novels, because they force us to attend to the concrete; they ask us to imagine possible relations and hence help us to understand our own. One could argue that it is metaphoric, in that it forces us to see similarities and differences in a fluid way between past and projected human interactions. Ethics requires us not only to see someone *as* a student, or *as* an Asian, or *as* a female but *as* a person.

At the heart of a contemporary definition of good, which he claims begins with Montaigne, Charles Taylor finds in what he calls the affirmation of the ordinary life a 'care' value which has decisively replaced the two more traditional conceptions of reason, the inward-looking procedural notion that we called subjective and others have called deontic, and the functional one that we called objective or consequentialist and others have termed utilitarian. The shift to the ordinary life sounds much like Oakeshott's (1975) insistence that morality functions in the vernacular rather than through cerebral academic theories.

I do not believe that the tripartite model of consequences/consistency/care simply presents a new fashionable theory to replace the major traditional theories of ethics. Rather, it accepts what people would have found useful in those theories in a genuinely postmodern and inclusive way and tries to incorporate their views into a modern world-view that is coping with constant change and review. It is not a theory in itself because most theories aim at being certain and consistent. Rather, it provides traditional frames which allow us to reflect temporarily.

Taylor concludes in his history of ethics that the world is devoid of absolute meaning, but that we can delve into our inner being to fashion an ethical self. That is similar to Weber's solution, that each individual must accept responsibility for their own actions and choose a particular stance for themselves, that is, choose to be a morally responsible individual. Foucault would say that this individual is not possible, or at least cannot be separated out from the discursive resources available to us in our particular situation. He warns against accepting subjectivity as a foundation of moral action, because it ignores the power structures that influence the apparently intuitive perception of things as ethical or not.

TWO IS BETTER THAN ONE, AND THREE IS BETTER THAN TWO

Most postmodernists view a subject as an entity that is produced by and produces social codes. An intentional agent requires a subject that perceives itself as having some degree of autonomy and efficacy in the world. Lorraine Code (1991: 115) argues that there are two contemporary views of the subject: the humanist subject – a unified rational self-interested agent like that proposed by Weber – and the postmodern or poststructuralist subject – a connected self with no coherent account of freedom, responsibility or authenticity. These opposing views of the subject set up a binary opposition that must be resolved dialectically. Dialectical logic dictates that opposites be synthesized in a new, truer concept that embraces the truths of each side of the opposition – hence the dialectical subject.

The postmodernists provide a justification for pushing previous cultures together and watching the interactions of different belief systems as they collide, hoping through the collision to provide new insights and new alternatives. That is partly what I hope will happen in groups of people discussing the issues raised in this book. People with different views will not only arrive at different decisions but for different reasons and their differences do not form a modernist dichotomy of good or bad actions but different ones which require reconciliation or compromise rather than a binary dialectic (Hekman 1995: 89). That was one of my reasons for choosing three frames rather than two. Consistency and consequences share the reflective capacity to abstract using language, when contrasted with care. Care has in common with consistency the subjective mode, even though it is concerned with how a person feels or reacts rather than how they think. Care has in common with the consequences mode the 'objective' capacity to 'take care' or 'being careful' in the sense of being aware of the possible impact of external realities of the situation. But they interact as two terms of a metaphor do, not separately or abstractly like the terms of an analogy, but fluidly and contextually with consideration of one aspect affecting the quality of the other two.

DECONSTRUCTION, DIFFÉRANCE AND THE DIFFEREND

What consequences does our tripartite model of ethics have for reason and our capacity to think about morality? Foucault argues that we have finally broken down the line between 'is' and 'ought' and that it is no longer possible to separate the fine line between truth and understanding. He argues that we *do* in fact live in a different world from that theorized by the moderns, not that we *should* live in such a world or that we should do thus and so to achieve that world. He argues that the Cartesian subject upheld by Kant, and even Kohlberg, is not adequate to describe the situation of subjects in our society, that knowledge is no longer grounded in a widely accepted meta-narrative, and that power is dispersed rather than concentrated. This situation creates a very different role for the intellectual, the creator of theories of this world, and also a very different form of resistance (Hekman 1995: 145).

Lyotard had argued that, like it or not, we live in a world devoid of meta-narratives, lacking a groundless ground for knowledge. But he then goes on to ask how we can be said to know anything at all. In *The Differend*, he pursues this enquiry in a specifically ethical context, asking how we can live in the postmodern world as moral beings. How can we behave as if we had a theory, or guiding structure of rational beliefs, when we can logically have no ground for such a theory? He assumes the impossibility of avoiding conflicts and the absence of a universal genre of discourse. His answer is that cognition, ethics and politics are all in play when one phrase is linked to another. Like Wittgenstein, he believes that discourses have rules and that there exist genres of discourse that fix the rules of linkages for other discourses (Lyotard 1988: 29). If we accept Lyotard's picture of knowledge as a game, then ethics becomes a social drama/game in which there are different rules, different games in the different institutions. There are 'orders in the army, prayer in the church, denotation in the schools, narration in families, questions in philosophy, performativity in businesses' (Lyotard 1988: 17).

Just as the foundations of ethics have shifted from the ideal forms of logic, through the practical consequences to the romanticism of narrative, Lyotard claims that our foundation of knowledge is being changed in computerized societies. Where traditionally there had been two forms of knowledge – the scientific and the narrative, corresponding roughly to Habermasian technical and social media – in a postmodern culture, the grand narratives of science and the arts have lost their credibility, whether it is for the people, or for a higher good. The fading of the grand narratives, says Lyotard, results in a shift from the end product to the means producing these ends. Computerization of knowledge will be a large part of society's attempts to achieve what he calls paralogical ideas, ideas that constantly challenge our logics or structures through which we understand the world and each other. The mass of imaginative or paralogical ideas available through information technology will generate new ideas, new statements. That is one of my agendas in presenting readers with scenarios that nudge their imagination to reflect and in presenting the three aspects of ethics, each of which challenges the other two.

This places discussion about ethics not at the realm of what we *should* do, but what we *do*, so that like Foucault we become more like historians of the present. To do this requires us to be open to the community within which we are practising. Some people conceive of school discipline as a simple way of focusing on individual behaviour to guarantee superficial peace and order in the class and do not endow it with an important moral function. As we noted in Chapter 2, and in many places in this book, from a moral point of view externally imposed impersonal requirements can be seen as barbaric – as a tyranny of complicated rules.

I distinguished between prudence and ethics by saying that in ethics the interests of the other had to be considered. We are deliberately operating as social beings. At the beginning of Chapter 1 I asked you as reader to consider a situation that you felt was unfair. A common response from students has been that the teacher never listens to them because they are girls or members of an ethnic minority. I can remember the invisibility of my comments when I was the only female member of an academic council, and my feeling of frustration when a male professor would make the same point that I had just made and he would be given ownership of the idea. I at first considered that maybe I was at fault, that I had not made my point clearly enough, but then became aware that most people present did not *expect* a woman to make a contribution to academic debate. I became adept at asserting the point loudly and reclaiming possession by saying, 'I'm glad that Professor X agreed with my earlier point.' Is this an ethical issue? I would like to say that my assertion was not merely egotistical attention-seeking, that it was more an attempt to change the behaviour of the group and have it working more cooperatively as a whole inclusive one. I do not hold those 'deaf' people to blame for their inattention to difference, unless it is a sort of Arendtian indifference for which they are culpable. They were not intentionally harming others. They were, after all, doing the bracketing out that is necessary if we are to make sense of an infinitely complex world. The male professors inhabit a different life-world which is confronted by 'the other' and they would prefer to ignore it than have to confront their own assumptions. Gilligan and Bernstein discuss 'unfairness and not listening' (Gilligan *et al.* 1990: 147–61). What an open community of inquiry would aim at is equal respect for persons and fair consideration of all ideas. In other words, it would operate like an inclusive curriculum.

Kemmis (1995: 24) has looked a little more closely at these peculiar complexities of individual practices in a group. Using Bourdieu's understanding of social practices to blur the distinction between the objective and the subjective traditions on the one hand and the individual/social dimension on the other, he provides a matrix to look at the individual and the social through the objective and subjective perspectives I introduced in Chapter 1 and in so doing allows us to look at how we come to understand ethics (see Table 10.1).

Vygotsky criticized the Piagetian model because the individual child, the subjective agent in box 3, could not construct their own rules without the social acquisition of languages from box 4. I had, by implication, placed Wren's deontic mode in box 3 and his ethical modes in box 2, and then, possibly simplistically, I had allocated the consistency and conse-

Table 10.1 Individual social dimensions of the subject/object

Perspective	Focus	
	The individual	*The social*
Objective	(1) Practice as individual behaviour, seen in terms of performances, events and effects	(2) Practice as social interaction, e.g. ritual, system-structured
Subjective	(3) Practice as intentional action, shaped by meaning and values	(4) Practice as socially structured, shaped by discourses, tradition

quences positions to these as well. It may be that consistency cannot be just located in box 3 because to build a logical structure one has to acquire socially the concepts that enable the structures to be constructed. As the consequences and consistency positions become consolidated through shared conventions into individual and social theories, they slide into boxes 1 and 2 because, through discussion and trial-and-error practice, we eliminate subjective error.

Kemmis (1995: 23) argues that we need not only to distinguish between subjective/objective and the individual/social distinctions but to note that, on their own, each of these are false dichotomies. We can escape from the partiality of each by seeing the two sides of the dichotomies not as opposites, any one of which can be true, but as dialectically related, that is, as mutually constitutive aspects of one another, both of which are necessary to achieve a more comprehensive perspective on practice. I have already suggested that this is true of the interpersonal and intra-personal models of ethics.

It appears that we set up these distinctions only as hypothetical constructs which we are continually modifying to suit our shared purposes. Kemmis tries to capture Bourdieu's emphasis on the reflexive quality of thought by being reflexive *both* in reaching beyond the partial focus of the individual or the social, *and* in reaching beyond objectivist and subjectivist perspectives. This is the ongoing dynamics of ethics which makes it impossible to reach an absolute status. The evolving interplay between our experienced conceptions and our ideal ethical concepts involve a double dialectic of the mutually constitutive relationships between the individual and the social, and between objective and subjective perspectives (see Table 10.2).

Kemmis noted that Bourdieu's understanding of social practices blurred the distinction between the objective and the subjective traditions on the one hand and the individual/social dimension on the other. 'He seems to confound a focus on the individual with the objectivist perspective of empiricism on the one side and a focus on the group with a subjectivist perspective of phenomenology on the other' (Kemmis 1995: 24). A similar theme underlies Vygotsky's criticism of the Piagetian model, for the child cannot construct his own rules without the social acquisition of language. Perhaps this is true of many of the ethical theorists I have summarized above. Wren's deontic and ethical modes, for instance, belong to the objective and subjective categories respectively, and in my earlier discussion I had allocated consistency and consequences positions to these as well. But as these two positions become socially consolidated into theories, they are seen as objective relative to the more subjective care position. We can map ethical understanding onto this more complex diagram.

Table 10.2 Dialectical practices

Perspective	Focus		
	The individual	*The social*	*Both reflexive–dialectical view of individual–social relations and connections*
Objective	(1) Practice as individual behaviour, seen in terms of performances, events and effects: behaviourist and most cognitivist approaches in psychology	(2) Practice as social interaction: ritual, 'system-structured' structure-functionalist and social systems approaches	
Subjective	(3) Practice as intentional action, shaped by meaning and values: psychological *verstehen* (empathetic understanding) and most constructivist approaches	(4) Practice as socially structured, shaped by discourses, tradition: interpretive, aesthetic–historical *verstehen* and poststructuralist approaches	
Both: reflective–dialectical view of subjective/objective relations and connections			(5) Practice as socially and historically constituted, and as reconstituted by human agency and social action: critical theory: critical social science

Ethical practice as individual behaviour to be studied objectively

This first perspective sees it primarily from the outside, as individual behaviour to which such 'subjective' processes as intention, duty and reasons for acting are irrelevant. Those adopting this perspective frequently understand the science of behaviour as objective and apply this view of understanding practice. For instance, in classroom management many teachers are encouraged to use reinforcing strategies such as Canter's assertive discipline and measure their success by an observable decrease in disruptive or deviant behaviour or an increase in compliant behaviour. Inquiry from this perspective usually adopts correlational or quasi-experimental methods, is likely to use descriptive or inferential statistics and adopts an instrumental view of the relationship between the researcher and the researched, in which the field being studied is understood in the 'third person' (as objects whose behaviour is to be changed). The consequences of any behaviour are relatively predictable, given certain precedent conditions. The larger the sample measured, the more likely changes in behaviour are to become predictable, because idiosyncrasies and personalities are smoothed out. So this perspective is likely to be adopted in large administrative systems and in conjunction with the measurement of norms of ethical behaviour.

Ethical practice as a group behaviour ritual, to be studied objectively

The second perspective also views ethical practice from the outside but sees it in terms of the social group. Those adopting this perspective also understand the study of group behaviour as objective. Those who work in social psychology or who adopt structure functionalist perspectives in sociology tend to describe ethical practices as though they had the status of laws or formalistic rituals. The community, whether is it is defined geographically, ethnically or racially, is viewed as a consistent group, a relatively uniform whole whose members are atomistic units and whose identity is defined in terms of the social group. Inquiry from this perspective is also likely to adopt correlational or quasi-experimental methods, to use descriptive or inferential statistics and adopt an instrumental view of the relationship between the researcher and the researched, in which the field being studied is understood as objects whose behaviour is to be changed. Whether in epidemiology or in educational systems the research question is likely to be one asked by people administering systems who want to change them by changing system inputs, processes and outputs. A causal mechanism of consequences, or at least of explanation and prediction, is similarly presumed.

A government educational policy that promises extra funding to those who join the national unified scheme, or threatens a clawback in funding if student numbers decline, has as its underlying assumption a punishment–reward system which we placed at the very top of the Kohlbergian scale, presuming a fairly uncomplicated pleasure/pain behavioural response on an institutional rather than an individual scale.

Ethical practice as individual action to be studied from the perspective of the subjective

The third perspective attempts to understand practice from the inside, from the perspective of the individual practitioner. On this view human action (including practice) cannot be understood as mere behaviour – it must be seen as shaped by the values, intentions and judgements of the practitioner. It requires the exercise of human judgement by people choosing to act in certain situations, and must involve understanding motives, intentions, values and meanings. Although it is called subjective, it is as capable of laying claim to be scientific in its approach. Some clinical, humanistic and Gestalt psychologies belong to this tradition although they are generally categorized as phenomenological. Even where the patterns that allow us to process meaning are thought to be physiologically based (as with Gestaltists such as Koffka and Arnheim), judgement is still required to match the phenomenal perceptions to a 'template' in the brain, but that judgement could well be located in what some recent psychologists (Churchlands) have defined as neural nets. Karl Popper (1972) equally tried to locate the values that allow us to make a reasoned response inside a 'preference gene'. In a proposed book on metaphor, I will argue that this naturalization of metaphorical transfer of meaning allows us to construct our theories.

While I do not espouse the scientific tradition of research for this frame, I would place what I have called the subjective aspect of ethics, the so-called deontological or rule-following tradition, within this frame because there must be internalized rules to guide one's voluntary actions whether they can be discovered in brain cells or not. Research must somehow get inside the head of the 'subject' who makes such judgements. It is largely done by self-report, which assumes that the researched is a knowing, responsible and autonomous subject, a person similar to the researcher in being able to make decisions about how to act in the situations in which they find themselves and talk about their actions and reasons for acting. It generally adopts qualitative methods (including autobiographical, idiographic and phenomenological methods).

Ethical practice as responsible social action or tradition

This will require us to look at practice as socially structured over time, as Foucault had shown, shaped by discourses and tradition. It therefore embraces the interpretive, aesthetic–historical, *verstehen* and poststructuralist approaches. To regard ethical practice from a view that values meaning over truth is necessary if we want to explain how shared conventions allow us to internalize rules for our behaviour. To discuss ethical decision-making as though it was a purely individual matter would be to ignore the shaping of our actions through the shared conventions of language. We see a situation as ethical or not; we describe an identical physical act as bullying or righteous. In the preceding chapters, the selection of any situation as an ethical one appropriate for discussion has reflected my way of seeing it, the meaning that certain behaviours have for me. That meaning is not idiosyncratic or random. Before I can commit it to words, I must presume that others will understand what I am saying.

Practice as socially and historically constituted, and as reconstituted by human agency and social action; critical theory, critical social science

Kemmis tries to capture Bourdieu's emphasis on the reflexive quality of thought by being reflexive *both* in reaching beyond the partial focus of the individual or the social, *and* in reaching beyond objectivist and subjectivist perspectives.

> In the study of practice, and object of study which is inherently dynamic, productive and reconstructive, even as it reconstitutes the world in familiar ways, it seems to me that we need a way of comprehending it that explicitly recognises the double dialectic (of the mutually-constitutive relationships between the individual and the social, and between objective and subjective perspectives). Hence I have preferred the label 'reflexive/dialectical' in attempting to describe what Bourdieu regarded as a third tradition and I represent in my table as a fifth.
>
> (Kemmis 1995: 24)

The social meanings that govern our descriptions and perceptions of our external world are codified not only in language, but in abstract formulations that guide our practice. We are in a growing spiral of awareness that grows out of our own reflections on our basic presumptions, reflections that must be formed partially out of socially discursive systems.

In Chapter 1 I considered the influence of regulations and laws on our daily practices in schools, and looked at less overt social systems that govern our actions. Wittgenstein (1969: §105) said:

> All testing, all confirmation and disconfirmation of a hypothesis takes place already within a system. And this system is not a more or less arbitrary and doubtful point of departure for all our arguments: no, it belongs to the essence of what we call an argument. The system is not so much the point of departure, as the element in which arguments have their life.

The systems are real, in the sense that our actions governed by them affect our emotional and physical worlds. Only by becoming aware of them can we begin to change them if necessary.

Wittgenstein (1980: §§96–8) uses a vivid metaphor to capture the impossibility of grounding moral judgements in absolute certainty or constructing an ethical theory. Instead of looking for the ultimate reasons for doing good, we have to step back and look at what we actually do: like Gilligan, he believes that we gain our moral certainty from our awareness of what we *do*. Our language games, our forms of life, the systems we construct both individually and socially, says Wittgenstein (1969), are like water flowing through a riverbed. The riverbed determines the direction of the water that flows through it, just as the fixed beliefs that are central to our form of life determine what we mean by an argument, proof and evidence. The riverbed may shift over time; propositions that were once fluid may harden, and others that were hard may become fluid. But despite these changes, it is nevertheless the case that at any given time the riverbed provides the ground of our language games, our form of life. When we search for some indubitable ground of our reasons, the riverbed is the hard rock that we hit, causing our spade to turn; it is the end of reasons and the beginning of our intuitive concept of self. Moral beliefs are not arbitrary. If I had different moral beliefs, I would be a different person: I cannot fully understand what my riverbed or form of life would be if I had a different set of beliefs, because moral beliefs are so central to who I am.

The philosopher C.S. Peirce was opposed to the privileging of the knowing subject above the acting subject but, like those in the consequences and consistency bracketing, he places more emphasis than Gilligan or Wittgenstein on the power of persuasion through language. Like Wittgenstein and Foucault, Peirce wants to destroy the myth of the given and the illusion of truth as the certainty of our mental representations. He agrees that all our beliefs are interwoven with our practices. 'A belief which will not be acted upon ceases to be a belief' (Peirce 1931–58: 3.77). This is incorporated in the Kantian position that an autonomous person is consistent in beliefs and actions. Mind is situated and finds its embodiment in the symbolic and social medium of language *and* in that of practice. Like Habermas, Peirce believes that discussion and reasoning will bring people to an agreement if those people have adequate experience. He does not conceive of such discussion as a contest (1931–58: 5.406) in which one side seeks to overpower the other rhetorically; it appears rather as a cooperative search for truth by means of the publicly open exchange of arguments. Only then is a discussion able to serve as a 'test of dialectical examination' (Peirce 1931–58: 5.392).

Where he differs from Habermas or Wittgenstein is in his persistence in searching for 'truth'. He expects ultimately, as Kant did, that eventually all statements about the world would fit into a unified coherent scheme, complicated as it would be, that would contain no contradictions. The whole power problem which lies at the base of ethics emerges again. If people who act morally are capable of employing different moral discourses, how do the marginalized voices or the minority views resist giving way to the moral discourses of those in power, those of the dominant world-view? Are each as basic as a Wittgensteinian riverbed? The problem with whistle-blowing is that it is pragmatically very difficult to get a voice without power heard, even if it is morally reasonable or has evidence to back it up. Gilligan discovered that both men and women can speak in both the justice and care voices. But if women can and do speak in the justice voice, why should we be so concerned with the care voice? We have been arguing that part of constructing a self involves having a moral voice. Then different selves will have different kinds of voices and there cannot be one paradigm or system for either morality and subjectivity.

Hekman discusses Gadamer's attempt to solve this problem. Gadamer argues that, because all understanding occurs in language, in the complex web of meanings that constitute our linguistic ability, aesthetic understanding in particular is self-understanding and relates to the whole of our existence. The scientific notion of truth to which Peirce subscribes is based, he argues, on a prejudice against prejudice. For Gadamer (1975: 239–40), 'prejudice' comes from the pre-understandings that inform our language and make meaning possible, the bedrock of the riverbed of which Wittgenstein spoke. Scientific knowledge, in his view, tries to deny the characteristic prejudice of knowledge to move away from it into an abstraction of objectivity. Art is, on the other hand, located and hermeneutic in character, not abstracted from locatedness as most scientific theories are. Gadamer's notion of prejudice is not as closed as our common usage of the word. This hermeneutic horizon is flexible and open: it allows, and even requires, critique and examination. There cannot be an enclosure in language, because every language is unlimited. 'Precisely the experience of finitude and particularity of our being – a finitude manifest in the diversity of languages – opens the road to the infinite dialogue in the direction of ontological truth' (Gadamer 1976: 15–16). In the earlier chapters of this book, I proposed that the 'foundation' of ethics, insofar as we could have one, might well be a Heideggerian or Eriksonian notion of care, and this is consistent with Gadamer's prejudice in that the qualities of openness and attention are kept to the forefront. Such prejudice, however, must, if it is to be ethical, maintain this openness, the continual self-critique – the only way to begin to act ethically to people of different values is to remain open to the possibility that they have any good ideas or better solutions to interacting as persons. The basis of this is prejudged, but open. It requires openness, trust and, perhaps, optimism.

FLYING BY THE NET OF LANGUAGE

Donald Davidson used a striking phrase, 'flying by the net of language', in an unpublished article which I cannot now locate. It is a neat summary of our attempt to tie together our subjective and objective worlds by being responsive to it, and responsible to other people's constructions of it. The phrase is deliberately ambiguous. In its first sense: our actions and practices depend on our having a net of language, that is they fly with the aid of language which binds them together so that we can make sense of them while at the same time. For Wittgenstein, Peirce and Gadamer the limits of our language remain the limits of the world. Learning processes are ultimately unable to break away from a semiotic circle of signs that are given interpretations by us.

In the second sense, we could not escape the net of language which limits and constrains our experiences at the conventional levels, caught up in absolute principles and scientific theories held to be fact, unless we could also fly past those nets through non-linguistic practices. In each of the hierarchies of ethics we have been considering, there is a presumption that somehow we can bootstrap ourselves up both using language and moving beyond it to a post-conventional level. The consequentialist view is the one that is least able to explain how we do this because it tends to atomize people, to count them as objects and single units operating in chains of cause and effect rather than having independent minds. This is why, in Chapter 1, I had the consequences view taper off as the subjective aspects developed linguistic 'control' over the objective world. Peirce tried to expand the world of symbolic forms beyond the borders of linguistic forms of expression, but he still needed to relate these intentionally employed indices and icons within a logically related structure of some sort to enable practice and experience to be meaningful. Habermas tries to overcome this idealism by reminding us of the consequences of our interpretations – that all languages are porous and every newly disclosed aspect to the world remains an empty projection as long as its fruitfulness does not also *prove its worth* in learning processes that are made possible by the changed perspective on the world (Habermas 1992: 106). He also develops the notion of a life-world, which is semiotically constructed from bottom up, and forms a network of implicit meaning structures that are sedimented in signs which, although non-linguistic, are nonetheless accessible to interpretation. The situations in which participants to an interaction orient themselves are overflowing with cues, signals and tell-tale traces; at the same time they are marked by stylistic features and expressive characteristics that can be intuitively grasped and which reflect the spirit of the society, the tincture of the age, the physiognomy of a city or social class (Habermas 1992: 107). This deciphering of implicit meaning structures is a holistic mode of experience. I am not as sure as Peirce and Dewey that it is simply a matter of accumulated practice or habit. Peirce's notion of habit extends far beyond the human world to include animal, vegetable and mineral (Peirce 1931–58: 5.492). It is the understanding of meaning that requires the learning subject to take care, to be open to the experience. But this openness to making sense of non-linguistic experiences is one of the marks of the moral subject.

It may be true, as Foucault argued (1993: 222–3), that the self is nothing other than a historical correlation of the technologies of language built into our history. But because there are multiple truths in our society, not a single grand narrative, by looking at how truths are constructed by discourses and how those discourses change over time, we become aware of different discourses. If we care about our connections with others, we become *critically* aware. Through the continual appearances of subjugated knowledges 'of these localized popular knowledges, these disqualified knowledges . . . criticism performs its work' (Foucault 1980: 82).

Hekman (1995) skilfully links these points back to issues of power. For Foucault, power is not localized in a single source. It circulates like blood through capillaries, permeating every aspect of the body politic. From McLaren's (1993) point of view, the situation is no different in schools. Power is embedded in the practices as well as in those in authority. Discourses of truth produced by the experts so revered in bourgeois society create institutions of power that govern both bodies and minds. Disciplinary power is inseparable from the production of truth in bourgeois society. The age of the universal intellectual, the person who relies on universal truths and arguments to ground their principles, and pronounce on the global order of things, however, is retreating (Foucault 1980: 126) and giving way to a 'specific intellectual', the intellectual who is concerned with local and immediate forms of power and oppression (1980: 128–9).

WHAT COUNTS AS MORAL MATURITY?

On Foucault's account, the mature person is not the universal intellectual who has mastered all the philosophical theories outlined above, and generalizes to a universal theory from their writings, as Nozick (1989) started to do. When we reflect on the language games of others, either in conversation with them or by reading the writings of other reflective philosophers, there is always a moral/political dimension to our analysis, but it is particular and historical rather than universal and absolute.

The goal of the intellectual's analysis of games of truth is to 'reinterrogate the obvious and the assumed, to unsettle habits, ways of thinking and doing, to dissipate accepted familiarities, to evaluate rules and institutions and . . . to participate in the formation of a political will' (Dallmayr 1984: 30). If this seems negative, a logic of dissent, it is no more than the critical reflection required by an ethic of care, to transcend the systems grounded in tradition. What has been created by discourse can also be overthrown by discourse, but it is not done by appealing to universal truths or by reference to a transcendent subject, but by exploring the gaps and silences within discourse itself and by applying a discourse where it does not belong to effect a political and psychological disruption.

Gilligan (1982: 165) argues that moral maturity is marked by an increasing tolerance that moves beyond absolutes. This is not dissimilar to the Piagetian or Kohlbergian post-conventional level at which there is a transition from a belief that knowledge is absolute and answers clearly right or wrong to an understanding of the contextual relativity of both truth and choice. Kohlberg's notion of acting according to principles can be postmodern if there is a recognition that there can be different and equally valid conceptions of the basic concepts or principles. His notion of autonomy requires that the autonomous person is aware of the possibility of alternatives within which to make a choice.

Where a discourse is grounded in care, it can be 'dislocated' by pointing out the consequences, or the consistency. Where a discourse is grounded in the assumption of universal truths, it can be 'relocated' by grounding it in actual or predicted consequences and the holistic reaction of care. The dominant moral discourse of the West is repressive if it defines only one moral truth and excludes other moral voices from the realm of the moral. The aspects of care, consistency and consequences are not abstractly different or distinct from one another. As I showed in Chapter 1, they are distinctions that we make for certain purposes, but they are all interdependent and mutually supportive. What Foucault calls 'the freeing of difference' requires 'thought without contradiction, without dialectics, without negation, thought that accepts divergence; affirmative thought whose instrument is distinction; thought of the multiple – of the nomadic and dispersed multiplicity that is not limited or confined by the constraints of similarity' (Foucault 1977: 185).

Ethics is a way of living with others that allows resistance to domination. While we are living within relations of power, it is impossible to move outside the practices of power without thinking about them. 'The problem is not trying to dissolve [practices of power], in the utopia of a perfectly transparent communication, but to give oneself the rules of law, the techniques of management and also the ethics, the *ethos*, the practice of self which would allow these games to be played with a minimum of domination' (Foucault 1986: 129).

If we are to be consistent with our own advocated process of reflecting on everything, we have to consider whether our whole discussion of persons is a collective myth. Skinner said that our notion of freedom was a false illusion; some Marxists have said that we have no individual will but rather a collective consciousness. However, the freedom to choose self-consciously is already built into our understanding of what it means to be a person. Ethics begins by presuming respect for persons, and defines persons as being responsible autonomous beings. Our earlier discussion of whether students or animals had rights, that is whether they were to be legitimately considered as persons before they had the capacity to choose freely and rationally, indicates that we believe reason-ableness to be at least one of the markers of adulthood, if not maturity. Reasonableness presumes a conscious capacity to reflect, think and act independently.

From each position, our actions and values are determined by our history and/or our environment. If the self is little more than a reactive set of brain chemicals adapting to ongoing sensory irritations, then we do have to throw ethical principles away. Evers and Lakomski (1991: 185) argue that distinctions between ethical claims and empirical claims should be abolished from a perspective of social behaviourism in which individual decisions are less important than social expectations. But even they concede that in confronting a welter of conflicting moral viewpoints and the sheer complexity of administrative decision-making, the norma-tive framework for educational administrators is provided by the general requirement that decision and action should be, in the long term, educa-tive; the growth of knowledge should be promoted. This is a shared social convention and, as such, open to abuse of power. Ethical decisions need to move beyond existing conventions and theories, and therefore to move, as Foucault would desire, beyond institutions of power.

SETTING UP A COMMUNITY OF ETHICAL INQUIRY

I have been discussing how postmodern literature, critical theory and management theory have made us aware that many of our actions, particularly when they are institutionalized as in schools, have implicit structures which embed and maintain existing power relations (Illich, Foucault). They are real, in the sense that our actions affect our emotional and physical worlds. Only by becoming aware of them can we begin to change them if necessary.

We cannot make Kemmis's subjective/objective social/individual matrix (Table 10.1) as complicated as our lived reality – as I have argued elsewhere (Haynes 1996), a map cannot be isomorphic with reality, even where they become as complicated as Nozick's (1989) 48-dimensional polyhedron of ethics. If we exhaust the theoretical structures we have built, there is nothing we can do but say with Wittgenstein when we have reached bedrock, and our spade is turned, 'This is simply what I do.' Such matrices are only intellectual games if they are not useful in focusing our attention on differences that we need to maintain to discuss aspects of ethical practice. It would be too easy to place the caring aspects into box 2 or 3, because it seems in its holism to embrace all four, both in initiating a focus on any one of them and also in transcending each of them. Yet the fluidity of lines between the three frames that I presented in this book precludes taking refuge in any one of them. As the metaphor of the Borromean knot informs us, they are held together only if all three are borne in mind.

The consistency model is the traditional philosophical mode of reflection or self-consciousness which critically stands aside from both the problem, or one's personal stance, the intellectual distancing for which Peters and Gilligan criticize it, and the consequentialist model is framed within a scientific genre which objectifies persons as things. Even within the philosophical or reflective mode, there has to be something that impels the reflection. Remember that we resolved the dialectic between the subjective and objective aspects of consistency and consequences by showing how at the level of universalizability they became almost identifiable. That would make the subjective one higher on a developmental model of ethics because it includes the other and moves beyond it. Similarly, Noddings (1984) and Ruddick (1980, 1989) assert the superiority of the women's moral voice over the masculine voice of logical consistency. Gilligan, while wanting to retain the separate integrity of an ethic of care and an ethic of justice, sees them as ultimately converging in shared assumptions.

> While an ethic of justice proceeds from the premise of equality – that everyone should be treated the same – an ethic of care rests on the premise of nonviolence – that no one should be hurt. In the representation of maturity, both perspectives converge in the realization that just as inequality adversely affects both parties in an unequal relationship, so too violence is destructive for everyone involved. This dialogue between fairness and care not only provides a better understanding of relations between the sexes but also gives rise to a more comprehensive portrayal of adult work and family relationships.
>
> (Gilligan 1982: 174)

I believe that in emphasizing response rather than reason, Gilligan, with many other feminine writers (A.C. Baier 1987), is moving to what Foucault, in an interview, called appropriately 'power and sex', described as a 'freeing of difference'. It requires 'thought without contradiction, without dialectics; affirmative thought whose instrument is distinction; thought of the multiple – of the nomadic and dispersed multiplicity that is not limited or confined by the constraints of simi-larity' (1977: 185). Friedman suggests (1987: 106) that the best way to care for persons is to respect their rights. He also says that Kohlberg tacitly concedes the collapsing of justice and care in his famous Heinz dilemma (1987: 198) because it works only as a moral dilemma if it is Heinz's wife who is sick, demonstrating the necessity of this caring relationship to morality. Each of these perspectives requires us to engage in conversa-tion with those who appear to be different, one of the essential components of setting up a genuinely open community of inquiry.

Both Kohlberg and Gilligan share a belief that the self is constructed out of rational reflection, in a sort of bootstrapping manner, and when we engage in conversation with someone whom we believe shares a slightly different 'rational' structure from our own, we are forced to reflect on our own assumptions. The whole deconstruction of 'self' suggests that feminist ethics and traditional ethics are each socially conditioned to a certain extent, but that we can choose to construct a different ethic to guide our actions. We are already presuming a multi-layered hierarchical model in which through reflection we are setting up structures that are socially defined as much as personally defined, even when it is primarily a responsive model. Our ethical matrix cannot be uni-dimensional, standing only on one leg of the three-legged stool, but must rather take the form of a balanced and evolving hierarchy, a spiral built up of cumulative public evidence, private reflection and personal response.

Because both Gilligan and Noddings each present a more situational response to ethical decision-making than Kohlberg and Kant, they can provide a means of moving beyond an essentially static ethical matrix of subjective and objective reason. The dualistic subjective/objective matrix is essentially modernist. From a postmodern point of view, objective and subjective views of ethics are still locked into the analytic frame of modernist science. The assumptions underlying it are still those of atom-istic realism as opposed to experiential realism (Lakoff 1989), namely that you can lock them into a static matrix. But to organize one's responses into an analytic frame may not be as demeaning as the postmodernists would have us believe. It may be the only way that we can make social meaning out of our personal constructions, the only way to consolidate a self.

One cannot objectively view the consequences of an action without the help of a schema or internalized structure of concepts which relates the consequences to the action. One cannot objectively calculate the greatest good for the greatest possible number and arrive at a 'correct' answer. More importantly a felicific calculus of one's act cannot be carried out objectively on the basis of one's knowledge of possible conse-quences, because that would make those who are ignorant less ethical than those who can estimate the consequences. Furthermore, no one person could know all the possible long- or short-term consequences of an act.

The subjective model as expressed by Kant has similarly been justifiably criticized by many for its intellectual abstraction which makes the most clever person, the person who can justify their actions logically, the most principled and therefore the most moral. The foundationalist assumption that the most consistent universal structure is the most ethical one is to make the assumption that the dominant world-view is the best one. For all its system, it is too clever for its own good – in this Peters was right. Additionally it lacks any reference to the ethical dimension of empathetic response which drives it. Emotion, motivation, personality and biography have been kept out of sight in a purely cognitive decontextualized paradigm that focuses on universal structures of moral judgement.

For Derrida, language functions as a mode of location for determining the meaning of the reality/event. Much of what we perceive is located neither in the external world nor in the internal one, but is part of a unified event that we perceive from the aspect of our own location. In other words, the reality exists, but the meaning of the reality is not out there or in here: the meaning of the reality is located in language. As Davidson (1985: 473) has pointed out, we connive with our language to make it, and us, seem special. The theories of ethics that most of us have been trained in, basically the objective view and the subjective view, have been composed by men (Spender 1990). So the ethic of care espoused by Gilligan and Noddings is often spoken of as if it were a feminine contrapuntal theory which denied or at least defied the first two masculine theories. I have argued in this book that this is not the case. In some senses, the ethic of care depends upon the linguistic foundations of utilitarianism and Kantian philosophy, even where it appears to slide past them. It, like many of the feminine writings I have referred to, is attempting to place back into the ethical frame some aspects of morality for which traditional theories have no ethical language.

Noddings (1993: 51) sees caring as a type of critical theory which requires the other frames for activation:

> [Caring] is activated when we are challenged to justify our recommendations in light of the practicalities of contemporary schooling. Critics ask: How can any teacher do what caring requires? For care theorists, this challenge does not force retreat. Instead it triggers a deep and devastating critique of the present structures of schooling . . . when we adopt caring as our moral orientation, we are also led to examine our own practices as teachers.

In all of these the traditional conceptions of care, consistency and consequences ground any discussion of morals in an ethical triad upon which the construction of a rational self depends. The autonomy of the self, not only in teaching, is always tightly bound up with *justice* for each *individual*, the *knowledge* of the *consequences* of one's actions and *solicitude* for the *other*. Teachers can exercise professional judgement and provide a moral model for students if they are aware of these three aspects of ethics.

Appendix A

What ought I to do?

Answer 'Yes', 'No' or 'It depends' to the following questions. If the latter, look closely at the things on which your answer depends, that is, what do you think would be relevant to your decision? What do these salient features reveal about the basis for your ethical decision? Which is foremost in your mind in deciding your answer – consistency, consequences or care? Are you consistent across answers? Can you justify the inconsistency? Can you identify a moral code that justifies your answer? If not, what does? Do you appeal to intuitions, principles, rules, codes or regulations to justify your response? Which is overriding in most cases?

1 At a staff meeting, your deputy principal makes some offensive remarks. Do you express your true feelings and risk offending him/her?

2 A student tells you in confidence that another teacher made sexual advances to him/her. Do you report it to his/her parents?

3 You want to quit education to make more money in private business, but decide to put it off until 1 April so that you can get your Christmas holiday pay. The principal is counting on you to get the April camp organized. Do you tell him of your intention to leave?

4 You have been working in Kambalda, and the Education Department pays return air fares once a year home to Perth. You decide to use the money to take a trip to Singapore instead. Do you inform the Education Department of your destination?

5 You lose an exciting and lucrative job opportunity because of a social justice policy of hiring minorities. Do you feel resentful?

6 In the car park, you accidentally dent the superintendent's car. Do you leave a note taking responsibility?

7 It is getting dark as you leave the school grounds and you notice a long-haired dirty student lying in a pool of vomit behind the toilet block. No one else is around. Do you try to help the student?

8 Another administrator wants to copy and swap some expensive computer software with you. You know it is illegal. Do you swap?

9 Your uncle is in the building industry. He offers to build you a new garage for nothing if you can help to secure him a lucrative contract with the Education Department to build a new school. Do you agree to help put his name forward?

10 The maths teacher has a severe case of bad breath. Do you mention it to him/her?

11 You suspect that a parent is abusing his child. Your attempts to discuss it with the child, the parents and other teachers have been rebuffed. Do you notify the authorities?

12 You have been attending educational management lectures all year. An acquaintance, who rarely shows up, asks to photocopy your notes. Do you consent?

13 A parent wants his severely retarded child in your already over-crowded classroom on the grounds that it will enhance his social skills and self-esteem. Do you allow the child to join the class?

14 Because it is forbidden to smoke on school grounds, you reach the staff room with a sigh of relief, shut the door and light up that cigarette. The teacher next to you is coughing and showing discomfort. Do you finish your cigarette?

15 It is the last day before Christmas holidays. You have no classes to teach and there is no one around the car park. Do you leave school early?

16 You have just designed and implemented a new health curriculum in a private school. The Curriculum Council recommends changes that will more easily meet the demands of your local community. Do you reject their suggestions for change?

17 You are physically attractive, but not coping very well with the mortgage repayments or the marking load. Someone offers you a lot of money to work at night for an 'escort service'. Do you accept?

18 One of your students, whom you know comes from a broken home, is carrying an expensive watch which you suspect is stolen. Do you go up to him/her and ask how she/he came to have the watch?

19 You have discovered a means whereby you can make a false insurance claim on the school computer and appropriate it at no loss to the school for your own personal use without detection. Do you use it?

20 One of your colleagues has sunk into a depression and behaves in a thoroughly unattractive manner. Do you distance yourself until he/she gets it together again?

21 A friend asks you to write a reference. You feel that your friend is poorly qualified for the job. Do you refuse?

22 An Aboriginal parent tells you that maths in Year 6 is a complete waste of time and that he wishes his daughter to be given exemption from attending the compulsory classes on equity grounds. Do you say 'Yes' or 'No'?

23 In order to be eligible for a well-paid teaching position at a private school you must profess to the values of a religion that is not your own faith. Do you lie in order to get the position?

24 You know your tax agent trusts you and will not ask to see receipts. Do you inflate the amount you spent on your professional library to get a larger rebate for studies?

25 A parent wants to get her child into the gifted and talented class. You owe the parent a favour and you have not much faith in the IQ test results anyway. Do you misrepresent the child's IQ score to get him/her in?

26 You know that a student who has not been concentrating in class has been taking drugs. The student's parent is a prominent politician and asks how the child is progressing. Do you avoid any mention of the drugs?

27 You are discussing euthanasia in class. Do you make your own views known to the class?

28 A 14-year-old student asks you to buy him a copy of *Penthouse* with his money. Do you?

29 Parents on the school council have protested about the obscene language in one of the English texts. Do you allow it to remain on the syllabus on the grounds that the parents are being unnecessarily protective?

30 Two science teachers are arguing noisily about the merits of the student profiles in the national curriculum. Do you interrupt to try to prevent them arguing further?

31 You are a primary school teacher. A pupil is trying very hard but has a long history of failure. Do you fail the student for below-standard work?

32 One of the junior teachers in your school has quietly left town for an unofficial holiday. His/her principal calls you at home and says he/she has an urgent message. Do you tell where the teacher can be reached?

33 The parents on the school council say that they will withdraw their children if condom-vending machines are placed in the toilets. Do you install the machines anyway?

34 A close friend will be interviewed for a job with your supervisor. You have confidential information that will help him/her to get the job. Do you supply it?

35 You know you are attractive to the opposite sex. Do you use your sex appeal to get ahead in your career?

36 You and your best friend are in the same teaching area. You hear of an excellent, little-known opportunity for which you think you will apply. Do you inform your friend?

37 Your lecturer has forgotten about a book that he/she loaned you. You want the book and cannot get another copy. Do you keep it?

38 You discover that the artist-in-residence is HIV positive. Do you try to have him/her removed from the school?

39 You have gone to see a nude show with business associates. The next day the class asks you how you spent the evening. Do you tell the truth?

40 You are not physically ill, but you are emotionally exhausted. Do you

telephone work to say that you are sick and need a replacement for a couple of days?

41 You suspect that the senior English teacher is an alcoholic and has a bottle of Scotch hidden behind the class set of *Hamlet*s. Do you mention it to the other English teachers?

42 Your brightest Year 12s want to go to the art gallery by themselves in school hours. Do you give permission for them to be out of school?

43 You are applying for a job that requires experience that you don't have. Do you claim that you do?

44 You discover that the social studies teacher is not only a practising homosexual but that he has been talking to his students about discrimination on the basis of sexual preference. Do you inform the principal?

45 You have a pair of twins, one precocious, the other slow. Do you hold back the progress of the brighter one so that the other will not feel inferior?

46 You have just signed for a six-month relief contract when you are offered an excellent permanent position elsewhere. Do you break the contract and take the full-time job?

47 Your Year 10 class ask you if you have ever smoked marijuana. You did once or twice. Do you admit it?

48 You do not hire a teacher because he/she has a personal hygiene problem. The teacher asks why the job was lost. Are you honest?

49 You are unmarried. You sense a mutual attraction between you and one of your upper school students. Do you keep a professional distance until the course ends?

50 One of the top officials in your educational system has listed in his/her CV a degree which you know he/she sat but did not pass. The official has been a dedicated and effective public servant for years. Do you call the press?

Code of ethics – Australian College of Education

(revised November 1987)

PREAMBLE

The Australian College of Education, in its Memorandum of Association, states that it is formed to 'create a fellowship of those engaged in education which will foster educational thought and practice and set before itself and the community the ethics of high professional responsibility'. The concluding words of that sentence invite a statement of professional ethics. While it is recognized that members of the College exhibit a wide diversity of belief, there is present in the community of educators a sufficient measure of agreement on values to permit a statement of broad principles regarding professional conduct to function both as guidance and ideals for members.

THE BASIC CONSIDERATIONS FOR A TEACHER

At every level of education the teacher is taking a part in the process of initiating members of society into its structures and functioning and of imparting to them knowledge, skills, values and attitudes necessary for understanding themselves and the reality in which they live, and for finding self-fulfilment within it. Since our society, to a high degree, preserves, adapts and enriches itself through being constantly transformed, teachers are inevitably involved both in transmitting its culture and in presenting a critique of that culture in the light of changing social needs and advances in learning.

Teachers should recognize that education is lifelong and that therefore their teaching of their pupils should be consistent with the further stages to be expected in the pupil's personal development and growth in knowledge and skills.

Teachers have an obligation to keep abreast of advances in learning and in theories and strategies of teaching, and to be aware of changing social needs and of broad cultural outlooks. They are responsible for what they teach and for the way in which they relate to students. In this they should show a respect for the individuality of students; they should also endeavour to promote maturity and responsibility in their students.

While the teacher essentially has a unique relationship with each pupil, nevertheless no teacher works alone. Teachers need to draw on others who are sources of information and techniques to work with students, with other teachers, with those who organize educational institutions and systems and, where students are children, with their parents.

TEACHER AND STUDENTS

At all levels of education the relationship between teacher and students is basic to the educational process. Teachers should seek to establish themselves and their students' confidence and trust grounded in mutual respect. They should not exploit students nor should they show undue partiality in response to them. Honesty, integrity and a high regard for the uniqueness of each student should characterize the relationships. Because teachers hold this position of trust and confidence with respect to students, society expects of them a high standard of conduct at all times.

Teachers of children should bear in mind the special relationship between parent and child and, until it is proper to treat the child as an adult, should seek the active cooperation of the parent in securing the students' welfare and development. In this, teachers should respect the parent's religious and moral beliefs.

TEACHER AND SOCIETY

A teacher's responsibility for the initiation of members of society into its cultures will involve not only the teaching of knowledge and understanding held to be of worth but also the development of commitment to its highest values. In this society these include freedom, equality, respect for persons, consideration of the common interest, belief in the human capacity to base actions on reason and in the possibility of change by peaceful means.

Within a general agreement on values, different groups in society will place different emphases. In matters where public opinion is strongly divided it will be the teacher's responsibility to teach respect for different positions and understanding of the arguments upon which these positions are based. Beyond this, it is even more important to encourage a growing commitment to reason, in which the human considerations of sympathy and forbearance will play their part, in the making of value judgements.

TEACHER AND PROFESSION

Those who enter the teaching profession should recognize that it makes great demands: it requires constant striving for improvement in everything that helps and encourages students' growth and learning, and requires all the support possible that can be given to colleagues. Colleagues should be treated with respect without discrimination on grounds of status, sex, race, colour, national origin or religious or political belief and such respect should be encouraged in others.

Good education requires collaboration between teachers, administrators and others contributing at all levels to the educational task; professionalism therefore includes not only the obligation to lead and show initiative, but to cooperate.

Experienced teachers have a special responsibility to assist new entrants to the profession in settling into an unfamiliar organization and to help them in their continuing professional development.

The health and effectiveness of the profession largely depend on the quality of channels of communication. Members of the profession should use such channels as exist and where these are inadequate, seek to establish them so that information, ideas, suggestions and explanations flow freely. This would facilitate cooperation and the resolution of differences.

Where, in serious issues, a disagreement cannot be resolved, or a teacher is unable to accept a direction properly given, she or he should consider resigning rather than acting against personal convictions or sense of personal integrity.

Glossary

This glossary consists of short definitions of a number of some ethical terms appearing in this book. Where a term is closely associated with a particular writer, that writer's name is given in parentheses.

action   A decision or movement that is done consciously, intentionally, as opposed to a behaviour, which can be done automatically, out of habit or immediate unthinking response. 'Action' presumes mind and intention; 'behaviour' does not.

algorithm   A rule that must be carried out precisely, or it has no application, as in formal systems of logic or mathematics, or some games, like chess.

altruism   Description of action aimed at producing good for someone other than the person acting. Contrasted with *egoism*.

amoral   Applied to a person living without any concern for moral rules. Not the same as *immoral*; used for the deliberate breaking of moral rules.

aporia   A shock to our structures of thinking which may leave us temporarily stunned, not knowing how to go on, but which is sometimes necessary to help us look at things under a new aspect (Derrida).

a priori   A conclusion reached by reason alone, 'prior to' experience. Kant used the term to apply to those concepts such as time, space and causality which he thought were necessary for the formation of logical speech. Contrasted with *a posteriori*, which is a conclusion reached on the basis of experience, usually located in the sensed world. Quine has argued that this distinction, along with others, should be abandoned, and that we operate within a seamless web of beliefs in which our logical structures evolve alongside our experiences.

arete   Usually translated as 'virtue' but it is closer to a notion of quality or excellence. Aristotle believed that there were two kinds of *arete* – moral and intellectual. Pirsig believed that '*arete*' or 'quality' was the end which bound reason and belief together, a notion of the Good.

authoritarianism   The theory that good and evil, right and wrong, are whatever some authority (usually God, but it could be the Pope, the Bible or the school principal) asserts that they are.

autonomy   Literally self-governed, that is, not impelled to act by impulse or regulation or pressure from any external source. The opposite of heteronomy, which is governed by many external forces.

axiology   The philosophical discipline devoted to the study of values in general.

blame   To censure someone; to pass on moral notions of fault for a misdeed.

categorical imperative   A command without qualifications or conditions and therefore the fundamental principle of moral action (Kant). Also known as *the moral law*. Kant has given three formulations of this which supply the form, the content, and the link between form and content respectively:

1 Act as if you were legislating for everyone (the *universalizability* of 'ought').
2 Act so as to treat human beings always as ends and never merely as means.
3 Act as if you were a member of a realm of ends, that is, you should act as a member of a community of persons, all of whom make moral decisions (equality of respect for persons).

coercion   The use of physical or psychological force, rather than reason, to constrain or restrain others.

compulsion   Literally, 'pulling with', therefore forcing or using pressure to come or go or proceed. Related to 'compulsory' where no choice is possible.

conduct   Action in which the agent makes moral decisions. Like 'action' contrasted with 'behaviour', which does not involve such decisions.

conscience   A special faculty which each human is said to possess, which decides between right and wrong and internally condemns that person when he or she violates its dictates. Sometimes viewed as a marker of internal inconsistencies or contradictions of principle.

deontics   A model that emphasizes notions of duty, right and wrong rather than consequences.

deontology   The view that intentioned action, and its rightness or wrongness, arising from a sense of obligation or duty rather than from the consequences of action, is the main concern of ethics (Kant).

duty   An act that a person morally ought to do, the same as *moral obligation*.

egalitarianism   The theory that each individual, as such, has an equal right to happiness or the means thereto.

eudamonia   The highest good in life for Aristotle, usually translated as *happiness*, but also as *vital well-being, living well and doing well*. The main difference between 'eudamonia' and 'hedonistic happiness or pleasure' is that the former is attributed in terms of some kind of objective evaluation in terms of reasons which others could find acceptable, a sort of consquentialist commonwealth, whereas the latter is attributed merely in terms of the kind of life that the possessor *wants* to hold onto.

evolutionary ethics   Any theory that attempts to draw conclusions about what is good from the facts of evolution. Often associated with doctrines of 'the survival of the fittest', it is a naturalist theory.

excuse   A statement offered to extenuate an action, or plead innocence. Occasionally used as a pretence, as opposed to a reason.

existentialism   A literary and philosophical position, mainly twentieth century, which emphasizes individual responsibility, claiming that we exist as unique human beings who must make choices and construct meaning in a world that is morally 'absurd' (Sartre, Camus, Nietzsche).

extrinsic good   Instrumentally good, or good simply as a means to some other end. Contrasts with 'intrinsic good'.

fatalism   The belief that an individual's destiny is fixed and that the individual can do nothing to alter it. Not the same as determinism.

felicific calculus   A method of calculating pleasures and pains in order to determine what one should do. Moral arithmetic. Also known as *hedonistic calculus* (Bentham, Mill).

free will   A theory that presumes that we are able to make real choices between alternative actions. Opposed to *determinism*.

golden mean   Ideal moral virtue (Aristotle). The midpoint (not mathematical) between two extremes, both of which are vices. The life of moderation.

golden rule   The biblical notion of doing unto others as you would they should do unto you (Leviticus 19.18), this rule has been approximated to the Kantian *categorical imperative*. The New Testament version is 'Act lovingly towards your neighbour, for he is like yourself' (Matthew 19:19).

guilt   Awareness of a personal failure of duty, delinquency or some moral or legal offence.

happiness   Enjoyment of pleasures, security from pains (Bentham).

hedonism   The theory that pleasure is the only thing that is intrinsically good or good in itself (Bentham, Mill).

heteronomy   The character of a will that is moved to act by forces outside itself, particularly desires. Heteronomous action has no moral worth according to Kant.

heuristic   From the Greek notion of 'finding out', it has been applied to a system of education in which pupils are trained to find out for themselves. In ethics, it is usually used to mean an open-ended strategy like an ethical code as opposed to the formalism of a law or *algorithm*.

hierarchical responsibility   Originally applied to the orders of angels, but transferred to any human or political system in which the rules emanate from the top.

humanism   The view that all human values exist in this world and this life.

ideal utilitarianism   The theory that we ought always act in such a way as to produce the greatest amount of good possible, the good not being limited to pleasure (as with Bentham and Mill) but including other instrinsic goods as well (Moore).

idealism   In ethics the belief in and commitment to goods or ideals, but in metaphysics something quite different – the theory that the universe is totally mental, hence the denial of any physical or material reality.

inclination   Feeling or desire as a motive to action. Opposed to motivation by duty which is rational (Kant).

indeterminism   The theory that at least some events, in particular human actions that result from choices or decisions, are not the determined effects of antecedent causes.

instrumentalism   The theory that knowledge is valued for its usefulness in solving the practical problems that we face rather than its truth.

intrinsic good   Good in itself or good as an end. Contrasts with *extrinsic good*.

linguistic turn   A phrase generated by Rorty, to refer to the shift in interest from truth towards meaning in the twentieth century.

maxim   A principle or general rule like 'nothing can come from nothing', or 'knowledge is power'. Maxims in themselves are non-moral, but they become moral if an individual formulates them to explain their actions. Kant used it to apply to those situations in which the individual can will that the maxim should be universally adopted or acted upon by everybody (universalizability). See *categorical imperative*.

meliorism   A belief, midway between optimism and pessimism, that the world may be made better by human effort (Dewey).

meta-ethics   Inquiry into the domain of ethics itself, which asks questions about the meaning of ethical concepts or methodologies of ethics, in what ways ethical knowledge is possible or the place of reason in the justification of ethical actions.

moral sense   A special feeling, which is part of our emotional nature, that causes us to view some situations and actions with approval and others with disapproval (Hume).

naturalism   The theory that all ethical concepts can be defined in terms of empirical or testable concepts. Thus ethics can be reduced to a natural or empirical science (Quine).

naturalist ethics   The belief that ethics arises out of a natural need to solve problems and has its root in and is a plan of action rather than an essential or metaphysical truth (Dewey).

naturalistic fallacy   Arising from the belief that goodness is unanalysable in non-ethical terms, this states that it is a mistake to define good in terms of things or attributes other than what it is (Moore). Commonly stated as 'one cannot derive an ought from an is'.

normative   Concerning norms, standards, common values, what we ought to do. Ethics is a normative inquiry. Contrasts with *descriptive*.

objectivism   The theory that there are moral truths that hold regardless of how anyone feels about them. These are concepts of ethics such as honesty, promise-keeping, goodness, justice.

oxymoron   An apparent contradiction in terms, like military intelligence, or ethical management.

practical reason   Reason that is used to tell us what we ought to do both in a prudential and ethical sense and to motivate us to do it (Aristotle, Kant).

precept   A rule to be followed. An imperative (Kant, Hare).

psychological hedonism   The theory (Mill) that all action aims at attaining pleasure for the agent.

punishment   A penalty inflicted to ensure the application and enforcement of a law, rule or practice, usually retributive.

relativism   Ethical beliefs are relative to a particular person, group or time rather than absolute.

resistance   According to McLaren (1993: 146), oppositional student behaviour that has both symbolic, historical and lived meaning and which contests the legitimacy, power and significance of school culture in general and instruction in particular.

sanction   A way of inducing individuals to perform acts they do not want to do, by applying various kinds of pressure (Bentham). In modern usage, any consideration that operates to enforce obedience to any law or rule of conduct.

self-determinism   A theory that holds that, although our acts are all determined, the self is often the determining agent. A position between free will and standard determinism.

self-realization   The theory that the good for human beings lies in the realization of their highest potential (Aristotle).

social contract   A theory that attempts to justify civil society and its power by the argument that every citizen 'signs' an implicit social contract to abide by the laws in order to enjoy the benefits of living in a civilized community (Rawls).

subjectivism   The theory that moral standards depend on the feelings of the individual. Hence, no action is right or wrong in itself (Hume).

teleology   The view that the main concern of ethics is with the ends or goals of human action and with their goodness or badness (Aristotle, Bentham, Mill, Moore, Nozick, national curriculum writers).

utilitarianism   The theory that the rightness or wrongness of actions must be judged solely by their contribution to the 'greatest amount of happiness (pleasure) for the greatest number of people'. Utilitarianism is thus a form of hedonism and can be measured by looking at the possible consequences of an action, without reference to personal intentions or duty (Bentham, Mill, Barrow, Singer).

virtue   An acquired, desirable quality of character. Excellent performance of a distinctive function, like a good musician or a good teacher (Aristotle). Voluntary observance of recognized moral laws.

will   An inclination or desire that moves us to act purposefully.

will to power   The belief that every individual has a basic drive to gain power and that the best people are those who make this will effective as opposed to any notion of a social contract or rational community (Nietzsche).

Bibliography

ACLU (American Civil Liberties Union of Washington) (1995) Letter to Dr Don R. O'Neil, Bellevue School District, Washington, 25 May; Transmitted <http://k12.cnidr.org: 90/paulkim.html> : 95–05–26.

Adams, R. (1985) 'Involuntary sins', *Philosophical Review*, 94: 3–31.

Aiken, W. and La Follette, H. (eds) (1980) *Whose Child? Children's Rights, Parental Authority and State Power*, Totowa, NJ: Rowman & Littlefield.

Altieri, C. (1981) *Act and Quality: A Theory of Literary Meaning and Humanistic Understanding*, Amherst: University of Massachusetts Press.

——(1990) *Canons and Consequences: Reflections on the Ethical Force of Imaginative Ideals*, Evanston, IL: Northwestern University Press.

Anonymous (1996) Unpublished class assignment for E421 Gender and Education, Murdoch University.

Anscombe, G.E.M. (1981) *Ethics, Religion and Politics*, Oxford: Blackwell.

Apple, M. (1982) *Education and Power*, Boston: Routledge & Kegan Paul.

——(1986) 'National reports and the construction of inequality', *British Journal of Sociology of Education*, 7, 2: 171–90.

——(1988) *Teachers and Texts: Political Economy of Class and Gender Relations in Education*, New York: Routledge, Chapman & Hall.

Arendt, H. (1958) *The Human Condition*, Chicago, IL: University of Chicago Press.

——(1963) *Eichmann in Jerusalem*, London: Faber & Faber.

——(1970) *On Violence*, London: Penguin.

——(1978) *The Life of the Mind*, New York: Harcourt Brace Jovanovich.

Argyris, C. (1964) *Integrating the Individual and the Organisation*, New York: Wiley.

——(1982) *Reasoning, Learning and Action: Individual and Organisational*, San Francisco: Jossey Bass.

Aristotle (1905) *Politics*, trans. B. Jowett, Oxford: Clarendon Press.

——(1969) *Nicomachean Ethics*, London: Penguin.

Arnheim, R. (1970) *Visual Thinking*, London: Faber.

Arnot, M. and Weiler, K. (eds) (1993) *Feminism and Social Justice in Education: International Perspectives*, London: Falmer Press.

Audi, R. (1991) 'Responsible action and virtuous character', *Ethics*, 101: 301–21.

Austin, J. (1956–7) 'A plea for excuses', *Proceedings of the Aristotelian Society*, 57: 1–30.

——(1975) *How to Do Things with Words* (2nd edn), Oxford: Clarendon Press.

Ayer, A.J. (1984) *Freedom and Morality and Other Essays*, Oxford: Clarendon Press.

Baier, A.C. (1982) 'Caring about caring', *Synthèse*, 53, November.

——(1985a) *Postures of the Mind: Essays on Mind and Morals*, Minneapolis: University of Minnesota Press.

——(1985b) 'What do women want in a moral theory?', *Nous*, 19: 53–63.

——(1987) 'The need for more than justice', in M. Hanen and K. Nelson (eds) *Science, Morality and Feminist Theory*, Calgary: University of Calgary Press, pp. 41–56.

——(1995) *Moral Prejudices*, Cambridge, MA: Harvard University Press.

Baier, K. (1995) *The Rational and the Moral Order: The Social Roots of Reason and Morality*, Chicago: Open Court.

Ball, S. (1993) 'Educational policy, power relations and teachers' work', *British Journal of Educational Studies*, 41, 2: 106–21.

Barrow, R. (1975) *Moral Philosophy for Education*, London: Allen & Unwin.

——(1981) *The Philosophy of Schooling*, Sussex: Wheatsheaf Books.

——(1982) *Injustice, Inequity and Ethics: A Philosophical Introduction to Moral Problems*, Sussex: Wheatsheaf Books.

——(1991) *Utilitarianism: A Contemporary Statement*, Brookfield: E. Elgar.

Bateson, M.C. (1994) *Peripheral Visions: Learning Along the Way*, New York: HarperCollins.

Baumrin, B. and Freedman, B. (eds) (1983) *Moral Responsibility and the Professions*, New York: Haven Publications.

Baumrind, D. (1986) 'Sex differences in moral reasoning', *Child Development*, 57: 511–21.

Beauchamp, T.L. and Childress, J. (1984) 'Morality, ethics and ethical theories', in P. Sola (ed.) *Ethics, Education and Administrative Decisions*, New York: Peter Lang.

Beck, L.G. (1994) *Reclaiming Educational Administration as a Caring Profession*, New York: Teachers College Press.

Beck, L.G. and Murphy, J. (1993) *Understanding the Principalship: Metaphorical Themes*, New York: Teachers College Press.

Bellenky, M., Clinchy, B., Goldberger, N. and Tarule, J. (1986) *Women's Ways of Knowing*, New York: Basic Books.

Benhabib, S. (1992) *Situating the Self: Gender, Community and Postmodernism in Contemporary Ethics*, London: Routledge.

——(1995) *Feminist Contentions: A Philosophical Exchange*, London: Routledge.

Benhabib, S. and Cornell, D. (eds) (1987) *Feminism as Critique*, Cambridge: Polity Press.

Benhabib, S. and Dallmayr, F. (eds) (1990) *The Communicative Ethics Controversy*, Cambridge, MA: MIT Press.

Benn, S.I. (1958) 'An approach to the problems of punishment', *Philosophy*, XXXIII: 325–6.

Benn, S.I. and Peters, R.S. (1959) *Social Principles and the Democratic State*, London: Allen & Unwin.

Bentham, J. (1982) *An Introduction to the Principles of Morals and Legislation*, ed. J.H. Burns and H.L.A. Hart, London: Methuen.

Berger, P. and Luckmann, T. (1967) *The Social Construction of Reality*, New York: Anchor Books.

Bernstein, R.J. (1992) *The New Constellation*, Cambridge, MA: MIT Press.

Bettelheim, B. (1967) *The Empty Fortress: Infantile Autism and the Birth of the Self*, New York: Free Press.

Bishop, S. and Weinsweig, M. (1979) *Philosophy and Women*, Belmont, CA: Wadsworth.

Blum, L. (1980) *Friendship, Altruism and Morality*, Boston: Routledge & Kegan Paul.

——(1986) 'Iris Murdoch and the domain of the moral', *Philosophical Studies*, 50: 343–67.

——(1987) 'Particularity and responsiveness', in J. Kagan and S. Lamb (eds) *The Emergence of Morality in Young Children*, Chicago: University of Chicago Press, pp. 306–37.

——(1988) 'Gilligan and Kohlberg: implications for moral theory', *Ethics*, 98, 3: 472–91.

Blustein, J. (1991) *Care and Commitment: Taking the Personal Point of View*, Oxford: Oxford University Press.

Boonin, L. (1983) 'Guilt, shame and morality', *Journal of Value Inquiry*, 17: 295–304.

Bottery, Mike (1990) *The Morality of the School: The Theory and Practice of Values in Education*, London: Cassell.

Bourdieu, P. (1977) *Outline for a Theory of Practice*, Cambridge: Cambridge University Press.

Brabeck, M.M. (ed.) (1989) *Who Cares? Theory, Research and Educational Implications of the Ethic of Care*, New York: Praeger.

Brand, M. (1971) 'The language of not doing', *American Philosophical Quarterly*, 8: 45–53.

Broudy, H.S. (1981) *Truth and Credibility: The Citizen's Dilemma*, New York: Longman.

Brown, L.M. and Gilligan, C. (1992) *Meeting at the Crossroads: Women's Psychology and Girls' Development*, Cambridge, MA: Harvard University Press.

Buber, M. (1961) *Between Man and Man*, trans. R. Gregor Smith, London: Collins.

Burbules, N. (1992) *Dialogue in Teaching*, New York: Teachers College Press.

——(1996) 'Difference', unpublished manuscript, delivered at AARE Conference Singapore in December 1996.

Burbules, N.C. and Densmore, K. (1991) 'The limits of making teaching a profession', *Educational Policy*, 5: 44–63.

Butler, J. (1990) *Gender Trouble: Feminist Theory and the Subversion of Identity*, New York: Routledge.

Campbell, R. and Christensen, B. (1996) 'Heidegger', in *A Dictionary of Philosophy*, ed. Thomas Mautner, Oxford: Basil Blackwell, pp. 183–5.

Card, C. (ed.) (1991) *Feminist Ethics*, Lawrence: University of Kansas Press.

Carr, W. (1989) *Quality in Teaching: Arguments for a Reflective Profession*, London and New York: Falmer Press.

Chambers, I. (1990) *Border Dialogues: Journeys in Postmodernity*, London: Routledge.

Chazan, B. (1985) *Contemporary Approaches to Moral Education*, New York: Teachers College Press.

Chodorow, N. (1978) *The Reproduction of Mothering*, Berkeley: University of California Press.

——(1986) 'Toward a relational individualism: the mediation of self through psychoanalysis', in T. Heller, M. Sosua and D. Wellberg (eds) *Reconstructing Individualism*, Palo Alto, CA: Stanford University Press.

——(1994) *Femininities, Masculinities, Sexualities: Freud and Beyond*, Lexington: University Press of Kentucky.

Chubb, J.E. (1988) 'Why the current wave of school reform will fail', *The Public Interest*, 90: 28–19.

Churchlands, P.M. (1984) *Matter and Consciousness*, Cambridge, MA: MIT Press.

Clark, D.L. and Meloy, J.M. (1989) 'Renouncing bureaucracy: a democratic structure for leadership in schools', in T.J. Sergiovanni and J.H. Moore (eds)

Schooling for Tomorrow: Directing Reforms to Issues that Count, Boston, MA: Allyn & Bacon, pp. 272 –94.

Clarke, P.B. (ed.) (1994) *Citizenship*, London: Pluto Press.

Clarke, S. and Simpson, E. (eds) (1989) *Anti-theory in Ethics and Moral Conservatism*, Albany, NY: SUNY Press.

Code, L. (1988) 'Experience, knowledge and responsibility', in M. Whitford and M. Griffiths (eds) *Feminist Perspectives in Philosophy*, Bloomington: Indiana University Press, pp. 187–204.

——(1991) *What Can She Know? Feminist Theory and the Construction of Knowledge*, Ithaca, NY: Cornell University Press.

——(1995) *Rhetorical Spaces: Essays on Gendered Locations*, Ithaca, NY: Cornell University Press.

Colby, A. and Kohlberg, L. (1987) *The Measurement of Moral Judgement*, New York: Cambridge University Press.

Coleman, J.S. (1967) *The Concept of Educational Opportunity*, Baltimore, MD: Johns Hopkins University Press.

Collins, P.H. (1990) *Black Feminist Thought: Knowledge, Consciousness and the Politic of Empowerment*, Boston, MA: Unwin Hyman.

Cooper, D.E. (1980) *Illusions of Equality*, London: Routledge & Kegan Paul.

Cooper, N. (1987) 'On evading responsibility', *Journal of Applied Ethics*, 4: 89–94.

Cornell, D. (1991) *Beyond Accommodation: Ethical Feminism, Deconstruction and the Law*, New York: Routledge.

——(1993) *Transformations: Recollective Imagination and Sexual Difference*, New York: Routledge.

Cornell, D., Rosenfeld, M. and Carlson, D.G. (eds) (1992) *Deconstruction and the Possibility of Justice*, New York: Routledge.

Court, R. (1996) 'It's a matter of respect', *The West Australian*, 27 January, p. 1.

Curtis (1995) 'School rules' published for school parents by Trinity College, Perth.

Dallmayr, F.R. (1981) *Twilight of Subjectivity: Contributions to a Post-individualistic Theory of Politics*, Amherst: University of Massachusetts Press.

——(1984) *Language and Politics*, Notre Dame, IN: University of Notre Dame Press.

Davidson, D. (1963) 'Actions, reasons and causes', *Journal of Philosophy*, 60: 685 –700.

——(1985) 'Rational animals', in E. LePore and B. McLaughlin (eds) *Actions and Events*, New York: Basil Blackwell, p. 473.

Day, M. (1996) 'Ban on cane backed', *The West Australian*, 27 January, p. 3.

Dennett, D. (1984) *Elbow Room: The Varieties of Free Will Worth Having*, Cambridge, MA: Harvard University Press.

——(1987) *The Intentional Stance*, Cambridge, MA: MIT Press.

——(1993) *Consciousness Explained*, London: Penguin.

Derrida, J. (1973) *Writing and Difference*, trans. Alan Bass, London: Routledge & Kegan Paul.

Dewey, J. (1922) *Human Nature and Conduct*, New York: Holt Rinehart & Winston.

——(1932) *Ethics*, New York: Henry Holt.

——(1959) *Moral Principles in Education*, New York: Philosophical Library.

Downie, R.S. (1964) *Government Action and Morality*, London: Macmillan.

——(1990) 'Professions and professionalism', *Journal of Philosophy of Education*, 24: 147–59.

Downie, R.S., Loudfoot, E.M. and Telfer, E. (eds) *Educational and Personal Relationships*, London: Methuen.

Downie, R.S. and Telfer, E. (1969) *Respect for Persons*, London: Allen & Unwin.

Dreyfus, H. (1986) *Mind over Machine: The Power of Human Intuition and Expertise in the Era of the Computer*, New York: Free Press.

Dreyfus, H. and Rabinow, P. (1982) *Michel Foucault: Beyond Structuralism and Hermeneutics*, Chicago, IL: University of Chicago Press.

Dunlap, D.M. and Goldman, P. (1991) 'Rethinking power in schools', *Educational Administration Quarterly*, 27, 1: 5–29.

Durkheim, E. (1973) *Moral Education: A Study in the Theory and Application of the Sociology of Education*, trans. E.K. Wilson and H. Schnurer, New York: Free Press.

Dworkin, G. (1988) *The Theory and Practice of Autonomy*, Cambridge: Cambridge University Press.

Dworkin, R. (1979) *Taking Rights Seriously*, Cambridge, MA: Harvard University Press.

Edgerton, R. (1985) *Rules, Exceptions and Social Order*, Berkeley: University of California Press.

EDWA (1993) *Social Justice in Education: Policy and Guidelines for the Education of Students with Disabilities*, Perth: WA Government Printer.

Elmer-Dewitt, P. (1995) 'Porn on the Internet', *Time*, 10 July, 48–56.

Emler, N. and Reicher, S. (1987) 'Orientations to institutional authority in adolescents', *Journal of Moral Education*, 16, 2: 108–16.

Emmet, D. (1967) *Rules, Roles and Relations*, New York: St Martin's Press.

Erikson, E.H. (1964) *Insight and Responsibility: Lectures on the Ethical Implications of Psychoanalytic Insight*, New York: Norton Press.

——(1968) *Identity, Youth and Crisis*, New York: Norton Press .

——(1977) *Toys and Reasons: Stages in the Ritualization of Life*, New York: W.W. Norton.

Evers, C. and Chapman, J. (eds) (1995) *Educational Administration*, London: Allen & Unwin.

Evers, C. and Lakomski, G. (1991) *Ways of Knowing in Educational Administration: Contemporary Methodological Controversies in Educational Administration Research*, Oxford and New York: Pergamon.

Feinberg, J. (1970) *Doing and Deserving: Essays in the Theory of Responsibility*, Princeton, NJ: Princeton University Press.

Feinberg, J. and Gross, H. (eds) (1975) *Punishment: Selected Readings*, Encino, CA: Dickenson Press.

Fenstermacher, G. (1990) 'Some moral considerations of teaching as a profession', in J.I. Goodlad, R. Soder and K.A. Sirotnik (eds) *The Moral Dimensions of Teaching*, San Francisco, CA: Jossey Bass, pp. 130–51.

Ferguson, K.E. (1984) *The Feminist Case Against Bureaucracy*, Philadelpia: Temple University Press.

Flanagan, O. and Jackson, K. (1987) 'Justice, care and gender: the Kohlberg–Gilligan debate revisited', *Ethics*, 97: 622–37.

Flanagan, O. and Rorty, A. (eds) (1990) *Identity, Character and Morality: Essays in Moral Psychology*, Cambridge, MA: MIT Press.

Flew, A. (1954) 'The justification of punishment', *Philosophy*, XXIX: 293–4.

——(1976) *Sociology, Equality and Education: Philosophical Essays in Defence of a Variety of Differences*, London: Macmillan.

——(1989) *Equality in Liberty and Justice*, London and New York: Routledge.

Flores, A. (1983) 'Collective responsibility and professional roles', *Ethics*, 92: 537–45.

Foot, P. (1967) *Theories of Ethics*, Oxford: Oxford University Press.

——(1978) *Virtues and Vices*, Berkeley, CA: University of California Press.

Foucault, M. (1972) *The Archaeology of Knowledge*, trans. A.M. Sheridan Smith, New York: Pantheon Books.

——(1973) *The Order of Things: An Archaeology of the Human Sciences*, New York: Pantheon Press.

——(1977) *Discipline and Punish*, trans. A Sheridan, New York: Pantheon.

——(1978) *The History of Sexuality*, trans. Robert Hurley, New York: Random House.

——(1980) *Power/Knowledge*, New York: Pantheon.

——(1986) *The Care of the Self*, New York: Pantheon.

——(1993) 'About the beginnings of the hermeneutics of the self', *Political Theory*, 21, 2: 53–72.

Fowler, R. (1991) *The Dance with Community: The Contemporary Debate in American Political Thought*, Lawrence: University of Kansas Press.

Frankena, W.K. (1963) *Ethics*, Englewood Cliffs, NJ: Prentice-Hall.

Frankfurt, H. (1988) *The Importance of What We Care About: Philosophical Essays*, New York: Cambridge University Press.

Fraser, E., Hornsby, J. and Lovibond, S. (1992) *Ethics: A Feminist Reader*, Oxford: Blackwell .

Fraser, N. (1989) *Unruly Practices: Power, Discourse and Gender in Contemporary Social Theory*, Minneapolis: University of Minnesota Press.

French, M. (1986) *Beyond Power: On Men, Women and Morals*, London: Sphere; Cape: Abacus.

Freud, S. (1925) 'Some psychical consequences of the anatomical distinction between the sexes', *Collected Works*, vol. XIX , pp. 412–13.

Friedman, M. (1987) 'Beyond caring: the de-moralisation of gender', in M. Hanen and K. Nelson (eds) *Science, Morality and Feminist Theory*, Calgary: University of Calgary Press, pp. 87–110.

Frye, M. (1983) *The Politics of Reality*, Timansburg, NY: Crossing Press.

Fuller, F. (1969) 'Concerns of teachers: a developmental conceptualization', *American Educational Research Journal*, 6: 207–26.

Fuller, R.C. (1992) *Ecology of Care: An interdisciplinary Analysis of the Self and Moral Obligation*, Louisville, KY: Westminister/John Knox.

Fuller, T. (ed.) (1989) *The Voice of Liberal Education: Michael Oakeshott on Education*, New Haven: Yale University Press.

Fuss, D. (1989) *Essentially Speaking*, New York: Routledge.

——(ed.) (1991) *Inside/Out: Lesbian Theories, Gay Theories*, New York: Routledge.

Gadamer, Hans-Georg (1975) *Truth and Method*, New York: Continuum.

——(1976) *Philosophical Hermeneutics*, trans. D.E. Linge, Berkeley: University of California Press.

Gallop, J. (1988) *Thinking Through the Body*, New York: Columbia University Press.

Gardner, H. (1993) *Frames of Mind: The Theory of Multiple Intelligences*, London: Fontana.

Gass, William H. (1957) 'The case of the obliging stranger', *Philosophical Review*, 66, 2: 193–204.

Gaylin, W. (1976) *Caring*, New York: Knopf.

Geach, P.T. (1976) *Reason and Argument*, Oxford: Basil Blackwell.

Geertz, C. (1983) *Local Knowledge: Further Essays in Interpretive Anthropology*, New York: Basic Books.

Gewirth, A. (1978) *Reason and Morality*, Chicago, IL: Chicago University Press.

Gibson, R.F. (1986) 'Corporations, persons and moral responsibility', *Journal of Thought*, 21: 17–86.

Giddens, A. (1984) *The Constitution of Society*, Cambridge: Polity Press.

——(1991) *Modernity and Self-identity: Self and Society in the Late Modern Age*, Stanford: Stanford University Press.

Gilligan, C. (1982) *In a Different Voice: Psychological Theory and Women's Development*, Cambridge, MA: Harvard University Press.

——(1987) 'Moral orientation and moral development', in E. Kittay and D. Meyers (eds) *Women and Moral Theory*, Lanham, MD: Rowman & Littlefield, pp. 19–33.

Gilligan, C., Lyons, N. and Hammer, T. (eds) (1990) *Making Connections*, Cambridge, MA: Harvard University Press.

Gilligan, C., Ward, J.V. and Taylor, J.M. (eds) (1988) *Mapping the Moral Domain: A Contribution of Women's Thinking to Psychological Theory and Education*, Cambridge, MA: Harvard University Press.

Giroux, H. (1981) *Ideology, Culture and the Process of Schooling*, Philadelphia: Temple University Press.

Giroux, H. and Purpel, D. (1983) *The Hidden Curriculum and Moral Education: Deception or Discovery*, Berkeley, CA: McCutcheon.

Glatzer, N.N. (1966) *The Way of Response: Martin Buber*, New York: Schocken.

Glendon, M.A. (1991) *Rights Talk: The Impoverishment of Political Discourse*, New York: Free Press.

Glover, J. (1970) *Responsibility*, Harmondsworth: Penguin.

Goldinger, M. (ed.) (1974) *Punishment and Human Rights*, Cambridge: Cambridge University Press.

Goodlad, J.I., Soder, R. and Sirotnik, K.A. (eds) (1990) *The Moral Dimensions of Teaching*, San Francisco, CA: Jossey Bass.

Grassian, V. (1981) *Moral Reasoning*, Englewood Cliffs, NJ: Wadsworth.

Haan, N. (ed.) (1983) *Social Science as Moral Inquiry*, New York: Columbia University Press.

Habermas, J. (1978) *Knowledge and Human Interests*, trans. J. Shapiro, London: Heinemann.

——(1987) *Theory of Communicative Action*, vol. 2: *Lifeworld and System: A Critique of Functionalist Reason*, trans. T. McCarthy, Boston, MA: Beacon.

——(1989–90) 'Justice and solidarity; on the discussion concerning "stage 6"', *Philosophical Forum*, 21, 1–2: 32–52.

——(1990) *Moral Consciousness and Communicative Action*, Cambridge, MA: MIT Press.

——(1992) *Postmetaphysical Thinking*, trans. W.M. Hohengarten, Cambridge, MA.: MIT Press.

Hacking, I. (1984) 'Winner take less', *New York Review of Books*, 31, 28 June.

——(1995) *Rewriting the Soul: Multiple Personality and the Sciences of Memory*, Princeton: Princeton University Press.

Handy, C. (1986) *Understanding Organisations*, Harmondsworth: Penguin.

Hanen, M. and Nelson, K. (eds) (1987) *Science, Morality and Feminist Theory*, Calgary: University of Calgary Press.

Haraway, D. (1991) *Simians, Cyborgs and Women: The Reinvention of Nature*, New York: Routledge.

——(1992) *Primate Visions: Gender, Race and Nature in the World of Modern Science* (2nd edn), New York: Routledge.

Hardin, G. (1977) 'Lifeboat ethics: the case against helping the poor' in W. Aiken and H. La Follette (eds) *World Hunger and Moral Obligations*, Englewood Cliffs, NJ: NIL, pp. 11–21.

Hare, R.M. (1952) *The Language of Morals*, Oxford: Clarendon Press.

——(1981) *Moral Thinking: Its Levels, Method and Point*, Oxford: Clarendon.

Hart, H.L.A. (1968) *Punishment and Responsibility*, Oxford: Clarendon.

Harvey, D. (1989) *The Condition of Postmodernity*, Oxford: Basil Blackwell.

Hauerwa, S. and MacIntyre, A. (eds) (1983) *Revisions: Changing Perspectives in Moral Philosophy*, Notre Dame, IN: University of Notre Dame Press.

Hawes, Rachel (1995) 'School's hair rule deemed discriminatory', *The Australian* , 8 March, p. 5.

Haynes, F. (1989) 'On equitable cake-cutting', *Educational Philosophy and Theory*, 21: 12–22.

——(1994) 'Male dominance and the mastery of reason', *Thinking*, 11, 4: 18–24.

——(1996) 'Mapping the curriculum', unpublished paper, delivered at AARE Conference, Singapore.

Heidegger, M. (1927) *Being and Time*, trans. J. Macquarrie and E. Robinson (1962), New York: Harper & Row.

——(1972) *What is Called Thinking?*, trans. J. Gray, New York: Harper Torchbooks.

Hekman, S.J. (1986) *Hermeneutics and the Sociology of Knowledge*, Cambridge: Polity Press.

——(1990) *Gender and Knowledge: Elements of a Postmodern Feminism*, Cambridge: Polity Press.

——(1995) *Moral Voices, Moral Selves: Carol Gilligan and Feminist Moral Theory*, Oxford: Polity Press.

Held, V. (1984) *Rights and Goods: Justifying Social Action*, New York: Free Press.

——(1993) *Feminist Morality: Transforming Culture, Society and Politics*, Chicago: University of Chicago Press.

Hobbes, T. (1973) *Leviathan*, London: J.M. Dent.

Holstein, C. (1976) 'Development of moral judgment: a longitudinal study of males and females', *Child Development*, 47: 51–61.

Howe, K.R. (1986) 'A conceptual basis for ethics in teacher education', *Journal of Teacher Education*, 37, 3: 5–11.

Hume, D. (1975) *Treatise of Human Nature, Book III: Enquiries Concerning the Principles of Morals*, ed. P.H. Nidditch, London: Clarendon.

Ife, J. (1995) *Community Development: Creating Community Alternatives – Vision, Analysis and Practice*, Melbourne: Longman Australia.

Illich, I. (1972) *Deschooling Society*, New York: Harper & Row.

Imre, R.W. (1982) *Knowing and Caring: Philosophical Issues in Social Work*, New York: University Press of America.

Johnson, O.A. (1994) *Ethics: Selections from Classical and Contemporary Writers* (7th edn), New York: Harcourt Brace College Publishers.

Jordon, J. (ed.) (1991) *Women's Growth in Connection*, New York: Guilford Press.

Jungwirth, H. (1991) 'Interaction and gender – findings of a micro-ethnographical approach to classroom discourse', *Educational Studies in Mathematics*, 22: 263–84.

Kagan, J. and Lamb, S. (eds) (1987) *The Emergence of Morality in Young Children*, Chicago, IL: University of Chicago Press.

Kant, I. (1969) *Foundations of the Metaphysics of Morals*, trans. Lewis White Beck, London: Hutchinson.

Kegan, R. (1982) *The Evolving Self: Problem and Process in Human Development*, Cambridge, MA: Harvard University Press.

Kelley, M. (1996) 'Convicted killer says she deserves to die', *The Australian*, 17 January, p. 7 .

Kelsey, M.T. (1981) *Caring: How Can We Love One Another?* , New York: Paulist Press.

Kemmis, S. (1995) 'Action research and communicative action', unpublished manuscript from Stephen Kemmis Research and Consulting.

Kessell, S. (1992) 'What's a tertiary education – and am I getting one?' *Campus Review Weekly*, 24 June, pp. 8–9.

Kirby, P., Paradise, L.V. and Protti, R. (1992) 'Ethical reasoning of educational administrators: structuring inquiry around the problems of practice', *Journal of Educational Administration*, 30: 25–32.

Kittay, E. and Meyers, D. (eds) (1987) *Women and Moral Theory*, Lanham, MD: Rowman & Littlefield.

Kleinberger, A. (1982) 'The proper object of moral judgement and of moral education', *The Journal of Moral Education*, 11, 3: 147–58.

Kleinig, J. (1973) *Punishment and Desert*, The Hague: Martinus Nijhoff.

——(1981) *Philosophical Issues in Education*, London: Croom Helm.

Knight, T. (1974) 'Powerlessness and the student role: structural determinants of school status', *Australian and New Zealand Journal of Sociology*, 10, 2: 12–17.

Koffka, K. (1935) *Principles of Gestalt Psychology*, London: Routledge.

Kohl, H. (1984) *Growing Minds: On Becoming a Teacher*, New York: Harper & Row.

Kohlberg, L. (1970) 'Education for justice: a modern statement of the platonic view', in T. Sizer and N. Sizer (eds) *Moral Education*, Cambridge, MA: Harvard University Press, pp. 57 – 83.

——(1981) *The Philosophy of Moral Development: Essays in Moral Development*, *vol. 1*, New York: Harper & Row.

——(1984) *The Psychology of Moral Development: Essays in Moral Development*, *vol. 2*, New York: Harper & Row.

Kovesi, J. (1978) *Moral Notions*, London: Routledge & Kegan Paul.

Kozol, J. (1991) *Savage Inequalities*, New York: Crown.

Kuhn, T.S. (1972) *The Structure of Scientific Revolutions*, Oxford: Oxford University Press.

Kymlicka, W. (1995) *Multicultural Citizenship: A Liberal Theory of Minority Rights*, Oxford: Oxford University Press.

Lacan, J. (1975) *Encore*, Paris: Editions de Seuil.

Lakoff, G. (1989) *Women, Fire and Dangerous Things*, Chicago, IL: Chicago University Press.

Lamore, C.E. (1987) *Patterns of Moral Complexity*, Cambridge: Cambridge University Press.

Larrabee, J. (ed.) (1993) *An Ethic of Care*, New York and London: Routledge.

le Guin, U. (1997) *The One Who Walks from Omelas*, London: Gollancz.

Leicester, M. and Taylor, M. (eds) (1992) *Ethics, Ethnicity and Education*, London: Kogan Page.

Lemay, E. and Pitts, J. (1994) *Heidegger for Beginners*, New York: Writers and Readers.

Lennon, K. and Whitford, M. (eds) (1994) *Knowing the Difference*, London: Routledge.

LePore, E. and McLaughlin, B. (eds) (1985) *Actions and Events*, New York: Basil Blackwell.

Levin, D.M. (1982) 'Moral education: the body's felt sense of value' , *Teachers' College Record*, 84, 2: 283–300.

Lickona, T. (ed.) (1976) *Moral Development and Behavior: Theory, Research and Social Issues*, New York: Holt Rinehart & Winston.

——(1991) *Educating for Character: How our Schools can Teach Respect and Responsibility*, New York: Bantam.

Lillie, W. (1948) *An Introduction to Ethics*, London: Methuen.

Lipman, M. (1985) *Lisa: Ethical Inquiry*, Lanham, MD: IAPC.

Lloyd, G. (1984) *The Man of Reason: 'Male' and 'Female' in Western Philosophy*, Minneapolis: University of Minnesota Press.

Locke, J. (1947) *Social Contract*, London: Oxford University Press.

——(1966) *Second Treatise on Civil Government*, London: J.M Dent.

Lovibond, S. (1983) *Realism and Imagination in Ethics*, Minneapolis: University of Minnesota Press.

Lyotard, J.F. (1984) *The Postmodern Condition: A Report on Knowledge*, trans. Geoff Bennington and Brian Massumi, Minneapolis: University of Minnesota Press.

——(1988) *The Differend*, trans G. van den Abbeele, Minneapolis: University of Minnesota Press.

MacIntyre, A. (1981, rev. edn 1985) *After Virtue: A Study in Moral Theory*, London: Duckworth.

——(1987) *Education and Values*, London: Institute of Education.

——(1990) *Three Rival Versions of Moral Enquiry: Encyclopaedia, Genealogy, and Tradition* (Gifford Lectures delivered in the University of Edinburgh in 1988), London: Duckworth.

Mackie, J.L. (1977, rep. 1990) *Ethics: Inventing Right and Wrong*, London: Penguin.

Marshall, J.D. (1975) 'Punishment and education', *Educational Theory*, XXV, 2: 148–55.

Mayeroff, M. (1971) *On Caring*, New York: Harper & Row.

MCEETYA (1994) *National Strategy for Equity in Schooling*, Carlton: Curriculum Corporation.

McLaren, P. (1993) *Schooling as a Ritual Performance*, London and New York: Routledge.

McNeil, L.M. (1986) *Contradictions of Control: School Structure and School Knowledge*, New York: Routledge & Kegan Paul.

Mead, G.H. (1934) *Mind, Self and Society*, Chicago, IL: University of Chicago Press.

——(1982) *The Individual and the Social Self*, Chicago, IL: University of Chicago Press.

Merleau Ponty, M. (1962) *The Phenomenology of Perception*, trans. Colin Smith, London: Routledge & Kegan Paul.

Merrill, R. (ed.) (1988) *Ethics/Aesthetics: Postmodern Positions*, Washington, DC: Maissonneuve Press.

Midgley, M. (1981) *Heart and Mind: The Varieties of Moral Experience*, New York: St Martin's Press.

——(1984) *Wickedness*, London: Routledge & Kegan Paul.

Mill, J.S. (1960) *On Liberty: Representative Government: On the Subjection of Women*, London: J.M. Dent.

——(1975) *Utilitarianism: On Liberty*, London: J.M. Dent.

Millman, J. and Darling-Hammond, L. (eds) (1989) *The New Handbook of Teacher Evaluation: Assessing Elementary and Secondary School Teachers*, Newbury Park, CA: Sage.

Minson, Jeffrey (1985) *Genealogies of Morals*, New York: St Martin's Press.

Montefiore, A. (ed.) (1973) *Philosophy and Personal Relations*, London: Routledge & Kegan Paul.

Moore, G.E. (1903) *Principia Ethica*, Cambridge: Cambridge University Press.

Murdoch, I. (1970) *The Sovereignty of the Good*, London: Routledge & Kegan Paul.

——(1983) 'Against dryness: a polemical sketch', in S. Hauerwa and A. MacIntyre (eds) *Revisions: Changing Perspectives in Moral Philosophy*, Notre Dame, IN: University of Notre Dame Press.

——(1993) *Metaphysics as a Guide to Morals*, London: Chatto & Windus.

Murphy, J. (ed.) (1990) *The Reform of American Public Education in the 1980s: Perspectives and Cases*, Berkeley, CA: McCutchan.

Nagel, T. (1970) *The Possibility of Altruism*, Oxford: Clarendon Press.

——(1979) *Moral Questions*, Cambridge: Cambridge University Press.

——(1986) *The View From Nowhere*, New York: Oxford University Press.

——(1991) *Equality and Partiality*, New York: Oxford University Press.

Noam, T.E. and Wren, G.G. (eds) (1993) *The Moral Self*, Cambridge, MA: MIT Press.

Noddings, N. (1984) *Caring: A Feminine Approach to Ethics and Moral Education*, Berkeley, CA: University of California Press.

——(1988) 'An ethic of caring and its implications for instructional arrangements', *American Journal of Education*, 96, 2: 215–30.

——(1992) *The Challenge to Care in Schools: Alternative Approaches to Education*, New York: Teachers College Press.

——(1993a) 'Caring: a feminist perspective', in K.A. Strike and P.L. Ternasky (eds) *Ethics for Professionals in Education: Perspectives for Preparation and Practice*, New York: Teachers College Press, pp. 43–53.

——(1993b) *Educating for Intelligent Belief or Unbelief*, New York: Teachers College Press.

——(1994) 'Conversation as moral education', *Journal of Moral Education*, 23, 2: 107–118.

——(1995) *Philosophy of Education*, Oxford: Westview Press.

Nozick, R. (1989) *The Examined Life*, New York: Simon & Schuster.

Nussbaum, M. (1986) *The Fragility of Goodness: Luck and Ethics in Greek Tragedy and Philosophy*, Cambridge: Cambridge University Press.

——(1990) *Love's Knowledge: Essays on Philosophy and Literature*, New York: Oxford University Press.

——(1992) 'Virtue revived', *Times Literary Supplement*, 3 July, pp. 9–11.

——(1993) 'Equity and mercy', *Philosophy and Public Affairs*, 22, 2: 83–125.

Nussbaum, M. and Sen, A. (eds) (1993) *The Quality of Life*, Oxford: Clarendon Press.

Nyberg, D. (1981) *Power Over Power*, Ithaca, NY: Cornell University Press.

——(1993) *The Varnished Truth: Truth-telling and Deceiving in Ordinary Life*, Chicago, IL: University of Chicago Press.

Oakeshott, M. (1962) *Rationalism in Politics*, New York: Basic Books.

——(1975) *On Human Conduct*, Oxford: Oxford University Press.

Okin, S.M. (1989) 'Reason and feeling in thinking about justice', *Ethics*, 96, 2: 229–49.

Pappas, G. (1993) 'Dewey and feminism: the affective and relationship in Dewey's ethics', *Hypatia*, 8, 2: 78–95.

Parfit, D. (1973) 'Later selves and moral principles', in A. Montefiore (ed.) *Philosophy and Personal Relations*, London: Routledge & Kegan Paul.

——(1984) *Reasons and Persons*, Oxford: Oxford University Press.

Pateman, C. (1989) *The Disorder of Women*, Stanford: Stanford University Press.

——(1995) *Democracy, Freedom and Special Rights*, Swansea: University of Wales Press.

Pateman, C. and Gross, E. (1986) *Feminist Challenges: Social and Political Theory*, Sydney: Allen & Unwin.

Peirce, C.S. (1931–58) *Collected Papers* (8 vols), ed. C. Hartshorne *et al.*, Cambridge, MA: Harvard University Press.

——(1981) *Human Rights*, New York: New York University Press.

Peters, R.S. (1970) *Ethics and Education*, London: Allen & Unwin.
——(1973) *Authority, Responsibility and Education*, London: Allen & Unwin.
——(1981) *Moral Development and Moral Education*, London: Allen & Unwin.
Phenix, Philip H. (1964) *Realms of Meaning: A Philosophy of the Curriculum for General Education*, New York: McGraw-Hill.
Philips, M. (1987) 'Rationality, responsibility and blame', *Canadian Journal of Philosophy*, 17: 141–6.
Piaget, J. (1932) *The Moral Judgement of the Child*, London: Routledge.
Pirsig, R.M (1974) *Zen and the Art of Motorcycle Maintenance*, London: Bodley Head.
——(1991) *Lila: An Inquiry into Morals*, London and New York: Bantam.
Plato (1984) *The Republic*, trans. Desmond Lee, Harmondsworth: Penguin.
Popper, K. (1962) *The Open Society and its Enemies*, London: Routledge & Kegan Paul.
——(1972) *Objective Knowledge*, Oxford: Clarendon.
Postman, N. (1988) *Conscientious Objections*, New York: Knopf.
——(1995) *The End of Education: Redefining the Value of School*, New York: Knopf.
Pritchard, M.S. (1981) *On Becoming Responsible*, Kansas: University Press of Kansas.
Purpel, D.E. (1989) *The Moral and Spiritual Crisis in Education: A Curriculum for Justice and Compassion in Education*, Granby, MA: Bergin & Garvey.
Purpel, D.E. and Shapiro, H.S. (eds) (1985) *Schools and Meaning: Essays on the Moral Nature of Schooling*, Lanham, MD: University Press of America.
Quine, Willard van Ormond *Word and Object*, Cambridge, MA: MIT Press.
Quinn, W. (1993) *Morality and Action*, Cambridge: Cambridge University Press.
Raphael, D.D. (1994, rev. edn) *Moral Philosophy*, Oxford: Oxford University Press
Rawls, J. (1955) 'Two concepts of rules', *Philosophical Review*, 64: 3–32.
——(1971) *A Theory of Justice*, Cambridge, MA: Harvard University Press.
——(1980) 'Kantian constructivism in moral theory', *Journal of Philosophy*, 77: 9.
——(1993) *Political Liberalism*, New York: Columbia University Press.
Reed, D. (1989) 'My kidney for my son', *Canberra Times*, 14 October.
Reid, L.A. (1962) *Philosophy and Education*, London: Heinemann.
——(1984) *Ways of Understanding*, London: Heinemann.
Ricoeur, P. (1981) *Hermeneutics and Human Stories: Essays in Interpretation*, Cambridge: Cambridge University Press.
——(1992) *Oneself as Another*, trans. K. Blamey, Chicago: Chicago University Press.
Rizvi, F. (ed.) (1985) *Working Papers in Ethics in Educational Administration*, Geelong: Deakin University Press.
——(1995) 'Ethics in educational administration', in C. Evers and J. Chapman (eds) *Educational Administration*, London: Allen & Unwin.
Rorty, A. (ed.) (1976) *The Identities of Persons*, Berkeley: University of California Press.
——(1988) *Mind in Action*, Boston: Beacon.
——(1990) 'Varieties of pluralism in a polyphonic society', *Review of Metaphysics*, 44: 3–20.
——(1991) 'King Solomon and Everyman: a problem in co-ordinating conflicting moral intuitions', *American Philosophical Quarterly*, 28: 181–95.
——(1992) 'The advantages of moral diversity', *Social Philosophy and Policy*, 9: 38–62 .
Rorty, R. (1967) *The Linguistic Turn*, Chicago, IL: Chicago University Press.

——(1979) *Philosophy and the Mirror of Nature*, Princeton: Princeton University Press.

——(1991) 'Feminism and pragmatism', *Michigan Quarterly Review*, 31, 2: 231–58.

Rouner, L. (ed.) (1993) *Moral Education*, Notre Dame, IN: University of Notre Dame Press.

Ruddick, S. (1980) 'Maternal thinking', *Feminist Studies*, 96, 2: 342–67.

——(1989) *Maternal Thinking*, Boston: Beacon.

Sacred Heart College (1993) 'Rules of the school', mimeo set of rules for parents.

Sawicki, J. (1991) *Disciplining Foucault: Feminism, Power and the Body*, New York: Routledge.

Scheffler, I. (1970) *Reason in Teaching*, Indiana: Bobbs-Merrill.

Schmier, L. (1995) 'Nightmare on ABC street', email posting on <EDPOLYAN%ASUACAD.BITNET@uga.cc.uga.edu>.

Schön, D.A. (1983) *Educating the Reflective Practitioner: How Professionals Think in Action*, New York: Basic Books.

——(1987) *Educating the Reflective Practitioner: Toward a New Design for Thinking and Learning in the Professions*, San Francisco, CA: Jossey Bass.

Scott, C.F. (1990) *The Question of Ethics: Nietzsche, Foucault and Heidegger*, Bloomington: Indiana University Press.

Scriven, M. (1966) 'Causes, connections and conditions in history', in W. Dray (ed.) *Philosophical Analysis and History*, New York: Harper & Row.

Secada, W. (ed.) (1989) *Equity in Education*, London: Falmer.

Sergiovanni, T.J. (1994) *Building Community in Schools*, San Francisco, CA: Jossey Bass.

Sergiovanni, T.J. and Moore, J.H. (eds) (1989) *Schooling for Tomorrow: Directing Reforms to Issues that Count*, Boston: Allyn & Bacon.

Shakeshaft, C. (1987) *Women in Educational Administration*, Newbury Park, CA: Sage.

Sharp, A.M. and Reed, R.F. (1992) (eds) *Studies in Philosophy for Children: Harry Stottlemeier's Discovery*, Philadelphia: Temple University Press.

Shor, Ira (1992) *Empowering Education: Critical Teaching for Social Change*, Chicago, IL: Chicago University Press.

Sichel, B.A. 'An ethics of care and institutional ethics committees', *Hypatia*, 4, 2: 45–56.

Siegal, Michael (1991) *Knowing Children: Experiments in Conversation and Cognition*, Hove: Lawrence Erlbaum Associates.

Singer, P. (1973) 'The triviality of the debate over "is–ought" and the definition of "moral"', *American Philosophical Quarterly*, 10: 51–6.

——(1979) *Practical Ethics*, Cambridge: Cambridge University Press.

——(1983) *The Expanding Circle: Ethics and Sociobiology*, London: Penguin.

——(1993) *How Are We to Live? Ethics in an Age of Self-interest*, New York: Prometheus.

Sizer, T.R. (1984) *Horace's Compromises: The Dilemma of the American High School*, Boston: Houghton Mifflin.

Sizer, T.R. and Sizer, N.F. (eds) (1970) *Moral Education*, Cambridge, MA: Harvard University Press.

Smiley, M. (1992) *Moral Responsibility and the Boundaries of Community*, London: Chicago University Press.

Sockett, H. (1990) 'Accountability, trust and ethical codes of practice', in J.I. Goodlad, R. Soder and K.A. Sirotnik (eds) *The Moral Dimensions of Teaching*, San Francisco, CA: Jossey Bass, pp. 224–50.

——(1993) *The Moral Base for Teacher Professionalism*, New York: Teachers College Press.

Sola, P. (ed.) (1984) *Ethics, Education and Administrative Decisions*, New York: Peter Lang.

Soltis, J. (1968) *An Introduction to the Analysis of Educational Concepts*, Reading, MA: Addison-Wesley.

Sommers, C. and F. (1989) *Vice and Virtue in Everyday Life: Introductory Readings in Ethics*, New York: Harcourt Brace Jovanovich.

Spender, D. (1980, 2nd edn 1990) *Man Made Language*, London: Pandora.

——(1987) *The Education Papers*, New York: Routledge & Kegan Paul.

Sprigge, T.L.S. (1974) 'Punishment and moral responsibility', in M. Goldinger (ed.) *Punishment and Human Rights*, Cambridge: Cambridge University Press.

Starratt, R.J. (1991) 'Building an ethical school: a theory for practice in educational leadership', *Educational Administration Quarterly*, 27, 2: 185–202.

Stout, J. (1988) *Ethics after Babel: The Languages of Morals and their Discontents*, Boston: Beacon.

Strike, K.A. (1982) *Educational Policy and the Just Society*, Chicago, IL: University of Illinois Press.

——(1989) 'The ethics of educational evaluation', in J. Millman and L. Darling-Hammond (eds) *The New Handbook of Teacher Evaluation: Assessing Elementary and Secondary School Teachers*, Newbury Park, CA: Sage.

——(1994) 'On the construction of public speech: pluralism and public reason', *Educational Theory*, 44, 1: 1–26.

Strike, K.A. and Egan, K. (eds) (1978) *Ethics and Educational Policy*, London: Routledge & Kegan Paul.

Strike, K.A., Haller, Emil J. and Soltis, Jonas F. (1988) *The Ethics of School Administration*, New York: Teachers College Press.

Strike, K.A. and Ternasky, P.L. (eds) (1993) *Ethics for Professionals in Education: Perspectives for Preparation and Practice*, New York: Teachers College Press.

Tannen, D. and Saville-Troil, M. (eds) (1985) *Perspectives on Silence*, Norwood, NJ: Ablex.

Taylor, C. (1989) *Sources of the Self: The Making of the Modern Identity*, Cambridge: Cambridge University Press.

——(1992) *Multiculturalism and 'the Politics of Recognition'*, Princeton, NJ: Princeton University Press.

Teichman, J. (1974) 'Wittgenstein on persons and human beings', in Godfrey Vesey (ed.) *Understanding Wittgenstein*, Royal Institute of Philosophy Lectures vol. 7, 1972–3, London: Macmillan, pp. 133 –48.

Telfer, E. (1980) *Happiness*, New York: St Martin's Press.

Thayer-Bacon, B. (1993) 'Caring and its relationship to critical thinking', *Educational Theory*, 43, 3: 323–40.

Thomas, J.C. (1992) 'The development of reasoning in children through the community of inquiry', in A. Sharp and R. Reed (eds) *Studies in Philosophy for Children: Harry Stottlemeier's Discovery*, Philadelphia: Temple University Press, pp. 96–104.

Toulmin, S. (1972) *Human Understanding*, Princeton, NJ: Princeton University Press.

——(1986) *The Place of Reason in Ethics*, Chicago, IL: University of Chicago Press.

Tronto, J. (1987) 'Women's morality: beyond gender differences to a theory of care', *Signs*, 12, 4: 644–63.

——(1993) *Moral Boundaries: A Political Argument for an Ethic of Care*, New York: Routledge.

Tyler, S. (1987) *The Unspeakable: Discourse, Dialogue and Rhetoric in the Postmodern World*, Madison: University of Wisconsin Press.

Ury, W., Brett, J.M. and Goldberg, S.B. (eds) (1988) *Getting Disputes Resolved: Designing Systems to Cut the Costs of Conflict*, San Francisco, CA: Jossey Bass.

Vesey, G. (ed.) (1974) *Personal Identity*, London: Macmillan.

——(1982) *Idealism, Past and Present*, Cambridge: Cambridge University Press.

Walker, L. (1984) 'Sex differences in the development of moral reasoning: a critical review', *Child Development*, 55: 677–91.

Walker, M. (1989) 'Moral understandings: alternative "epistemology" for a feminist ethics', *Hypatia*, 4, 2: 15–28.

Warnock, G. (1971) *The Object of Morality*, London: Methuen.

Warnock, M. (1960) *Ethics since 1900*, London: Oxford University Press.

——(1979) *Education: A Way Ahead*, Oxford: Basil Blackwell.

Weil, S. (1951) *Waiting for God*, New York: Putnam.

Weiler, K. (1988) *Women Teaching for Change*, South Hadley, MA: Bergin & Harvey.

Weinryb, E. (1980) 'Omissions and responsibility', *Philosophical Quarterly*, 30: 1–18.

Western Mining Corporation Limited (1995) *Code of Conduct: A Guide to Conduct of Employees of Western Mining Corporation Limited*, Adelaide: WMC.

White, J. (1994) *Education and the Good Life*, New York: Teachers College Press.

White, S.K. (1989) *The Recent Work of Jürgen Habermas*, Cambridge: Cambridge University Press.

——(1990) 'Heidegger and the difficulties of a postmodern ethics and politics', *Political Theory*, 18, 1: 80–103.

Whitford, M. and Griffiths, M. (eds) *Feminist Perspectives in Philosophy*, Bloomington: Indiana University Press.

Williams, B. (1993) *Shame and Necessity*, Berkeley: University of California Press.

Wilson, J. (1995) *Reflection and Practice: Teacher Education and the Teaching Profession*, London and Ontario: Althouse.

Wilson, James (1993) *The Moral Sense*, New York: Free Press.

Wilson, John (1970) *Moral Thinking*, London: Heinemann.

——(1973) *The Assessment of Morality*, Windsor: NFER.

Wilson, P. (1971) *Interest and Discipline in Education*, London: Routledge & Kegan Paul.

Witherell, C. and Noddings, N. (1991) *Stories Lives Tell: Narrative and Dialogue in Education*, New York: Teachers College Press.

Wittgenstein, L. (1969) *Philosophical Investigations*, London: Basil Blackwell.

——(1980) *Culture and Value*, ed. G.H. von Wright, Chicago, IL: University of Chicago Press.

Wollheim, R. (1976) *The Good Self and the Bad Self*, London: British Academy.

Wood, D. (1973) 'Honesty', in A. Montefiore (ed.) *Philosophy and Personal Relations*, London: Routledge & Kegan Paul, pp. 191–223.

Wren, T.E. (ed.) (1990) *The Moral Domain: Essays in the Ongoing Discussion between Philosophy and the Social Sciences*, Cambridge, MA: MIT Press.

——(1993) 'Open-textured concepts of morality and the self', in T.E. Noam and G.G. Wren (eds) *The Moral Self*, Cambridge, MA: MIT Press, pp. 78–95.

Wyshogrod, E. (1990) *Saints and Postmodernism: Revisioning Moral Philosophy*, Chicago, IL: Chicago University Press.

Yates, L. (1986) 'Theorizing inequality today', *British Journal of Sociology of Education*, 7, 2: 119–34.

——(1993) *The Education of Girls*, Hawthorn: ACER.

Young, I. (1986) 'The ideal of community and the politics of difference' , *Social Theory and Practice*, 12, 1: 1–26.
Young, I. and Allen, J. (1990) *Justice and the Politics of Difference*, Princeton: Princeton University Press.
Zimmerman, M. (1988) *An Essay on Moral Responsibility*, Totowa, NJ: Rowman & Littlefield.

Index